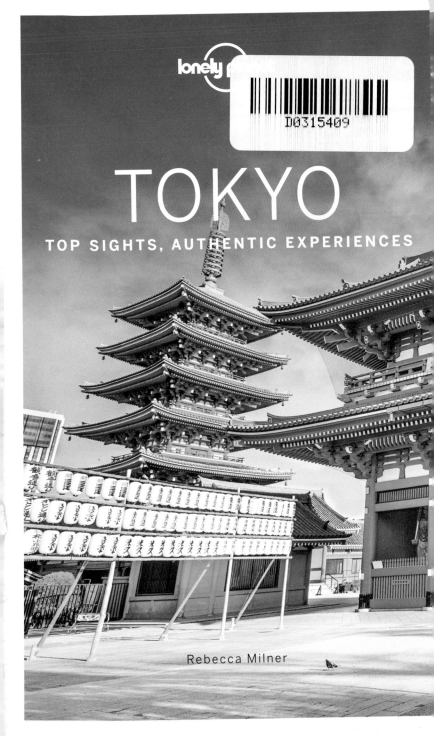

lonely planet

D0315409

TOKYO

TOP SIGHTS, AUTHENTIC EXPERIENCES

Rebecca Milner

Contents

Plan Your Trip

Top Experiences.....................35

Dining Out....................................119

Treasure Hunt 149

Bar Open 169

CLOCKWISE FROM TOP LEFT: SEAN PAVONE / SHUTTERSTOCK ©; SEAN PAVONE
/ SHUTTERSTOCK ©; MANUEL ASCANIO / SHUTTERSTOCK ©; TTSTUDIO
/ SHUTTERSTOCK ©; PANWASIN SEEMALA / SHUTTERSTOCK ©; WITAYA
RATANASIRIKULCHAI / SHUTTERSTOCK ©; MATT MUNRO / LONELY PLANET ©;
TAKASHI YASUI / 500PX ©; TOM BONAVENTURE / GETTY IMAGES ©; BIXPICTURE /
SHUTTERSTOCK ©; SEAN PAVONE / SHUTTERSTOCK ©; OLIOPI / SHUTTERSTOCK ©;

Plan Your Trip
This Year in Tokyo

2019

KAZUKO KIMIZUKA / GETTY IMAGES ©

Tokyo

From left: Sanja Matsuri festival (p10); Sumo tournament (p82); Chidori-ga-fuchi (p73) in cherry blossom season

From pop-culture events to festivals that have been taking place for centuries, there is always something going on in Tokyo. Like elsewhere in Japan, the seasons have special meaning, with every new bloom a reason for celebration.

2019

★ **Top Festivals & Events**

Hatsu-mōde January (p6)
Cherry Blossoms April (p9)
Sanja Matsuri May (p10)
Sumida-gawa Fireworks July (p12)
Kōenji Awa Odori August (p13)

Plan Your Trip
This Year in Tokyo

January

Tokyo is eerily quiet for O-shōgatsu (the first three days of the new year), but picks up as the month rolls on. Days are cold, but usually clear; sights are generally uncrowded.

🎎 Greeting the Emperor   2 Jan
The emperor makes a brief – and rare – public appearance in an inner courtyard of the Imperial Palace (p105) to make a ceremonial greeting.

☆ Sumo Tournament   13–27 Jan
The January *bashō* (grand sumo tournament) is the first chance of the year to see Japan's top wrestlers have at it. It's held at Ryōgoku Kokugikan (p82). Tournaments also take place in May and September.

🎎 Coming of Age Day   14 Jan
The second Monday of January is *seijin-no-hi*, the collective birthday for all who have turned 20 (the age of majority) in the past year; young women don gorgeous kimonos for ceremonies at Shintō shrines.

🎎 Hatsu-mōde   1 Jan
Hatsu-mōde, the first shrine visit of the new year, starts just after midnight on 1 January and continues through O-shōgatsu. Meiji-jingū (p41) is the most popular spot in Tokyo; it can get very, very crowded, but that's part of the experience. Above: Sensō-ji (p88), Asakusa

🛍 Setagaya Boro-ichi   15–16 Jan
Boro means 'old and worn'. At this market in residential Setagaya ward, hundreds of vendors converge to sell antiques and other sundry secondhand items. The market itself is also an antique: it's been happening for over 400 years. A second market is held 15 and 16 December.

⊙ Folk Crafts Exhibition   Jan–Feb
Catch an exhibition of *mingei* (Japanese folk crafts) at 21_21 Design Sight (p52) until 24 February.

2019

TIBOR BOGNAR / ALAMY STOCK PHOTO ©

02

February

February is the coldest month, though it rarely snows. Winter days are crisp and clear – the best time of year to spot Mt Fuji in the distance.

🎎 Setsubun   3 Feb
The first day of spring on the traditional lunar calendar signalled a shift once believed to bode evil. As a precaution, people visit Buddhist temples, toss roasted beans, and shout, *'Oni wa soto! Fuku wa uchi!'* ('Devil out! Fortune in!').

Above: Performers in devil costumes for Setsubun.

🎎 Shimo-Kitazawa Tengu Matsuri   early Feb
On the weekend nearest to Setsubun (which occasionally falls in late January), Shimo-Kitazawa hosts a parade with revellers dressed in *tengu* (devil) costumes.

👁 Roppongi Crossing   Feb–May
Mori Art Museum's (p110) once-every-three-years survey of contemporary Japanese art, Roppongi Crossing, runs from 9 Feb to 26 May.

👁 Plum Blossoms   late Feb
Ume (plum) blossoms, which appear towards the end of the month, are the first sign that winter is ending. Popular viewing spots include Koishikawa Kōrakuen and Yushima Tenjin.

MI7 / SHUTTERSTOCK ©

Plan Your Trip
This Year in Tokyo

March

Spring begins in fits and starts. The Japanese have a saying: sankan-shion – three days cold, four days warm.

✦ Tokyo Marathon　　3 Mar

Tokyo's biggest running event (www.marathon.tokyo; pictured above) happens on the first Sunday of March. Sign up the summer before; competition for slots is fierce.

☆ Anime Japan　　late Mar

Anime Japan (www.anime-japan.jp) has events and exhibitions for industry insiders and fans alike, at Tokyo Big Sight in Odaiba.

☆ Tokyo Haru-sai　　Mar–Apr

This month-long classical-music festival is held at venues around Ueno-kōen (p68).

❀ Hina Matsuri　　3 Mar

On and around Girls' Day, public spaces and homes are decorated with *o-hina-sama* (princess) dolls in traditional royal dress (pictured below).

2019

04

April

Warmer weather and blooming cherry trees make this quite simply the best month to be in Tokyo.

✿ Buddha's Birthday — 8 Apr

In honour of the Buddha's birthday, Hana Matsuri (flower festival) celebrations take place at temples. Look for the parade of children in Asakusa, pulling a white papier-mâché elephant.

Pictured above: ladles used to sprinkle water on a figure of the baby Buddha during the festival.

✿ Kannon-ura Ichiyo Sakura-matsuri Festival — mid-Apr

This annual spring event takes place on the second Saturday in April along the back-streets behind Sensō-ji (p88). The highlight is the procession of women dressed in the finery of Edo-era (1603–1868) courtesans.

✿ Earth Day — 20–21 Apr

Tokyo celebrates this international event over the nearest weekend to Earth Day (22 April) with a festival at Yoyogi-kōen (p46) that includes organic-food stalls, live music and workshops for kids.

◉ Cherry Blossoms — early Apr

From the end of March through the beginning of April, the city's parks and riversides turn pink and Tokyoites toast spring in spirited parties, called *hanami*, beneath the blossoms.

✿ Naki-zumo — 29 Apr

In Japan it's believed that crying babies grow big and strong. At this amusing festival, held at Sensō-ji, sumo wrestlers are brought in to pull faces at babies (in cute mini sumo outfits) to make them cry. The one who cries first, or loudest, is crowned the winner.

Plan Your Trip
This Year in Tokyo

PATARA / SHUTTERSTOCK ©

May

05

There's a string of national holidays at the beginning of May, known as Golden Week, which can make it hard to secure accommodation. Otherwise, with festivals and warm days, this is an excellent time to visit.

🎏 Children's Day   5 May
For the celebration also known as *otoko-no-hi* (Boys' Day), families fly *koinobori* (colourful banners in the shape of a carp), a symbol of strength and courage.

☆ Sumo Tournament   12–26 May
Another chance to see sumo live, at Ryōgoku Kokugikan (p82).

🎏 Sanja Matsuri   17–19 May
Arguably the grandest Tokyo *matsuri* (festival) of all, this event attracts around 1.5 million spectators to Asakusa-jinja (p91). The highlight is the rowdy parade of *mikoshi* (portable shrines) carried by men and women in traditional dress, which takes place on Sunday.

🎏 Tokyo Rainbow Pride   early May
Usually over Golden Week, Japan's LGBT community comes together for the country's biggest pride event (www.tokyorainbowpride.com), some years followed by a parade. It's not London or Sydney, but a spirited affair just the same.

🎏 Kanda Matsuri   mid-May
This is one of Tokyo's big three festivals, with a parade of *mikoshi* (portable shrines) put on by Kanda Myōjin around the streets of Kanda and Akihabara. It's held on the weekend closest to 15 May on odd-numbered years.

🎏 Design Festa   mid-May
Weekend-long Design Festa (www.design festa.com), held at Tokyo Big Sight in Odaiba, is Asia's largest art festival, featuring performances and thousands of exhibitors. There is a second event in November.

2019

JONATHON TREWAVAS / SHUTTERSTOCK ©

06

June

Early June is lovely, though by the end of the month, tsuyu (the rainy season) sets in.

🍷 **BeerFes Tokyo**   1–2 Jun
The chance to sample over 100 different craft beers from around Japan and the world happens the first weekend of June. And you get to sample as much as you want for 3½ hours (admission costs around ¥5000). Get details and tickets (it usually sells out) online: www.beerfes.jp.

⊙ **Fireflies**   Jun
June is the month for fireflies to light the night sky. The garden hotel Chinzan-so hosts evening events, as do parks and gardens on the outskirts of the city.

⊙ **Late Spring Blooms**   Jun
Rainy season in Tokyo can be a drag, but it does result in some glorious late-spring blooms. June sees irises bloom in gardens around Tokyo. Meiji-jingū Gyoen (pictured above; p41) is the most famous viewing spot. You'll also spot starbursts of hydrangea around town.

Plan Your Trip
This Year in Tokyo

July

07

When the rainy season passes in mid- to late July, suddenly it's summer – the season for lively street fairs and hanabi taikai (fireworks shows).

☘ Mt Fuji Climbing Season Jul–Aug
The most popular hiking route up Mt Fuji, the Yoshida Trail, opens 1 July. Other trails open 10 July. All are open until 10 September.

🎊 Tanabata 7 Jul
On the day the stars Vega and Altar (stand-ins for a princess and cowherd who are in love) meet across the Milky Way, children tie strips of coloured paper bearing wishes around bamboo branches. Look for decorations at youthful hang-outs such as Harajuku and Shibuya.

🎊 Mitama Matsuri 13–16 Jul
Yasukuni-jinja celebrates O-Bon early with a festival of remembrance for the dead that sees 30,000 illuminated *bonbori* (paper lanterns) hung in and around the shrine.

🎊 Sumida-gawa Fireworks 27 Jul
The grandest of the summer fireworks shows features 20,000 pyrotechnic wonders. Head to Asakusa early in the day to score a good seat. Check events listings for other fireworks displays around town.

☆ Summer Sonic mid-Aug
The Tokyo area's biggest music festival (www.summersonic.com) is this part-indoor, part-outdoor weekend-long bash at Makuhari Messe that draws big international and domestic artists.

🎊 Lantern Festivals Jul–Aug
Toro nagashi is a photogenic summer tradition, connected to O-Bon, where candle-lit paper lanterns are floated down rivers. It takes place from mid-July to mid-August; two big ones happen at Chidori-ga-fuchi (p73) and at Sumida-kōen in Asakusa.

JULIANNE HIDE / SHUTTERSTOCK ©

August

This is the height of Japan's sticky, hot summer; school holidays mean sights may be crowded.

🎎 Asagaya Tanabata　　early Aug
Asagaya holds a Tanabata festival with colourful lanterns strung up in its *shōtengai* (market streets), Pearl Centre, for several days.

🎎 O-Bon　　13–16 Aug
Several days in mid-August are set aside to honour the dead, when their spirits are said to return to the earth. Graves are swept, offerings are made, and *bon-odori* (folk dances) take place.

☆ Comiket　　mid-Aug
Twice annual Comiket (www.comiket.co.jp), also known as Comic Market, is a massive event for manga fans, where original self-published works are sold and many attendees come dressed as their favourite character. It happens again in December.

🎎 Kōenji Awa Odori　　late Aug
Kōenji Awa Odori (www.koenji-awaodori.com) is Tokyo's biggest *awa odori* (dance festival for O-Bon), with 12,000 participants in traditional costumes dancing their way through the streets. It takes place over the last weekend in August.

🎎 Asakusa Samba Carnival　　Late Aug
Tokyo's Nikkei Brazilian community and local samba clubs turn Kaminarimon-dōri into one big party (www.asakusa-samba.org). Held on a Saturday late in the month.

Plan Your Trip
This Year in Tokyo

09

September

Days are still warm, hot even – and the odd typhoon rolls through this time of year.

☆ **Tokyo Jazz Festival**   early Sep
Enjoy three days of shows by international and local stars at Tokyo's biggest jazz festival (www.tokyo-jazz.com), held at venues around the city.

☆ **Japan Media Arts Festival**   mid-Sep
The year's top animation, manga and digital installations go on display at the Japan Media Arts Festival (www.j-mediaarts.jp).

☆ **Sumo Tournament**   8–22 Sep
The final Tokyo sumo tournament of the year, held at Ryōgoku Kokugikan (p82).

☆ **Rugby World Cup**   Sep–Nov
The 2019 Rugby World Cup kicks off on 20 September at Tokyo Stadium. The final match will be held 2 November at Yokohama Stadium. You can count on matches being screened in bars around Tokyo.

☉ **Moon Viewing**   14 Sep & 14 Oct
Full moons in September and October call for *tsukimi*, moon-viewing gatherings. People eat *tsukimi dango – mochi* (pounded rice) dumplings which are round like the moon (pictured above).

☆ **Tokyo Game Show**   late Sep
Get your geek on when the Computer Entertainment Suppliers Association hosts Tokyo Game Show (http://tgs.cesa.or.jp), a massive expo at Makuhari Messe in late September.

BEEHAPPY28 / SHUTTERSTOCK ©

October

10

Pleasantly warm days and cool evenings make this an excellent time to be in Tokyo; many arts events take place this time of year.

☆ F/T   Oct–Nov
Tokyo's contemporary theatre festival (www.festival-tokyo.jp) takes place from October through mid-November at venues around the city, featuring works by local and international directors. Some events are subtitled.

◉ Design Touch   Oct–Nov
Held in and around Tokyo Midtown (p160), Design Touch is a series of public exhibitions and events around the theme of design, from mid-October through early November.

✾ Tokyo Grand
Tea Ceremony   late Oct
Held at Hama-rikyū Onshi-teien (p39), this is a big outdoor tea party (www.tokyo-grand-tea-ceremony.jp), with traditional tea ceremonies held in various styles, usually including one with English translation.

☆ Tokyo International
Film Festival   late Oct
Tokyo's principal film festival (www.tiff-jp.net) screens works from Japanese and international directors with English subtitles.

◉ Chrysanthemum
Festivals   late Oct
Chrysanthemums (pictured above) are the flower of the season (and the royal family). Dazzling displays are put on from late October to mid-November in Hibiya-kōen and at Meiji-jingū (p41).

✾ Halloween   31 Oct
Tokyo has gone mad for Halloween with thousands of costumed celebrants converging on Shibuya Crossing (p95). Shinjuku Ni-chōme and Roppongi see action, too.

Plan Your Trip
This Year in Tokyo

IRINA GUSEVA / SHUTTERSTOCK ©

November

11

Crisp and cool days, few crowds and pretty fall leaves.

🎊 Shichi-go-san   15 Nov
This adorable festival sees parents dress girls aged seven (*shichi*) and three (*san*) and boys aged five (*go*) in wee kimonos and head to Shintō shrines for blessings.

Below right: young girl dressed in kimono for Shichi-go-san blessings.

👁 Design Festa   mid-Nov
The off-the-wall DIY art fair that is Design Festa makes a repeat appearance this month, at Tokyo Big Sight.

☆ Tokyo Filmex   late Nov
Tokyo Filmex (www.filmex.net) focuses on emerging directors in Asia and screens many films with English subtitles.

👁 Maple Leaves   late Nov
The city's maples undergo magnificent seasonal transformations during *kōyō* (autumn foliage season); Rikugi-en (p109) and Koishikawa Kōrakuen have spectacular displays.

🎊 Tori-no-ichi   8 & 20 Nov
On 'rooster' days in November, 'O-tori' shrines such as Hanazono-jinja hold fairs called Tori-no-ichi (*tori* means 'rooster'). The day is set according to the old calendar, which marks days by the zodiac. Vendors hawk *kumade* – rakes that literally symbolise 'raking in the wealth'.

BENOIST / SHUTTERSTOCK ©

SASAKEN / SHUTTERSTOCK ©

December

Early December is pleasantly crisp, but as the month goes on the winter chill settles in. Commercial strips are decorated with seasonal illuminations.

☉ Golden Gingkos   early Dec
Tokyo's official tree, the *ichō* (gingko), turns a glorious shade of gold in late autumn; Ichō Namiki (Gingko Ave) in Gaienmae is the top viewing spot.

✿ Gishi-sai   14 Dec
Temple Sengaku-ji hosts a memorial service honouring the 47 *rōnin* (masterless samurai) who famously avenged their fallen master; locals dressed as the loyal retainers parade through nearby streets.

✗ Bōnenkai   late Dec
During the last weeks of the year, restaurants and bars are filled with Tokyoites hosting *bōnenkai* (end-of-the-year parties) with friends or colleagues. The boisterous mood takes the sting out of the newly chilled air, though be warned that tables may be hard to come by this time of year.

✗ Toshikoshi Soba   31 Dec
Eating buckwheat noodles on New Year's Eve, a tradition called *toshikoshi soba*, is said to bring luck and longevity – the latter symbolised by the length of the noodles.

☆ Comiket   late Dec
The massively popular winter edition of Comiket sees just as many attendees as the summer version – some 500,000.

✿ Joya-no-kane   31 Dec
Temple bells around Japan ring 108 times at midnight on 31 December, a purifying ritual called *joya-no-kane*. Sensō-ji (p88) draws the biggest crowds in Tokyo.

Plan Your Trip
Hotspots For...

CULTURE VULTURES

⊙ **Tokyo National Museum** Home to the world's largest collection of Japanese art. (p65)

☘ **Ohara School of Ikebana** Take a class in the Japanese art of flower-arranging. (p199)

⊙ **Contemporary Architecture** See the works of Japan's leading architects.

✕ **Sakurai Japanese Tea Experience** (p128) A deep dive into the Japanese cult of tea.

☆ **Kabukiza** Go in for a visual and dramatic feast at Tokyo's premier kabuki theatre. (p100)

PARTY PEOPLE

🍷 **A Night Out in Shimo-Kitazawa** Go on the ultimate Tokyo bar crawl in this artsy, eclectic 'hood. (p56)

⊙ **Cherry Blossoms** When the cherry trees bloom in spring, Tokyoites head to the parks for sake-drenched picnics. (p46)

✕ **Tokyo's Eating & Drinking Alleys** Grab a stool and raise a glass in an atmospheric old strip of bars and restaurants.

🍷 **Karaoke** Sing your heart out, and see why Japan is nuts for karaoke. (p112)

☆ **Unit** Catch a live music show or late-night DJ set at this fashionable venue. (p192)

FOODIES

⊙ Tsukiji Outer Market A pilgrimage site for chefs and home cooks alike, with lots of food to sample. (p36)

🛍 Akomeya Shop for packaged foods from around Japan at this beautiful food-stuffs boutique. (p160)

✕ Sushi Go for broke on a chef's tasting course, take lessons or experience the wonder of the conveyor-belt sushi restaurant.

✕ Ginza Kagari Join the queue at Tokyo's ramen shop du jour. (p139)

🍜 Tokyo Cooking Studio Soba-making lessons from a seasoned pro. (p198)

GLITZ & GLAMOUR

✕ Kikunoi Splurge on a meal of a lifetime at this famed kaiseki (haute cuisine) restaurant. (p138)

♨ Spa LaQua Soak away your troubles in this chic onsen (hot spring) complex. (p98)

🍸 Two Rooms Sundown cocktails on the terrace here are a must. (p116)

✕ Kozue Gaze over the city from this sky-high gourmet Japanese restaurant. (p124)

🛍 Shopping in Harajuku See the latest looks bubbling out of Harajuku's back streets. (p42)

OUTDOORSY TYPES

🥾 Mt Fuji Hoof it up Japan's iconic volcano in the summer months (or hunt for views year-round). (p58)

⊙ Rikugi-en Take a morning stroll through Tokyo's most beautiful landscape garden. (p109)

☆ Tokyo Dome Cheer on baseball powerhouse the Yomiuri Giants. (p198)

🥾 Yanaka Amble or (cycle!) through this charmingly vintage neighbourhood. (p70)

✕ Ohitotsuzen Tanbo Healthy meals featuring organic rice from the restaurant's own fields. (p125)

Plan Your Trip
Top Days in Tokyo

ENZOZO / SHUTTERSTOCK ©

West-Side Highlights

The neighbourhoods of Harajuku and Shinjuku, on the western edge of central Tokyo, make for a strong first impression: this is the Tokyo of skyscrapers and streets illuminated with many-coloured liquid-crystal lights; of bold architecture statements and even bolder fashion statements; and just enough tradition to give it all perspective.

Day

01

❶ Meiji-jingū

Tokyo's most famous Shintō shrine is shrouded in woods. It's a peaceful haven that feels worlds away from the city – though it is right in the thick of it. (And even more peaceful if you get here nice and early).

➲ Meiji-jingū to Omote-sandō

🏃 The broad boulevard Omote-sandō starts just across the street from the shrine entrance.

❷ Omote-sandō Architecture

Stroll down Omote-sandō to see the striking fashion boutiques, designed by Japan's leading contemporary architects, that line this wide, tree-lined boulevard.

➲ Omote-sandō to Maisen

🏃 The restaurant is a five-minute walk down a side street from Omote-sandō.

❸ Lunch at Maisen

Maisen is a Tokyo classic, serving up perfectly tender and crisp *tonkatsu* (breaded,

deep-fried pork cutlets) plus miso soup and cabbage salad in a cool old building that used to be a public bathhouse. (Bonus: lunch is a bargain.)

○ Maisen to Harajuku

✦ You're already here! Work your way back towards Harajuku Station along the side streets.

❹ Shopping in Harajuku

Harajuku is Tokyo's real-life catwalk, where the ultra-chic come to browse and be seen. Work your way through the snaking side alleys of Ura-Hara (the nickname for the side streets on either side of Omote-sandō), where the fashion, and the fashionistas, are edgier than on the main drag.

○ Harajuku to the Tokyo Metropolitan Government Building

🚃 Take the JR Yamanote line from Harajuku Station two stops north to Shinjuku, then walk 10 minutes to the government building from the west exit.

❺ Tokyo Metropolitan Government Building

The government building has observatories at 202m high that stay open until 11pm, so you can come for twinkling night views over the city. (Bonus: entry is free.)

○ Tokyo Metropolitan Government Building to the Park Hyatt

✦ It's just a five-minute walk from the city hall to the hotel.

❻ Drinks with a View

Choose between the sophisticated New York Bar, on the 52nd floor of the Park Hyatt hotel, or the excellent happy hour deal at Peak Bar, on the 41st floor. If you've still got steam, walk to the eastern side of Shinjuku Station, to see the crackling neon canyons of Tokyo's biggest and most colourful nightlife district.

From left: Meiji Jingū (p40); Prada Aoyama store (p55), Omote-sandō

Plan Your Trip
Top Days in Tokyo

TORWE_UITTENAI / GETTY IMAGES ©

Classic Sights of Central Tokyo

Spend your second day exploring Tokyo's more polished side in the central districts of Tsukiji, Ginza and Marunouchi. This area is home to many big-ticket attractions – the Imperial Palace, Tsukiji Outer Market, and the theatre, Kabukiza – as well as fine-dining and shopping options.

❶ Tsukiji Outer Market

Skip breakfast and head to Tokyo's iconic food market, where you can cobble together a morning meal of snacks from the market vendors. There are also stalls selling kitchen tools, tea and more. Come early before the market gets too crowded.

➡ Tsukiji Outer Market to Hama-rikyū Onshi-teien

🚶 It's an easy 10-minute walk from the market to the garden.

❷ Hama-rikyū Onshi-teien

From the bustling market, head to the quiet scenery of this classic landscape garden on the bay. There's a teahouse here, on an island in the middle of a placid pond, where you can have a pick-me-up bowl of bitter *matcha* tea.

➡ Hama-rikyū Onshi-teien to Kyūbey

🚕 Hop in a taxi; it should cost less than ¥1000. Otherwise, it's a 15-minute walk.

Day
02

❸ Lunch at Kyūbey

Splurge on lunch at this classy sushi counter, where you can indulge in a full tasting course of seasonal seafood. Bookings are only accepted for the first lunch seating at 11.30am; book well in advance or expect to queue for a later seating.

➲ Kyūbey to the Ginza Mitsukoshi

🏃 Work off lunch with a 10-minute stroll up Ginza's main drag, Chūō-dōri, to the department store.

❹ Mitsukoshi

Mitsukoshi is a quintessential Tokyo department store, with floors for pretty Japanese-style homewares, gourmet food products, and local and international fashion brands. It's the perfect place to start a shopping (or window-shopping) spree through stylish Ginza.

➲ Mitsukoshi to the Imperial Palace

🏃 It's a leisurely 15-minute walk from the department store to Hibiya then alongside the moat to the palace grounds.

❺ Imperial Palace

The majority of the compound, encased in a broad moat, remains off-limits to the general public, as it's the home of Japan's emperor. However, in the Imperial Palace East Garden you can admire the remains of the mammoth stone walls that once constituted Edo-jō, the largest fortress in the world.

➲ Imperial Palace to Kabukiza

🚇 Take the Hibiya line from Hibiya station two stops to Higashi-Ginza for the theatre.

❻ Kabukiza

Kabuki, a form of stylised traditional Japanese theatre, features stories based on popular legend and an all-male cast in dramatic make-up and decadent costumes. Catch a performance (or just a single act) at Kabukiza, Tokyo's principal kabuki theatre.

From left: Hama-rikyū Onshi-teien (p39); Imperial Palace (p104)

Plan Your Trip
Top Days in Tokyo

COVARDLION / SHUTTERSTOCK ©

The Historic East Side

Welcome to Tokyo's historic east side, which includes Ueno, long the cultural heart of Tokyo, with its park and museums; Yanaka, with its high concentration of traditional wooden buildings; and Asakusa, with its ancient temple and old-Tokyo atmosphere.

❶ Tokyo National Museum

Start with a morning at Japan's premier museum, which houses the world's largest collection of Japanese art and antiquities, including swords, gilded screens, kimonos and colourful *ukiyo-e* (woodblock prints). You'll need about two hours to hit the highlights.

↻ Tokyo National Museum to Ueno-kōen

🏃 The museum is on the edge of the park.

❷ Ueno-kōen

After the museum, take an hour or two to explore Ueno-kōen. Wend your way southward past the temples and shrines in the park, which include some of Tokyo's oldest standing buildings, to the large pond, Shinobazu-ike, choked with lotus flowers. There are cafes here, too.

↻ Ueno-kōen to Innsyoutei

🏃 The restaurant is in the park!

Day 03

PIYAWAN CHARGENLIMKUL / SHUTTERSTOCK ©

❸ Lunch at Innsyoutei

Innsyoutei, in a beautiful traditional structure that's over 140 years old, is one of the city's most charming lunch spots. It serves formal Japanese cuisine designed for the tea ceremony; bookings recommended.

➲ Innsyoutei to Yanaka

🚶 It's a 15-minute walk back through the park, to the northwest exit, where Yanaka begins.

❹ Walking in Yanaka

Yanaka is a neighbourhood with a high concentration of vintage wooden structures and more than a hundred temples. It's a rare pocket of Tokyo that miraculously survived the Great Kantō Earthquake and the allied fire-bombing of WWII to remain largely intact and a wonderful place to stroll.

➲ Yanaka to Sensō-ji

🚇 Take the Yamanote line from Nippori to Ueno then transfer for the Ginza subway line for Asakusa.

❺ Sensō-ji

The temple Sensō-ji was founded more than 1000 years before Tokyo got its start. Today the temple retains an alluring, lively atmosphere redolent of Edo (old Tokyo under the shogun). There are lots of shops selling traditional crafts and foodstuffs around here, too. Don't miss Sensō-ji all lit up from dusk.

➲ Sensō-ji to Oiwake

🚶 It's a 10-minute walk from the temple to the pub.

❻ Oiwake

Get a taste of entertainment old-Tokyo style at Oiwake, one of Tokyo's few remaining folk-music pubs. Here talented performers play *tsugaru-jamisen* (a banjo-like instrument) and other traditional instruments. Beer and classic pub food (like edamame) are served.

From left: Shinobazunoike Bentendo, Ueno-kōen (p68); Shop in Yanaka Ginza (p69)

Plan Your Trip
Top Days in Tokyo

Icons of Art & Pop Culture

On the agenda for your final day: culture, shopping and, most importantly, fun. This is a packed schedule, with a bit of running around, but it covers a lot of highlights – and some great souvenirs and photo ops in the process.

❶ Ghibli Museum

Take the train to the western suburb of Mitaka for a visit to the magical Ghibli Museum, created by famed animator Miyazaki Hayao (reservations necessary; we recommend getting in early at 10am). Afterwards walk through woodsy Inokashira-kōen to Kichijōji.

○ Ghibli Museum to Kikanbō

🚃 Take the JR Chūō line from Kichijōji to Kanda (25 minutes).

❷ Ramen at Kikanbō

Break for lunch at cult-favourite ramen shop Kikanbō, where you get to choose the level of spiciness and amount of noodles (careful: spicy really does mean spicy).

○ Kikanbō to Akihabara

🏃 It's a 10-minute walk, crossing the Kanda-gawa (Kanda River), or one stop on the JR Yamanote line, to Akihabara.

Day

04

BYENG / SHUTTERSTOCK ©

❸ Akihabara Pop Culture

In 'Akiba' you can shop for anime and manga; play retro video games at Super Potato Retro-kan; and ride go-karts – while dressed as video-game characters – through the streets (reserve ahead; international driving licence required).

○ Akihabara to Mori Art Museum

🚇 Take the Hibiya subway line from Akihabara to Roppongi, the nearest stop for the museum.

❹ Mori Art Museum

The excellent Mori Art Museum stages contemporary exhibits that include superstars of the art world from both Japan and abroad. Unlike most Tokyo museums, this one stays open until 10pm. Your ticket includes admission to Tokyo City View, the observatory on the 52nd floor of Mori Tower – if you want to get a last look of the city from this impressive vantage point.

○ Mori Art Museum to Shibuya Crossing

🚌 You can take the no 1 bus (¥210; 20 minutes), but a taxi will only cost about ¥1500 and is much easier.

❺ Shibuya Crossing

This epic intersection, lit by giant screens, has become synonymous with Tokyo. It's best seen in the evening when all the lights and signs are aglow. From here, the pedestrian traffic flows onto Shibuya Center-gai, the neighbourhood's lively main artery, lined with shops, cheap eateries and bars.

○ Shibuya Crossing to Karaoke-kan

🚶 The karaoke parlour is on Shibuya Center-gai, a five-minute walk from the crossing.

❻ Karaoke

End your last night with a time-honoured Tokyo tradition: singing yourself hoarse until the first trains start running again in the morning. Karaoke-kan is a classic Japanese karaoke parlour with tons of English-language songs from which to choose.

From left: Ghibli Museum (p92); Akihabara (p78)

Plan Your Trip
Need to Know

Daily Costs

Budget:
less than ¥8000

○ Dorm bed: ¥3000

○ Free sights such as temples and markets

○ Bowl of noodles: ¥800

○ Happy hour drink: ¥500

○ 24-hour subway pass: ¥600

Midrange:
¥8000–20,000

○ Double room at a business hotel: ¥14,000

○ Museum entry: ¥1000

○ Dinner for two at an *izakaya* (Japanese pub-eatery): ¥6000

○ Live music show: ¥3000

Top End:
more than ¥20,000

○ Double room in a four-star hotel: ¥35,000

○ Top-class sushi for two: ¥30,000

○ Orchestra seat for kabuki: ¥20,000

○ Taxi ride back to the hotel: ¥3000

Advance Planning

Three months before Purchase tickets for the Ghibli Museum; book a table at your top splurge restaurant.

One month before Book any tickets for sumo, kabuki and Giants games online; secure a spot on the Imperial Palace tour; scan web listings for festivals, events and exhibitions.

On arrival Look for free copies of *Time Out Tokyo, Tokyo Weekender* and *Metropolis* magazines at airports and hotels.

Useful Websites

Go Tokyo (www.gotokyo.org) The city's official website includes information on sights, events and suggested itineraries.

Lonely Planet (www.lonelyplanet.com/tokyo) Destination information, hotel bookings, traveller forum and more.

Time Out Tokyo (www.timeout.jp) Arts and entertainment listings.

Tokyo Food Page (www.bento.com) City-wide restaurant coverage.

Tokyo Cheapo (www.tokyocheapo.com) Hints on how to do Tokyo on the cheap.

Arriving in Tokyo

Narita Airport An express train or highway bus to central Tokyo costs around ¥3000 (one to two hours). Both run frequently from 6am to 10.30pm; pick up tickets at kiosks inside the arrivals hall (no advance reservations required). Fixed-fare taxis cost around ¥20,000.

Currency

Japanese yen (¥)

Language

Japanese

Visas

Visas are generally not required for stays of up to 90 days.

Money

Post offices and most convenience stores have international ATMs. Credit cards are accepted at major establishments, though it's best to keep cash on hand.

Mobile Phones

Purchase pre-paid data-only SIM cards (for unlocked smartphones only) online, at airport kiosks or electronics stores. For voice calls, rent a pay-as-you-go mobile.

Time

Japan Standard Time (GMT/UTC plus nine hours)

Tourist Information

Tokyo Tourist Information Center (p233) English-language information and publications.

For more, see the **Survival Guide** (p228)

When to Go

Spring and autumn are the best times to visit; August is hot and humid, but is also the month for summer festivals.

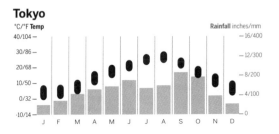

Tokyo

°C/°F **Temp**
40/104 —
30/86 —
20/68 —
10/50 —
0/32 —
-10/14 —

Rainfall inches/mm
— 16/400
— 12/300
— 8/200
— 4/100
— 0

J F M A M J J A S O N D

Haneda Airport Frequent trains and buses (¥400 to ¥1200, 30 to 45 minutes) to central Tokyo run frequently from 5.30am to midnight; times and costs depend on your destination in the city. There are only a couple of night buses. Budget between ¥6000 and ¥7000 for a cab.

Tokyo Station Connect from the *shinkansen* (bullet train) terminal here to the JR Yamanote line or the Marunouchi subway to destinations around central Tokyo.

Getting Around

Subway The quickest and easiest way to get around central Tokyo. Runs from 5am to midnight.

Train Japan Rail (JR) Yamanote (loop) and Chūō-Sōbu (central) lines service major stations. Runs from 5am to midnight.

Taxi Ubiquitous, and the only transport option that runs all night; unless you're stuck, taxis only make economical sense for groups of four.

Cycling A fun way to get around, though traffic can be intense. Rentals available; some hostels and ryokan (traditional Japanese inns) lend bicycles.

Walking Subway stations are close in the city centre; save cash by walking if you only need to go one stop.

What to Take

❍ Tokyo hotels can be tiny, so bring as small a suitcase as possible.

❍ You'll likely find yourself taking your shoes on and off at times and sitting on the floor, so it helps to have shoes that don't need lacing up. You might also want to pack socks even during sandal season (and second-guess that short skirt).

What to Wear

❍ Casual clothes are fine, but know that Tokyoites highly value a neat appearance.

❍ Some high-end restaurants and bars do have a dress code, but this usually just means no sleeveless shirts or sandals on men.

❍ There are no dress requirements for entering traditional Japanese religious sites.

Plan Your Trip
What's New

Above: Matcha tea set

Tokyo's Tourism Push

As the city prepares for the international spotlight during the 2020 Summer Olympics, more and more English is popping up in the form of navigational signs, apps, menus and brochures. More restaurants and shops are hiring English-speaking staff, too. Free city wi-fi, though still clunky, is improving.

Tsukiji Market Moving

After numerous delays, the date has been set for Tsukiji Market's move. From autumn 2018, the city's central wholesale market will operate out of a new facility in Toyosu. The popular Outer Market (p36), with its food stalls and kitchenware shops, is staying in Tsukiji.

New Experiences

One of the latest Tokyo crazes is racing around the city streets in go-karts – dressed like your favourite video-game character. MariCAR (p80) is the most popular operator. Another new trend is virtual-reality theme parks such as VR Zone Shinjuku (p200).

Tea & Sake

For years Tokyo was all about craft beer and coffee; now it's taking a second look at tea and sake – long seen as old-fashioned and uninteresting. New shops like Sakurai Japanese Tea Experience (p128) are giving *o-cha* (Japanese tea) new life; meanwhile bars such as Another 8 (p178) and Gem by Moto (p178) are part of the new wave of stylish sake bars.

Guesthouses Galore

The stylish hostels and guesthouses just keep coming. With new openings in central Tokyo neighbourhoods including Marunouchi and Roppongi, they're no longer confined to the east-side districts like Asakusa.

Plan Your Trip
For Free

Temples & Shrines

Shintō shrines are usually free in Tokyo and most Buddhist temples charge only to enter their *honden* (main hall) – meaning that two of the city's top sights, Meiji-jingū (p41) and Sensō-ji (p88) are free.

Parks & Gardens

Spend an afternoon people watching in one of Tokyo's excellent public parks, such as Yoyogi-kōen (p46) or Inokashira-kōen (p93). Grab a *bentō* (boxed meal) from a convenience store for a cheap and easy picnic.

Architecture

Prowl the city streets in search of the ambitious creations of Japan's leading architects. Omotesandō is great for this.

Festivals

Festivals are always happening in Tokyo – way more than we can list here; Go Tokyo (www.gotokyo.org) has a pretty comprehensive list. In the warmer months, festivals and markets, often hosted by Tokyo's ethnic communities and with live music, set up in Yoyogi-kōen (p46). And where there are festivals, there are usually street-food vendors.

24-hour Metro Pass

A great deal if you want to cram in the sights in a short stretch of time is Tokyo Metro's 24-hour pass (adult/child ¥600/300). You'll have to be strategic though, as the pass is only good for Tokyo Metro lines. For info see www.tokyometro.jp/en/ticket/value/index.html.

Discount Cards

The Grutto Pass (¥2200; www.rekibun.or.jp/grutto) gives you free or discounted admission to 92 attractions around town within two months – good value if you plan on visiting more than a few museums; all participating venues sell them. Also check hotel lobbies and TICs for discount coupons to city attractions.

JIRAT TEPARAKSA / SHUTTERSTOCK ©

Above: Tōkyū Plaza entrance (p54), Harajuku

Plan Your Trip
Family Travel

CLAIRE TAKACS / GETTY IMAGES ©

Sights & Activities

Tokyo is doable with little ones – it's a clean, well-run city after all – but it's better for older kids and teens, who will get a kick out of Tokyo's pop culture and neon streetscapes. Take them to explore the magical world of famed animator Miyazaki Hayao (*Ponyo, Spirited Away*) at the **Ghibli Museum** (p93) and to spot (and shop for) all their favourite characters at stores such as **Pokémon Center Mega Tokyo** (p154) and **KiddyLand** (p44). They'll also be able to participate in cultural activities, such as learning to make sushi rolls or their own woodblock prints. Young fashionistas will love shopping in Harajuku.

Unfortunately Tokyo's top sights – its museums, shrines and temples – don't make an effort to appeal to young visitors. Kids might enjoy the samurai armour and swords at the **Tokyo National Museum** (p65), and **Ueno Zoo** (p68) is nearby. The city does have lots of great parks, like **Yoyogi-kōen** (p46), **Inokashira-kōen**

(p93) and **Shinjuku-gyoen** (p73), for running around.

Karaoke is often associated with late-night drinking but can be a fantastic family activity. Major chain parlours usually have colourful rooms designed for kids (though regular rooms are fine, too – you can ask for a non-smoking one). Bonus: karaoke during the day is very cheap.

Also great fun: baseball games, seeing sumo wrestlers up close, amusement parks and introducing your kids to classic arcade games at **Super Potato Retro-kan** (p81).

Eating Out

Big chain restaurants (such as Jonathan's, Royal Host and Gusto) are the most family-friendly eating options: they have large booths, high chairs, non-smoking sections and children's menus. Unfortunately many central Tokyo restaurants are small, and often just not set up for littler ones (you might have to park the pram outside). This is the only issue though; kids will likely love the actual food: *gyōza* (dumplings),

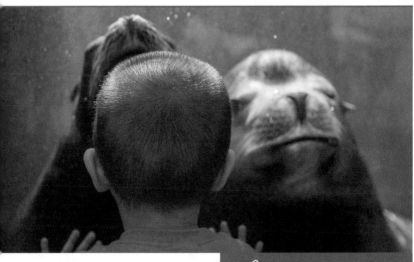

noodles, and sweets like *kakigōri* (flavoured shaved ice) and ice cream in flavours they may not have seen before. Convenience stores and bakeries are cheap, easy and ubiquitous sources of sandwiches and snacks.

Getting Around

You won't get much sympathy if you get on a crowded train during morning rush hour (7am to 9.30am) with a pram. If you must, children under 12 can ride with mums in the less-crowded women-only carriages. Otherwise the subway system is fairly child-friendly: priority seats exist for passengers who are pregnant or travelling with small children; most train stations and buildings in larger cities have lifts; and children between the ages of six and 11 ride for half-price on trains (under-sixes ride for free). Beware that side streets often lack pavements, though fortunately traffic is generally orderly in Tokyo.

Best Spots for Kids

Tokyo Disney Resort (p200)

Ghibli Museum (p93)

Tokyo Joypolis (p200)

Mokuhankan (p199)

Tokyo Dome (p198)

Need to Know

Resources If you're serious about touring Tokyo with tiny people, **Tokyo Urban Baby** (www.tokyourbanbaby.com) has the most comprehensive info, though it is not free.

Babysitting Babysitters (www.babysitters.jp) partners with many Tokyo hotels to provide English-speaking childcare workers.

Nappy Changing & Nursing Department stores and shopping malls always have nappy-changing facilities; newer ones have nursing rooms.

From left: Autumn leaves in Shinjuku-gyoen (p73); Face-to-face with sealions at Ueno Zoo (p68)

TOP EXPERIENCES

The very best to see & do

Tsukiji Outer Market

Tsukiji's Outer Market grew up organically around the neighbourhood's famed seafood and produce wholesale market, as a place for chefs to pick up anything else they might need, be it laver for wrapped sushi rolls, dried fish for making stock or a quick breakfast. While the wholesale market may be gone, this warren of tightly packed stalls with an old-Tokyo feel is staying put.

Great For...

❶ Need to Know

Tsukiji Outer Market (場外市場; Jōgai Shijō; 6-chōme Tsukiji, Chūō-ku; ⊙5am-2pm; ⓢHibiya line to Tsukiji, exit 1)

GUMPANAT THAVANKITDUMRONG / ALAMY STOCK PHOTO ©

After years of delay (and considerable controversy and protest), the metropolitan government decided to move Tsukiji's wholesale market to a new facility in Toyosu in 2018. But the city has no jurisdiction over the unofficial outer market (though they'd like to tidy it up a bit).

For most of its existence, the Outer Market was frequented only by food-industry professionals and a few zealous, in-the-know home cooks. In recent decades though, it has become an accidental hit – and one of Tokyo's top attractions. Restaurants that first opened to feed market workers now draw lines of tourists. Newer stalls have opened, aimed at this transient clientele. They sit alongside venerable old vendors, whose relationships with some of the city's top restaurants go back several generations.

Market Eats

Yamachō
Japanese ¥

(山長; Map p250; ☎03-3248-6002; 4-16-1 Tsukiji, Chūō-ku; omelette slices ¥100; ☻6am-3.30pm; ⓢHibiya line to Tsukiji, exit 1) Don't miss the delicious oblongs of sunshine-yellow egg on sticks sold at this venerable purveyor of *tamago-yaki* (Japanese rolled-egg omelettes). They come in a variety of flavours and you can watch them being expertly made as you line up to buy.

Kimagure-ya
Sandwiches ¥

(気まぐれ屋; Map p250; 6-21-6 Tsukiji, Chūō-ku; sandwiches ¥140-200; ☻5am-10am Mon-Sat; ⓢHibiya line to Tsukiji, exit 1) Locals adore the *ebi-katsu sando* (deep-fried prawn sandwiches) made by genial Matsubara-san out of a stall in his grandfather's old barber shop – and so will you. He also serves one

Tsukiji Outer Market

of the cheapest coffees (¥140) you'll find in Tokyo. The earlier you get here the better, as the sandwiches sell out fast.

Sushikuni   Japanese ¥¥
(鮨國; Map p250; ☑03-3545-8234; https://ameblo.jp/sushikuni; 4-14-15 Tsukiji, Chūō-ku; seafood rice bowls from ¥3000; ☺10am-3pm & 5-9pm Thu-Tue; ◍; ⑤Hibiya line to Tsukiji, exit 1) *Kaisen-don* (bowls of rice topped with raw fish) is a fish market staple and lots of shops in Tsukiji Outer Market sell it, but none are as good as Sushikuni. The toppings of rich, creamy *uni* (sea-urchin roe) and the salty pop of *ikura* (salmon roe) are generous and straight from the market. It's also open in the evenings.

Mosuke Dango   Sweets ¥
(モスケダンゴ; Map p250; ☑03-3549-8730; 4-14-18 Tsukiji, Chūō-ku; 3 for ¥450; ☺7am-3pm; ⑤Hibiya line to Tsukiji, exit 1) The original Mosuke, a street vendor, began making *dango* (dumplings) in 1898, back when the fish market was in Nihombashi. Today the eponymous shop makes *shōyu dango* (dumplings with soy sauce glaze) and *tsubuan dango* (dumplings made from chunky adzuki-bean paste) and more with organic adzuki beans from Hokkaidō and top brand Koshihikari rice from Niigata.

Shopping

In addition to dry goods like seaweed and green tea, the market has several shops selling specialist kitchenware items. Try **Tsukiji Hitachiya** (つきじ常陸屋; 4-14-18 Tsukiji, Chūō-ku; ☺8am-3pm Mon-Sat, 10am-2pm Sun; ⑤Hibiya line to Tsukiji, exit 1) for hand-forged knives, sturdy bamboo baskets and other great kitchen and cooking tools.

What's Nearby?

Hama-rikyū Onshi-teien   Gardens
(浜離宮恩賜庭園; Detached Palace Garden; Map p250; www.tokyo-park.or.jp/park/format/index028.html; 1-1 Hama-rikyū-teien, Chūō-ku; adult/child/senior ¥300/free/¥150; ☺9am-5pm; ⑤Ōedo line to Shiodome, exit A1) This beautiful garden, one of Tokyo's finest, was once part of a seaside villa owned by the shogun. The main features are a large duck pond with an island that's home to a charming tea pavilion, Nakajima no Ochaya (p141), as well as some wonderfully manicured trees (black pine, Japanese apricot, hydrangeas etc), some of which are hundreds of years old.

> ☑ **Don't Miss**
> A highlight of visiting the market is the food vendors, hawking freshly shucked oysters, deep-fried fish cakes and more.

FIIPHOTO / SHUTTERSTOCK ©

> ✕ **Take a Break**
> Grab a latte from nearby Turret Coffee (p141).

Chōzubachi (water basin for ritual ablutions)

Meiji-jingū

Tokyo's grandest Shintō shrine feels a world away from the city. The grounds are vast, enveloping the classic wooden shrine buildings and a landscaped garden in a thick coat of green.

Great For...

☑ **Don't Miss**

Festivals, ceremonies and events (all free!) are held here throughout the year; check the website for a schedule.

Meiji-jingū is dedicated to the Emperor Meiji and Empress Shōken, whose reign (1868–1912) coincided with Japan's transformation from isolationist, feudal state to modern nation. Constructed in 1920, the shrine was destroyed in WWII air raids and rebuilt in 1958; however, unlike so many of Japan's postwar reconstructions, Meiji-jingū has atmosphere in spades. In preparation for its centennial in 2020, Meiji-jingū is currently undergoing renovations. Some structures may be under wraps, but the shrine as a whole will remain open.

The Shrine

The shrine is secreted in a wooded grove, accessed via a long winding gravel path. At the entrance you'll pass through the first of several towering, wooden *torii* (shrine gates). These mark the boundary between

Ema (prayer boards)

⊙ Meiji-jingū

Yoyogi-kōen

Harajuku **Ⓢ** Meiji-jingūmae

Meiji-dōri

Takeshita-dōri

❶ Need to Know

Meiji-jingū (明治神宮; www.meijijingu. or.jp; 1-1 Yoyogi Kamizono-chō, Shibuya-ku; dawn-dusk; JR Yamanote line to Harajuku, Omote-sandō exit) FREE

✕ Take a Break

Coffee shop **Mori no Terrace** (杜の テラス; Map p246; ☏03-3379-9222; 1-1 Yoyogi Kamizono-chō, Shibuya-ku; coffee & tea ¥400; 9am-dusk; JR Yamanote line to Harajuku, Omote-sandō exit) is near the main gate.

★ Top Tip

The rule of photo taking here is this: if there's a roof over your head, it's a no-go.

the mundane world and the sacred one; as such, it's the custom to bow upon passing through a *torii*.

Just before the final *torii* is the *temizuya* (font), where visitors purify themselves by pouring water over their hands (purity is a tenet of Shintoism). To do so, dip the ladle in the water and first rinse your left hand then your right. Pour some water into your left hand and rinse your mouth, then rinse your left hand again. Make sure none of this water gets back into the font!

The main shrine, built of unpainted cypress wood, sparkles with a new copper-plated roof (part of the centennial restoration). To make an offering here (and, if you like, a wish), toss a coin – a ¥5 coin is considered lucky – into the box, bow twice, clap your hands twice and then bow again.

To the right, you'll see kiosks selling *ema* (wooden plaques on which prayers are written), along with racks where the plaques are strung. The same kiosks also sell *omamori* – charms for good health, success in school entrance exams and, our personal favourite, safe travel.

The Gardens

The shrine itself occupies only a small fraction of the sprawling forested grounds, which contain some 120,000 trees collected from all over Japan. Of this, only the strolling garden **Meiji-jingū Gyoen** (明治神宮御苑; Map p246; Inner Garden; ¥500; 9am-4.30pm, to 4pm Nov-Feb; JR Yamanote line to Harajuku, Omote-Sandō exit) is accessible to the public – the entrance is halfway down the gravel path to the shrine. There are peaceful walks, a good dose of privacy on weekdays and spectacular irises in June.

Street fashion stall, Takeshita-dōri

CARL FORBES / SHUTTERSTOCK ©

Shopping in Harajuku

Harajuku is the gathering point for Tokyo's diverse fashion tribes – the trendy teens, the fashion-forward peacocks and the polished divas. For shopping (and people watching), there's no better spot in Tokyo.

Great For...

☑ Don't Miss

Exploring Harajuku's maze-like (and surprise-filled) side streets.

Omote-sandō is the wide boulevard that cuts through Harajuku (between JR Harajuku Station and the Omote-sandō subway station); many European fashion houses have boutiques here. For edgier local stuff, head to the narrow streets on either side of the boulevard – the area known as Ura-Hara ('back' Harajuku). The pedestrian-only Cat Street (perpendicular to Omote-sandō) has a mish-mash of local and international boutiques.

Closer to Harajuku Station the shops tend to be more youth-oriented, while those closer to Omote-sandō Station are more sophisticated. This trend continues beyond Omote-sandō Station, in the upscale Aoyama district where the legends of Japanese fashion design – Issey Miyake, Yohji Yamamoto and Comme des Garçons – have their flagship boutiques.

❶ Need to Know

The JR Yamanote line stops at Harajuku. Subway stations Meiji-jingūmae and Omote-sandō are also convenient.

✕ Take Break

Refuel at Koffee Mameya (p130).

★ Top Tip

For serious shopping, avoid weekends, when Harajuku gets very crowded.

shocking today as it once did speaks volumes for her far-reaching success. This eccentric, vaguely disorienting architectural creation is her brand's flagship store.

Laforet Fashion & Accessories
(ラフォーレ; Map p246; www.laforet.ne.jp; 1-11-6 Jingūmae, Shibuya-ku; ⊘11am-9pm; ⓡJR Yamanote line to Harajuku, Omote-sandō exit) Laforet has been a beacon of cutting-edge Harajuku style for decades and lots of quirky, cult favourite brands still cut their teeth here (you'll find some examples at the ground-floor boutique, Wall). A range of looks are represented here from *ame-kaji* (American casual) to gothic (in the basement).

Comme des Garçons Fashion & Accessories
(コム・デ・ギャルソン; Map p246; www. comme-des-garcons.com; 5-2-1 Minami-Aoyama, Minato-ku; ⊘11am-8pm; ⓢGinza line to Omote-sandō, exit A5) Designer Kawakubo Rei threw a wrench in the fashion machine in the early '80s with her dark, asymmetrical designs. That her work doesn't appear as

Sou-Sou Fashion & Accessories
(そうそう; Map p246; ☎03-3407-7877; http:// sousounetshop.jp; 5-3-10 Minami-Aoyama, Minato-ku; ⊘11am-8pm; ⓢGinza line to Omote-sandō, exit A5) Kyoto brand Sou-Sou gives traditional Japanese clothing items – such as split-toed *tabi* socks and *haori* (coats with kimono-like sleeves) – a contemporary spin. It is best known for producing the steel-toed, rubber-soled *jika-tabi* shoes worn by Japanese construction workers in fun, playful designs, but it also carries bags, tees and super-adorable children's clothing.

House @Mikiri Hassin Fashion & Accessories
(ハウス@ミキリハッシン; Map p246; ☎03-3486-7673; http://house.mikirihassin.co.jp; 5-42-1 Jingūmae, Shibuya-ku; ⊘noon-9pm Thu-Tue; ⓢGinza line to Omote-sandō, exit A1) Hidden

deep in Ura-Hara (Harajuku's backstreet area), House stocks an ever-changing selection of avant-garde Japanese fashion brands. Contrary to what the cool merch might suggest, the sales clerks are polite and friendly – grateful, perhaps, that you made the effort to find the place. Look for 'ハウス' spelled vertically in neon.

Arts & Science · Fashion & Accessories
(Map p246; http://arts-science.com/; 101, 103, 105 & 109 Palace Aoyama, 6-1-6 Minami-Aoyama, Minato-ku; ◷noon-8pm; Ⓢ Ginza line to Omote-sandō, exit A5) Strung along the 1st floor of a mid-century apartment (across from the Nezu Museum) is a collection of small boutiques from celebrity stylist Sonya Park. Park's signature style is a vintage-inspired minimalism in luxurious, natural fabrics. Homewares, too.

Musubi · Arts & Crafts
(むす美; Map p246; ☏03-5414-5678; http://kyoto-musubi.com; 2-31-8 Jingūmae, Shibuya-ku; ◷11am-7pm Thu-Tue; ⓇJR Yamanote line to Harajuku, Takeshita exit) *Furoshiki* are versatile squares of cloth that can be folded and knotted to make shopping bags and gift wrap. This shop sells pretty ones in both traditional and contemporary patterns – sometimes in collaboration with designers or fashion brands. There is usually an English-speaking clerk who can show you how to tie them.

KiddyLand · Toys
(キデイランド; Map p246; ☏03-3409-3431; www.kiddyland.co.jp; 6-1-9 Jingūmae, Shibuya-ku; ◷11am-9pm; ⓇJR Yamanote line to Harajuku, Omote-sandō exit) This multi-storey toy emporium is packed to the rafters with

Yoyogi-kōen (p46)

character goods, including all your Studio Ghibli, Sanrio and Disney faves. It's not just for kids, either; you'll spot plenty of adults on a nostalgia trip down the Hello Kitty aisle.

Fake Tokyo   Fashion & Accessories
(Map p246; www.faketokyo.com; 6-23-12 Jingū-mae, Shibuya-ku; ◷noon-10pm; 🚃JR Yamanote line to Shibuya, Hachikō exit) This is one of the best places in the city to discover hot underground Japanese designers. It's actually two shops in one: downstairs is **Candy** (www.candy-nippon.com), full of brash, unisex streetwear; upstairs is **Sister** (http://

> ★ **Local Knowledge**
> Trends move fast in Harajuku. To keep up with the latest, follow @TokyoFashion on Twitter.

SIMON LONG / GETTY IMAGES ©

sister-tokyo.com), which specialises in more ladylike items, both new and vintage.

Pass the Baton   Vintage
(パスザバトン; Map p246; ☎03-6447-0707; www.pass-the-baton.com; 4-12-10 Jingūmae, Shibuya-ku; ◷11am-9pm Mon-Sat, to 8pm Sun; 🚇Ginza line to Omote-sandō, exit A3) There are all sorts of treasures to be found at this consignment shop, from 1970s designer duds to delicate teacups, personal castaways to dead stock from long defunct retailers. It's in the basement of Omotesandō Hills, but you'll need to enter from a separate street entrance on Omote-sandō.

6% Doki Doki   Fashion & Accessories
(ロクパーセントドキドキ; Map p246; www.dokidoki6.com; 2nd fl, 4-28-16 Jingūmae, Shibuya-ku; ◷noon-8pm; 🚃JR Yamanote line to Harajuku, Omote-sandō exit) Tucked away on an Ura-Hara backstreet, this bubblegum-pink store sells acid-bright accessories that are part raver, part schoolgirl and, according to the shop's name, 'six percent exciting'. We wonder what more excitement would look like! Anyway, it's 100% Harajuku.

Gallery Kawano   Clothing
(ギャラリー川野; Map p246; www.gallery-kawano.com; 4-4-9 Jingūmae, Shibuya-ku; ◷11am-6pm; 🚇Ginza line to Omote-sandō, exit A2) Gallery Kawano has a good selection of vintage kimonos in decent shape, priced reasonably (about ¥7000 to ¥25,000). The knowledgeable staff will help you try them on and pick out a matching *obi* (sash); they're less excited about helping customers who try things on but don't intend to buy. Crafty types can pick up kimono scrap fabric here, too.

RagTag   Clothing
(ラグタグ; Map p246; ☎03-6419-3770; www.ragtag.jp; 6-14-2 Jingūmae, Shibuya-ku;

> ★ **Top Tip**
> Combine a day of shopping with a tour of Omote-sandō's contemporary architecture.

⏱11am-8pm; 🚉JR Yamanote line to Harajuku, Omote-Sandō exit) This *risaikuru shoppu* ('recycle shop' – second-hand clothing shop) is stocked with labels loved by Harajuku kids, such as Comme des Garçons and Vivienne Westwood (for men and women).

Chicago Thrift Store   Vintage
(シカゴ; Map p246; www.chicago.co.jp; 6-31-21 Jingūmae, Shibuya-ku; ⏱10am-8pm; 🚉JR Yamanote line to Harajuku, Omote-sandō exit) Chicago is crammed with all sorts of vintage clothing, but best of all is the extensive collection of used kimono and *yukata*, priced very low, in the back. They have a few other stores in the neighbourhood, too.

What's Nearby
Takeshita-dōri   Area
(竹下通り; Map p246; 🚉JR Yamanote line to Harajuku, Takeshita exit) This is Tokyo's famously outré fashion bazaar, where trendy duds sit alongside the trappings of decades of fashion subcultures (plaid and safety pins for the punks; colourful tutus for the *decora;* Victorian dresses for the Gothic Lolitas). Be warned: this pedestrian alley is a pilgrimage site for teens from all over Japan, which means it can get packed.

Ukiyo-e Ōta Memorial Museum of Art   Museum
(浮世絵太田記念美術館; Map p246; ☎03-3403-0880; www.ukiyoe-ota-muse.jp; 1-10-10 Jingūmae, Shibuya-ku; adult/child ¥700-1000/free; ⏱10.30am-5.30pm Tue-Sun; 🚉JR Yamanote line to Harajuku, Omote-sandō exit) Change into slippers to enter the peaceful, hushed museum that houses the excellent *ukiyo-e* (woodblock print) collection of Ōta Seizo, the former head of the Toho Life Insurance Company. Seasonal, thematic exhibitions are easily digested in an hour and usually include a few works by masters such as Hokusai and Hiroshige. It's often closed the last few days of the month.

Yoyogi-kōen   Park
(代々木公園; Map p246; www.yoyogipark.info; 🚉JR Yamanote line to Harajuku, Omote-sandō exit) If it's a sunny and warm weekend afternoon, you can count on there being a crowd lazing around the large grassy expanse that is Yoyogi-kōen. You can also usually find revellers and noisemakers of all stripes, from hula-hoopers to African drum circles to a group of retro greasers dancing around a boom box. It's an excellent place for a picnic and probably the only place in the city where you can reasonably toss a frisbee without fear of hitting someone.

Nezu Museum   Museum
(根津美術館; Map p246; ☎03-3400-2536; www.nezu-muse.or.jp; 6-5-1 Minami-Aoyama, Minato-ku; adult/student/child ¥1100/800/free, special exhibitions extra ¥200; ⏱10am-5pm Tue-Sun; 🚇Ginza line to Omote-sandō, exit A5) Nezu Museum offers a striking blend of old and new: a renowned collection of Japanese, Chinese and Korean antiquities in a gallery

Crowds filling Takeshita-dōri

space designed by contemporary architect Kuma Kengo. Select items from the extensive collection are displayed in seasonal exhibitions. The English explanations are usually pretty good. Behind the galleries is a woodsy strolling garden laced with stone paths and studded with teahouses and sculptures.

Design Festa   Gallery
(デザインフェスタ; Map p246; ☏03-3479-1442; www.designfestagallery.com; 3-20-2 Jingūmae, Shibuya-ku; ⓒ11am-7pm; ☒JR Yamanote line to Harajuku, Takeshita exit) **FREE** Design Festa has been a leader in Tokyo's DIY art scene for nearly two decades. The madhouse building itself is worth a visit; it's always evolving. Inside there are dozens of small galleries rented by the day. More often than not, the artists themselves are hanging around, too.

Espace Louis Vuitton Tokyo   Gallery
(エスパス ルイ・ヴィトン東京; Map p246; www.espacelouisvuittontokyo.com; 7th fl, Louis Vuitton Omote-sandō, 5-7-5 Jingūmae, Shibuya-ku; ⓒnoon-8pm; ☒Ginza line to Omote-sandō, exit A1) **FREE** Atop Aoki Jun's Louis Vuitton boutique, this light-filled gallery plays host to installations (sometimes designed with the space in mind) from the collection of the luxury brand's well-endowed arts foundation.

✕ Take a Break
Escape the crowds into the hushed comfort of Montoak (p131).

★ Local Knowledge
Pop star and fashion icon Kyary Pamyu Pamyu (@pamyurin) is Harajuku's official ambassador of 'kawaii'.

Tokyo International Forum (p52)

Contemporary Architecture

Tokyo's willingness to experiment with contemporary architecture seems at odds with its practical approach to just about everything else. But of course, Japan's architects are among the most celebrated in the world and this city is their showcase. Tokyo has long been a source of inspiration for designers around the world; perhaps it will be for you, too.

Great For...

ℹ Need to Know

Sights are scattered around the city; several are free.

★ **Top Tip**

Tours of Reversible Destiny Lofts and Nakagin Capsule Tower happen a few times a month and must be booked in advance.

Architects in Japan

Japanese architecture really came into its own in the 1960s. Tange Kenzō (1913–2005) was the most influential architect of the age. He was influenced by both traditional Japanese forms and the aggressively sculptural works of French architect Le Corbusier. For decades in the mid to late 20th century, Tange was Tokyo's choice for monumental projects.

Concurrent with Tange were the 'metabolists', who promoted flexible spaces and functions at the expense of fixed forms. Design-wise, they were a radical bunch who produced a number of fascinating sketches and plans, the majority of which went unbuilt. Maki Fumihiko (b 1928) was the most realistic of the bunch; his buildings use geometric shapes in unexpected ways and make use of new and varied materials.

The next generation, which includes Andō Tadao (b 1941) and Itō Toyō (b 1941), continue to explore both modernism and postmodernism, while mining Japan's architectural heritage. Andō's works are heavy, grounded and monumental; his favourite medium is concrete. Itō's designs are lighter and more conceptual. Sejima Kazuyo (b 1956) and Nishizawa Ryue (b 1966) who helm the firm SANAA are noted for their luminous form-follows-function spaces.

Kengo Kuma (b 1954) has received a number of high-profile commissions lately – including the new National Stadium to be completed for the 2020 Tokyo Summer Olympics. He is considered Tange's successor in terms of impact, but not in style: Kengo is known for his use of wood and light.

Top Sights

The adjacent districts Harajuku and Aoyama are rich in contemporary architecture, mostly in the form of designer boutiques along Omote-sandō (p51), but Yoyogi National Stadium (p53) and Spiral Building (p53) are also here.

Tokyo Metropolitan Government Building   Notable Building

(東京都庁; Tokyo Tochō; Map p253; www.metro. tokyo.jp/ENGLISH/OFFICES/observat.htm; 2-8-1 Nishi-Shinjuku, Shinjuku-ku; ⊗observatories

Nakagin Capsule Tower (p52)

☑ Don't Miss

The view from the free observatory atop the Tokyo Metropolitan Government Building.

---

❶ Need to Know

Many museums are also worth a visit just for their design, such as the Nezu Museum (p46) and the Gallery of Hōryū-ji Treasures at the Tokyo National Museum (p65).

9.30am-11pm; S Ōedo line to Tochōmae, exit A4)
FREE Tokyo's seat of power, designed by
Tange Kenzō and completed in 1991, looms
large and looks somewhat like a pixelated
cathedral (or the lair of an animated villain).
Take an elevator from the ground floor of
Building 1 to one of the twin 202m-high
observatories for panoramic views over
the never-ending cityscape (the views are
virtually the same from either tower). On a
clear day (morning is best), you may catch
a glimpse of Mt Fuji to the west.

Archi-Depot   Gallery

(建築倉庫; Kenchiku Sōko; ☑03-5769-2133;
http://archi-depot.com; Warehouse Terrada,
2-6-10 Higashi-Shinagawa, Shinagawa-ku; adult/
student/child ¥2000/1000/free; ☉11am-8pm
Tue-Sun; ☒Rinkai line to Tennōzu Isle, exit B)
This is brilliant: a facility that lets architects
store the miniature models they make to
conceptualise buildings (thus preserving
them) and lets the public see them up
close. Many of the big names of Japanese
architecture are represented here (Ban
Shigero, Kuma Kengo). It looks very much
like a storage room too, with the models
sitting on rows of metal shelves (and not
behind glass). Information about the architects can be accessed through QR codes.
Archi-Depot is on bayside Tennōzu Isle,
which is awkward to get to by train; a taxi
here from Tsukiji or Ginza should cost
around ¥2500.

Omote-sandō   Area

(表参道; Map p246; S Ginza line to Omote-sandō,
exits A3 & B4, ☒JR Yamanote line to Harajuku,
Omote-sandō exit) This regal, tree-lined
boulevard was originally designed as the
official approach to Meiji-jingū. Now it's
a fashionable strip lined with high-end

boutiques. Those designer shops come in designer buildings, which means Omote-sandō is one of the best places in the city to see contemporary architecture. Highlights include the Dior boutique by SANAA (Nishizawa Ryue and Sejima Kazuyo) and the Tod's boutique by Itō Toyō.

21_21 Design Sight   Exhibition Space

(21_21デザインサイト; Map p252; ☏03-3475-2121; www.2121designsight.jp; Tokyo Midtown, 9-7-6 Akasaka, Minato-ku; adult/student/child ¥1100/800/free; ⏰11am-7pm Wed-Mon; ⑤Ōedo line to Roppongi, exit 8) An exhibition and discussion space dedicated to all forms of design, the 21_21 Design Sight acts as a beacon for local art enthusiasts, whether they be designers themselves or simply onlookers. The striking concrete and glass building, bursting out of the ground at sharp angles, was designed by Pritzker Prize–winning architect Andō Tadao.

Reversible Destiny Lofts   Architecture

(天命反転住宅; Tenmei Hanten Jūtaku; ☏0422-26-4966; www.rdloftsmitaka.com; 2-2-8 Ōsawa, Mitaka-shi; adult/child ¥2700/1000; ♿; ℝJR Sōbu-Chūō line to Mitaka, south exit) Designed by husband and wife Arakawa Shūsaku (1936–2010) and Madeleine Gins (1941–2014) and completed in 2005, this housing complex certainly strikes against the mould: Created 'in memory of Helen Keller' the nine units have undulating, ridged floors, spherical dens and ceiling hooks for hammocks and swings. All this is meant to create a sensory experience beyond the visual (though the building is plenty colourful). Inside access is by tour only (check the website); the guides can speak some English.

From JR Mitaka Station, take bus 51 or 52 (¥220, 15 minutes, every 10 to 15 minutes) from bus stop 2 on the station's south side and get off at Ōsawa Jūjiro (大沢十字路); you can see the building from the bus stop. Not all buses go this far, so show the driver where you want to go.

Nakagin Capsule Tower   Architecture

(中銀カプセルタワー; Map p250; 8-16-10 Ginza, Chūō-ku; ⑤Ōedo line to Tsukijishijō, exit A3) A Facebook campaign has been started by some residents and fans to save Kurokawa Kishō's early-1970s building, which is a seminal work of Metabolist architecture. The tower's self-contained pods, which can be removed whole from a central core and replaced elsewhere, are in various states of decay and the building is swathed in netting, but it's still a very impressive design.

Tokyo International Forum   Architecture

(東京国際フォーラム; Map p253; ☏03-5221-9000; www.t-i-forum.co.jp; 3-5-1 Marunouchi, Chiyoda-ku; ⏰7am-11.30pm; ℝJR Yamanote line to Yūrakuchō, central exit) FREE This

21_21 Design Sight

architectural marvel designed by Rafael Viñoly houses a convention and arts centre, with eight auditoriums and a spacious courtyard in which concerts and events are held. The eastern wing looks like a glass ship plying the urban waters; you can access the catwalks from the 7th floor (take the lift).

Also visit for the twice-monthly **Ōedo Antique Market** (大江戸骨董市; ☑03-6407-6011; www.antique-market.jp; 3-5-1 Marunouchi, Chiyoda-ku; ◎9am-4pm 1st & 3rd Sun of the month; ⑲ JR Yamanote line to Yūrakuchō, Kokusai Forum exit) and food trucks serving bargain meals and drinks to local office workers at lunch Monday to Friday.

Spiral Building   Architecture
(スパイラルビル; Map p246; ☑03-3498-1171; www.spiral.co.jp; 5-6-23 Minami-Aoyama,

Minato-ku; ◎11am-8pm; Ⓢ Ginza line to Omote-sandō, exit B1) **FREE** The asymmetrical, geometric shape of architect Maki Fumihiko's Spiral Building (1985) may not look very sinuous on the outside, but the name will make more sense upon entry. The patch-work, uncentred design is a nod to Tokyo's own incongruous landscape. The spiralling passage inside doubles as an art gallery.

✗ Take a Break
Sakurai Japanese Tea Experience (p128) is inside Spiral Building.

☑ Don't Miss
If you're visiting Sensō-ji (p88) look for Philippe Starck's Super Dry Hall (p91) across the river.

K SHUN / SHUTTERSTOCK ©

Walking Tour: Omote-sandō Architecture

Omote-sandō, a broad, tree-lined boulevard running through Harajuku, is known for its parade of upmarket boutiques designed by the who's who of (mostly) Japanese contemporary architects.

Start Tōkyū Plaza
Distance 1.5km
Duration One hour

2 Andō Tadao's deceptively deep **Omotesandō Hills** (2003; 表参道 ヒルズ; 4-12-10 Jingūmae,Shibuya-ku) is a high-end shopping mall spiralling around a sunken central atrium.

1 Tōkyū Plaza (2012; 東急プラザ; 4-30-3 Jingūmae,Shibuya-ku), is a castle-like structure by up-and-coming architect Nakamura Hiroshi. There's a spacious roof garden on top.

3 The flagship boutique for **Dior** (2003; 5-9-11 Jingūmae,Shibuya-ku), designed by SANAA (composed of Sejima Kazuyo and Nishizawa Ryūe), has a filmy, white exterior that seems to hang like a dress.

4 Meant to evoke a stack of clothes trunks, Aoki Jun's design for **Louis Vuitton** (2002) features offset panels of tinted glass behind sheets of metal mesh of varying patterns. Gallery **Espace Louis Vuitton Tokyo** (p47) is on the top floor.

6 Maki Fumihiko's **Spiral Building** (1985) is a postmodern landmark from an earlier era; there's an art gallery inside. (p53)

5 The criss-crossing strips of concrete on Itō Toyō's construction for **Tod's** (2004; 5-1-15 Jingūmae, Shibuya-ku) take their inspiration from the zelkova trees below.

JINGUMAE

URA-HARA

Take a Break...
Anniversaire Café (アニヴェルセル カフェ; http://cafe.anniversaire.co.jp; ⊘11am-10pm Mon-Fri, 9am-10pm Sat & Sun) has an attractive patio that is perfect for people watching.

Classic Photo Close-up of the bubbly facade of the Prada building.

7 Herzog and de Meuron designed this convex glass fish bowl for **Prada** (2003; 5-2-6 Minami-Aoyama, Minato-ku).

KITA-AOYAMA

Omote-sando

Omote-sando

Aoyama-dori

MINAMI-AOYAMA

FINISH

Shimo-kitazawa street

WORLD DISCOVERY / ALAMY STOCK PHOTO ©

A Night Out in Shimo-Kitazawa

For generations, Shimokita (as it's called here) has been a hang-out for musicians, artists and actors – it's among this city's last bastions of bohemia. Spend an evening here and raise your glass to (and with) the characters committed to keeping Shimokita weird.

Great For...

☑ **Don't Miss**

Making new friends – typically small Shimokita bars have a social vibe.

Ghetto   Bar

(月灯; 1-45-16 Daizawa, Setagaya-ku; ⊙8.30pm-late; 🚊Keiō Inokashira line to Shimo-Kitazawa, south exit) What are the odds that the characters for 'moon' and 'light' could be pronounced together as 'ghetto'? It's not unlike the uncommon synergy that comes together nightly as musicians, travellers and well-intentioned salarymen (and others) descend on this little bar in the rambling Suzunari theatre complex. By open until late we mean very, very late. No cover charge; drinks from ¥600.

Mother   Bar

(マザー; ☎03-3421-9519; www.rock-mother. com; 5-36-14 Daizawa, Setagaya-ku; ⊙5pm-2am Sun-Thu, 5pm-5am Fri & Sat; 🔖; 🚊Keiō Inokashi-ra line to Shimo-Kitazawa, south exit) Mother is a classic Shimo-Kitazawa bar with a soundtrack from the '60s and '70s and

❶ Need to Know

Shimo-Kitazawa (下北沢; Setagaya-ku; ℝKeiō Inokashira Line to Shimo-Kitazawa)

✕ Take a Break

Go for a meal at local pub fave *izakaya* Shirube (p131).

★ Top Tip

Shimokita nightlife really gets going late, and keeps going until morning.

an undulating, womb-like interior covered in mosaic tile. There's a good line-up of *shochu* drinks and cocktails (from ¥600) as well as Okinawan and Southeast Asian food on the menu. Don't miss the made-in-house 'mori' liquor, served from a glass skull. No cover.

Never Never Land   Bar

(ネヴァーネヴァーランド; 2nd fl, 3-19-3 Kitazawa, Setagaya-ku; ⊙6pm-2am; 🗐; ℝKeiō Inokashira line to Shimo-Kitazawa, north exit) Smoky, loud and filled with bohemian characters, Never Never Land is a long-running fixture on Shimokita's bar circuit. It's a good place to wind up when you're in need of food – the bar snacks are tasty Okinawan dishes. Cover is ¥200; food and drink from ¥500. Look for the twinkling lights in the window.

Trouble Peach   Bar

(トラブル・ピーチ; ☎03-3460-1468; 2nd fl, 2-9-18 Kitazawa, Setagaya-ku; cover ¥400; ⊙7pm-7am; 🗐; ℝKeiō Inokashira line to Shimo-Kitazawa, south exit) Pretty much everything here is chipped, frayed or torn – and none of it is artifice. This is a well-worn and well-loved bar, open for some 40-odd years, and still playing vinyl. It looks primed for demolition but has somehow managed to survive. Drinks from ¥600. Look for the neon sign by the tracks.

Shimo-Kitazawa Cage   Beer Garden

(下北沢ケージ; http://s-cage.com; 2-6-2 Kitazawa, Setagaya-ku; ⊙1-11pm; 🚼; ℝOdakyū line to Shimo-Kitazawa, south exit) Winning the award for most literal name, Shimo-Kitazawa Cage is a fenced-off cube under the Keiō Inokashira Line tracks. Get beers and snacks (from ¥400) from the Thai food kiosk and grab a picnic table. There's a night market every Wednesday and other one-off events. The Cage is a temporary space and will depart sometime in 2019.

Day Trip: Mt Fuji

Catching a glimpse of Mt Fuji (富士山; 3776m), Japan's highest and most famous peak, will take your breath away. Dawn from the summit? Pure magic (even when it's cloudy). Fuji-san is among Japan's most revered and timeless attractions. Hundreds of thousands of people climb it every year, continuing a centuries-old tradition of pilgrimages up the sacred volcano.

Great For...

ⓘ Need to Know

The official climbing season runs from 1 July to 10 September.

★ Top Tip

Check summit weather conditions before planning a climb at www.snow-forecast.com/resorts/Mount-Fuji/6day/top.

Climbing Mt Fuji

There are four trails up Mt Fuji: Yoshida, Subashiri, Gotemba and Fujinomiya. The mountain is divided into 10 'stations' from base (first station) to summit (10th); however, the trails start at the fifth station, which is accessible by road.

The **Yoshida Trail** is far and away the most popular route up the mountain, because buses run directly from Tokyo to the trailhead at the **Fuji Subaru Line Fifth Station** (at 2300m; sometimes called the Kawaguchi-ko Fifth Station or just Mt Fuji Fifth Station). It also has the most huts (with food, water and toilets).

For this hike, allow five to six hours to reach the top and about three hours to descend, plus 1½ hours for circling the crater at the top. When descending, make sure you don't wind up going down the Subashiri

Trail, which intersects with the Yoshida Trail at the 8th station. The Gotemba Trail is the steepest and takes the longest to climb.

Know Before You Climb

Make no mistake: Mt Fuji is a serious mountain and a reasonable amount of fitness is required. It's high enough for altitude sickness, and on the summit it can go from sunny and warm to wet, windy and cold remarkably quickly. Even if conditions are fine, you can count on it being close to freezing in the morning, even in summer. Visibility can rapidly disappear.

At a minimum, bring clothing appropriate for cold and wet weather, including a hat and gloves. If you're climbing at night, bring a torch (flashlight) or headlamp, and spare batteries. Water and food are available from mountain huts, but at a significant

Hikers viewing sunrise from Mt Fuji summit

mark-up (and you'll need cash); mountain huts also have toilets (¥200).

Descending the mountain is much harder on the knees than ascending; hiking poles will help. To avoid altitude sickness, be sure to take it slowly and take regular breaks. If you're suffering severe symptoms, you'll need to make an immediate descent.

Timing Your Climb

Most climbers aim to get to the top just before dawn, but not too much before dawn (because it will be cold and windy). One strategy, the most popular, is to start out around 9pm or 10pm and climb through

the night. The other is to start in the afternoon, sleep for a bit in a mountain hut halfway up the mountain and then begin again in the early morning hours. This is the safer approach, as it gives you more time to acclimatise to the altitude.

It's a very busy mountain during the two-month climbing season. You won't be bounding up it so much as staring at the back of the person in front of you for hours. To avoid the worst of the crush head up on a weekday, or start earlier during the day. And definitely don't climb during the mid-August Obon holiday.

Authorities strongly caution against climbing outside the regular season, when the weather is highly unpredictable and first-aid stations on the mountain are closed. Once snow or ice is on the mountain, Fuji becomes a very serious and dangerous undertaking and should only be attempted by those with winter mountaineering equipment and plenty of experience. Do not climb alone; a guide will be invaluable.

Mountain Huts

Conditions in mountain huts are spartan: a blanket on the floor sandwiched between other climbers. Booking ahead is highly recommended; Fuji Mountain Guides (p62) can assist with reservations (for a ¥1000 fee). Let huts know if you need to cancel at the last minute; no-shows are still expected to pay.

Fujisan Hotel   Hut ¥
(富士山ホテル; 🗓late Jun–mid-Sep 0555-24-6512, reservations 0555-22-0237; www.fujisanhotel.com; per person with/without 2 meals from ¥8350/5950; ☺) One of the largest and most popular rest huts open on Mt Fuji during the climbing season, the Fujisan Hotel is at the 8th station where the Yoshida and

> ☑ **Don't Miss**
>
> Watching the sunrise from the summit is a profound, once-in-a-lifetime experience.

NONCHANON / SHUTTERSTOCK ©

> ✕ **Take a Break**
>
> Mountain huts offer hikers simple hot meals in addition to a place to sleep. Most huts allow you to rest inside as long as you order something.

Subashiri trails meet. There's usually some English-speaking staff here. Bookings are accepted from 1 April and are highly recommended. Credit cards accepted.

Taishikan   Hut ¥

(太子館; ☎0555-22-1947; www.mfi.or.jp/w3/home0/taisikan; per person incl 2 meals from ¥8500) One of several rest huts open during the climbing season on Mt Fuji, located at the 8th station of the Yoshida trail. There is usually some English-speaking staff here, and vegetarian or halal meals are available if requested in advance. Reservations accepted from 1 April. Cash only.

Equipment Rental

Want to climb Mt Fuji, but don't want to invest in (or schlep) all the requisite gear? **Yamadōgu Rental** (やまどうぐレンタル屋; ☎050-5865-1615; www.yamarent.com; 6th fl, 1-13-7 Nishi-Shinjuku, Shinjuku-ku; ☉noon-7pm Mon-Sat, 6.30am-7pm every day Jul & Aug; ☒JR Yamanote line to Shinjuku, west exit) can set you up with individual items (shoes, poles, rain jacket etc) or a full kit including a backpack (from ¥10,500 for two days). Most of the gear is from Japanese outdoor brand Montbell. Reserve in advance online.

Tours

It's certainly not necessary to use a tour operator when climbing in-season, though it can make arranging logistics easier from abroad. Another perk is that they may lead you to a route other than the Yoshida Trail, meaning less frustrating crowds.

Fuji Mountain Guides   Hiking

(☎042-445-0798; www.fujimountainguides.com; 2-day Mt Fuji tours per person ¥47,520) Aimed at foreign visitors, these excellent tours are run both in and out of season by highly experienced and very professional American bilingual guides. Transport to and from Tokyo, mountain guide, two meals and one night in a mountain hut is included; gear rental is available for extra.

Discover Japan Tours   Hiking

(www.discover-japan-tours.com; tours per person from ¥10,000) Reputable company running self-guided overnight treks to/from Shinjuku, timed for sunrise arrival, on summer Saturdays, with a stop at a public hot spring on the way back. Groups of up to six can arrange a private tour (¥55,000) any day of the week.

Fuji Five Lakes

Outside the climbing season, you can hunt for views of Mt Fuji in the Fuji Five Lake region, where placid lakes, formed by ancient eruptions, serve as natural reflecting pools. Kawaguchi-ko is the most popular lake, with plenty of accommodation, eating and hiking options around it. The other lakes are Yamanaka-ko, Sai-ko, Shōji-ko and Motosu-ko.

Canoes on the bank of Lake Shōji-ko at sunrise

Several hiking trails through the foothills, open year-round, offer rewarding vistas – and are far less of a slog than climbing the actual mountain. Ask for a map at the **Kawaguchi-ko Tourist Information Center** (📞0555-72-6700; ⏱8.30am-5.30pm).

Getting There & Around

During the climbing season, Keiō Dentetsu Bus (https://highway-buses.jp) runs direct buses (¥2700, 2½ hours; reservations necessary) from the **Shinjuku Bus Terminal** (バスタ新宿; Busuta Shinjuku; 📞03-6380-4794; http://shinjuku-busterminal.co.jp; 5-24-55 Sendagaya, Shibuya-ku; 🚆 🚉JR Yamanote line to Shinjuku, new south exit) to Fuji Subaru Line Fifth Station, for the Yoshida Trail. The other trails are best accessed as part of a tour or with private transportation.

Year-round, buses run between Shinjuku and Kawaguchi-ko (¥1750, 1¾ hours).

Keisei Bus (www.keiseibus.co.jp) makes two runs daily between Narita Airport and Kawaguchi-ko (¥4400; 3½ hours). From roughly mid-April to early December (weather permitting), buses travel from Kawaguchi-ko to the Fuji Subaru Line Fifth Station (one way/return ¥1540/2100, one hour), so even if you can't climb you can still get up close to the hulking volcano.

To really explore the Fuji Five Lakes area, we recommend renting a car.

★ Local Knowledge

There is a Japanese saying, 'He who climbs Mt Fuji once is a wise man, he who climbs it twice is a fool'.

❶ Need to Know

See the 'Official Web Site for Mt Fuji Climbing' (www.fujisan-climb.jp) for maps and detailed climbing info.

STRUCTURESXX / SHUTTERSTOCK ®

NONNAKRIT / SHUTTERSTOCK ©

Tokyo National Museum

This is the world's largest collection of Japanese art, home to gorgeous silk kimonos, evocative scroll paintings done in charcoal ink, earthy tea-ceremony pottery and haunting examples of samurai armour and swords.

Great For...

☑ **Don't Miss**

The gilded Buddhas of the Gallery of Hōryū-ji Treasures.

Established in 1872, The Tokyo National Museum is divided into several buildings. Visitors with only a couple of hours should hone in on the Honkan (Main Gallery) and the Gallery of Hōryū-ji Treasures. There are English explanations throughout.

Honkan (Main Gallery)

The Honkan houses the Japanese art collection. Second-floor galleries are arranged by era; first-floor galleries are arranged by medium, offering a deeper dive into traditional arts such as lacquerware, metalwork and ceramics.

The building was designed by Watanabe Jin in what is known as the Imperial Style, which mixes modernist ideas and materials with native Japanese forms (like the sloping tiled roof). For a couple of weeks in spring and autumn, the garden, with five **vintage teahouses**, is opened to the public.

Buddhist statue, Tokyo National Museum

❶ Need to Know

Tokyo National Museum (東京国立博物館; Map p254; Tokyo Kokuritsu Hakubutsukan; ☎03-3822-1111; www.tnm.jp; 13-9 Ueno-kōen, Taitō-ku; adult/child & senior/student ¥620/free/410; ⊗9.30am-5pm Tue-Thu & Sun, to 9pm Fri & Sat; ⍰JR lines to Ueno, Ueno-kōen exit)

✕ Take a Break

There are restaurants in the Gallery of Hōryū-ji Treasures and in the Tōyōkan.

★ Top Tip

Allow two hours to take in the highlights, a half-day to do the whole Honkan in depth or a whole day to see everything.

temporary exhibitions; these can be fantastic, but note that they cost extra and often lack the English signage found throughout the rest of the museum.

Gallery of Hōryū-ji Treasures

The stunning **Gallery of Hōryū-ji Treasures** (法隆寺宝物館) – oddly moody for a museum – displays masks, metalwork and sculptures from the Hōryū-ji (in Nara Prefecture, dating from 607 and one of Japan's earliest temples). Most impressive is the spot-lit first-floor exhibition of 48 gilt Buddha statues, each only 30cm to 40cm tall and all slightly different. The spare, elegant building (1999) was designed by Taniguchi Yoshio.

Heiseikan

Accessed via a passage on the 1st floor of the Honkan, the **Heiseikan** (平成館) houses the **Japanese Archaeological Gallery**, full of pottery, talismans and articles of daily life from Japan's palaeolithic and neolithic periods. The second floor is used for

Tōyōkan

The Tōyōkan (Gallery of Asian Art) houses the museum's collection of Buddhist sculptures from around Asia, Chinese ceramics and more, offering a bigger picture of art in the region over the last few millennia. The three-storied building, also by Taniguchi Yoshio, has been renovated recently and showcases its holdings beautifully.

Kuroda Memorial Hall

Kuroda Seiki (1866–1924) is considered the father of modern Western-style painting in Japan. The **Kuroda Memorial Hall** (黒田記念室; ☎03-5777-8600; www.tobunken.go.jp/kuroda/index_e.html; 13-9 Ueno-kōen, Taitō-ku; ⊗9.30am-5pm Tue-Sun; ⍰JR lines to Ueno, Ueno-kōen exit) **FREE**, a 1928-vintage annex to Tokyo National Museum, displays

LEO DAPHNE / ALAMY STOCK PHOTO ©

Tokyo National Museum

HISTORIC HIGHLIGHTS

It would be a challenge to take in everything the sprawling Tokyo National Museum has to offer in a day. Fortunately, the Honkan (Japanese Gallery) is designed to give visitors a crash course in Japanese art history from the Jōmon era (13,000–300 BC) to the Edo era (AD 1603–1868). The works on display here are rotated regularly, to protect fragile ones and to create seasonal exhibitions, so you're always guaranteed to see something new.

Buy your ticket from outside the main gate then head straight to the Honkan with its sloping tile roof. Stow your coat in a locker and take the central staircase up to the 2nd floor, where the exhibitions are arranged chronologically. Allow two hours for this tour of the highlights.

The first room on your right starts from the beginning with **ancient Japanese art ❶**. Be sure to pick up a copy of the brochure *Highlights of Japanese Art* at the entrance.

Continue to the **National Treasure Gallery ❷**. 'National Treasure' is the highest distinction awarded to a work of art in Japan. Keep an eye out for more National Treasures, labelled in red, on display in other rooms throughout the museum.

Moving on, stop to admire the **courtly art gallery ❸**, the **samurai armour and swords ❹** and the *ukiyo-e* and **kimono ❺**.

Next, take the stairs down to the 1st floor, where each room is dedicated to a different decorative art, such as lacquerware or ceramics. Don't miss the excellent examples of **religious sculpture ❻** and **folk art ❼**.

Finish your visit with a look inside the enchanting **Gallery of Hōryū-ji Treasures ❽**.

Ukiyo-e & Kimono (Room 10)
Chic silken kimono and lushly coloured *ukiyo-e* (woodblock prints) are two icons of the Edo-era (AD 1603–1868) *ukiyo* – the 'floating world', or world of fleeting beauty and pleasure.

Japanese Sculpture (Room 11)
Many of Japan's most famous sculptures, religious in nature, are locked away in temple reliquaries. This is a rare chance to see them up close.

MUSEUM GARDEN
Don't miss the garden if you visit in spring and autumn during the few weeks it's open to the public.

Heiseikan & Japanese Archaeology Gallery

Research & Information Centre

Hyōkeikan

Kuro-mon

Main Gate

Gallery of Hōryū-ji Treasures
Surround yourself with miniature gilt Buddhas from Hōryū-ji, one of Japan's oldest Buddhist temples, founded in 607. Don't miss the graceful Pitcher with Dragon Head, a National Treasure.

Courtly Art (Room 3-2)
Literature works, calligraphy and narrative picture scrolls are displayed alongside decorative art objects, which allude to the life of elegance led by courtesans a thousand years ago.

Samurai Armour & Swords (Rooms 5 & 6)
Glistening swords, finely stitched armour and imposing helmets bring to life the samurai, those iconic warriors of Japan's medieval age.

Honkan (Japanese Gallery) 2nd Floor

Honkan (Japanese Gallery) 1st Floor

National Treasure Gallery (Room 2)
A single, superlative work from the museum's collection of 88 National Treasures (perhaps a painted screen, or a gilded, hand-drawn sutra) is displayed in a serene, contemplative setting.

Museum Garden & Teahouses

Honkan (Japanese Gallery)

Tōyōkan (Gallery of Asian Art)

GIFT SHOP

The museum gift shop, on the 1st floor of the Honkan, has an excellent collection of Japanese art books in English.

Dawn of Japanese Art (Room 1)
The rise of the imperial court and the introduction of Buddhism changed the Japanese aesthetic forever. These clay works from previous eras show what came before.

Folk Culture (Room 15)
See artefacts from Japan's historical minorities – the indigenous Ainu of Hokkaidō and the former Ryūkyū Empire, now Okinawa.

some of his key works. The most famous of his paintings, including *Reading* (1891) and *Lakeside* (1897), are in a room that only opens a few times a year; check the website for a schedule.

What's Nearby?

The Tokyo National Museum sits on the edge of **Ueno-kōen** (上野公園; Map p254; http://ueno-bunka.jp; Ueno-kōen, Taitō-ku; 🚃 JR lines to Ueno, Ueno-kōen or Shinobazu exit), a park with cultural facilities, shrines, temples and Tokyo's zoo. There's also a large pond here, with giant lotuses that bloom in summer. A short walk away, the neighbourhood Yanaka has smaller museums and galleries.

Ueno Tōshō-gū   Shinto Shrine

(上野東照宮; Map p254; ☎03-3822-3455; www.uenotoshogu.com; 9-88 Ueno-kōen, Taitō-ku; ¥500; ⊙9am-5.30pm Mar-Sep, to 4.30pm Oct-Feb; 🚃 JR lines to Ueno, Shinobazu exit) This shrine inside Ueno-kōen was built in honour of Tokugawa Ieyasu, the warlord who unified Japan. Resplendent in gold leaf and ornate details, it dates from 1651 (though it has had recent touch-ups). You can get a pretty good look from outside the gate, if you want to skip the admission fee.

Ueno Zoo   Zoo

(上野動物園; Map p254; Ueno Dōbutsu-en; ☎03-3828-5171; www.tokyo-zoo.net; 9-83 Ueno-kōen, Taitō-ku; adult/child/senior ¥600/free/300; ⊙9.30am-5pm Tue-Sun; 🚃 JR lines to Ueno, Ueno-kōen exit) Japan's oldest zoo, established

---

Don't Miss

The Tokyo National Museum's Kuromon (Black Gate), transported from the Edo-era mansion of a feudal lord.

Asakura Museum of Sculpture

PHILLIP MAGUIRE / SHUTTERSTOCK ©

in 1882, is home to animals from around the globe, but the biggest attractions are the giant pandas that arrived from China in 2011 – Rī Rī and Shin Shin. Following several disappointments, the two finally had a cub, Xiang Xiang, in 2017. There's also a whole area devoted to lemurs, which makes sense given Tokyoites' love of all things cute.

Ameya-yokochō   Market

(アメヤ横町; Map p254; www.ameyoko.net; 4 Ueno, Taitō-ku; ⊙10am-7pm, some shops close Wed; ℝJR lines to Okachimachi, north exit) Step into this partially open-air market paralleling and beneath the JR line tracks, and ritzy, glitzy Tokyo feels like a distant memory. It got its start as a black market, post-WWII, when American goods were sold here. Today, it's packed with vendors selling everything from

fresh seafood and exotic cooking spices to vintage jeans and bargain sneakers (and more). See p166 for recommendations of where to shop here.

Asakura Museum of Sculpture, Taitō   Museum

(朝倉彫塑館; Map p254; www.taitocity.net/ taito/asakura; 7-16-10 Yanaka, Taitō-ku; adult/ child ¥500/250; ⊙9.30am-4.30pm Tue, Wed & Fri-Sun; ℝJR Yamanote line to Nippori, north exit) Sculptor Asakura Fumio (artist name Chō-so; 1883–1964) designed this atmospheric house himself. It combined his original home and garden with a large studio that incorporated vaulted ceilings, a 'sunrise room' and a rooftop garden with wonderful neighbourhood views. It's now a reverential museum with many of the artist's signature realist works, mostly of people and cats, on display.

SCAI the Bathhouse   Gallery

(スカイ ザ バスハウス; Map p254; ☎03-3821-1144; www.scaithebathhouse.com; 6-1-23 Yanaka, Taitō-ku; ⊙noon-6pm Tue-Sat; ⓢChiyoda line to Nezu, exit 1) FREE This 200-year-old bathhouse has for several decades been an avant-garde gallery, showcasing Japanese and international artists in its austere vault-ed space. Closed in-between exhibitions.

Yanaka Ginza   Area

(谷中銀座; Map p254; ℝJR Yamanote line to Nippori, north exit) Yanaka Ginza is pure, vintage mid-20th-century Tokyo, a pedestrian street lined with butcher shops, vegetable vendors and the like. Most Tokyo neighbourhoods once had stretches like these (until supermarkets took over). It's popular with Tokyoites from all over the city, who come to soak up the nostalgic atmosphere, plus the locals who shop here.

Meerkat in Ueno Zoo

KOREA PANDA / SHUTTERSTOCK ©

★ Top Tip

Spend the morning at the Tokyo National Museum and the afternoon exploring Ueno-kōen or nearby Yanaka.

Walking Tour: Yanaka

Yanaka, long beloved by local artists, is a charming part of Tokyo. There are lots of temples and old wooden buildings, creating a sense that time stopped several decades ago.
Start Tokyo National Museum
Distance 3km
Duration Two hours

NISHI-NIPPORI

FINISH
7 Yanaka Ginza

Classic Photo Yanaka Ginza from the Yūyake Dandan 'Sunset Stairs'.

7 The classic mid-20th-century shopping street, **Yanaka Ginza** (p69), has food vendors and craft stores.

2 See the works of long-time Yanaka resident and painter Allan West at his studio, **Edokoro** (p166).

3 This ancient, thick-trunked **Himalayan cedar tree** is a local landmark.

4 At **Enju-ji** (延寿寺; 03-3265-1021; http://nichika-do.jp;1-7-36 Yanaka,Taitō-ku; 10am-4pm; [S] Chiyoda line to Nezu, exit 1), Nichika-sama, the 'god of strong legs', is enshrined; the temple is popular with runners.

4 **3** **2**

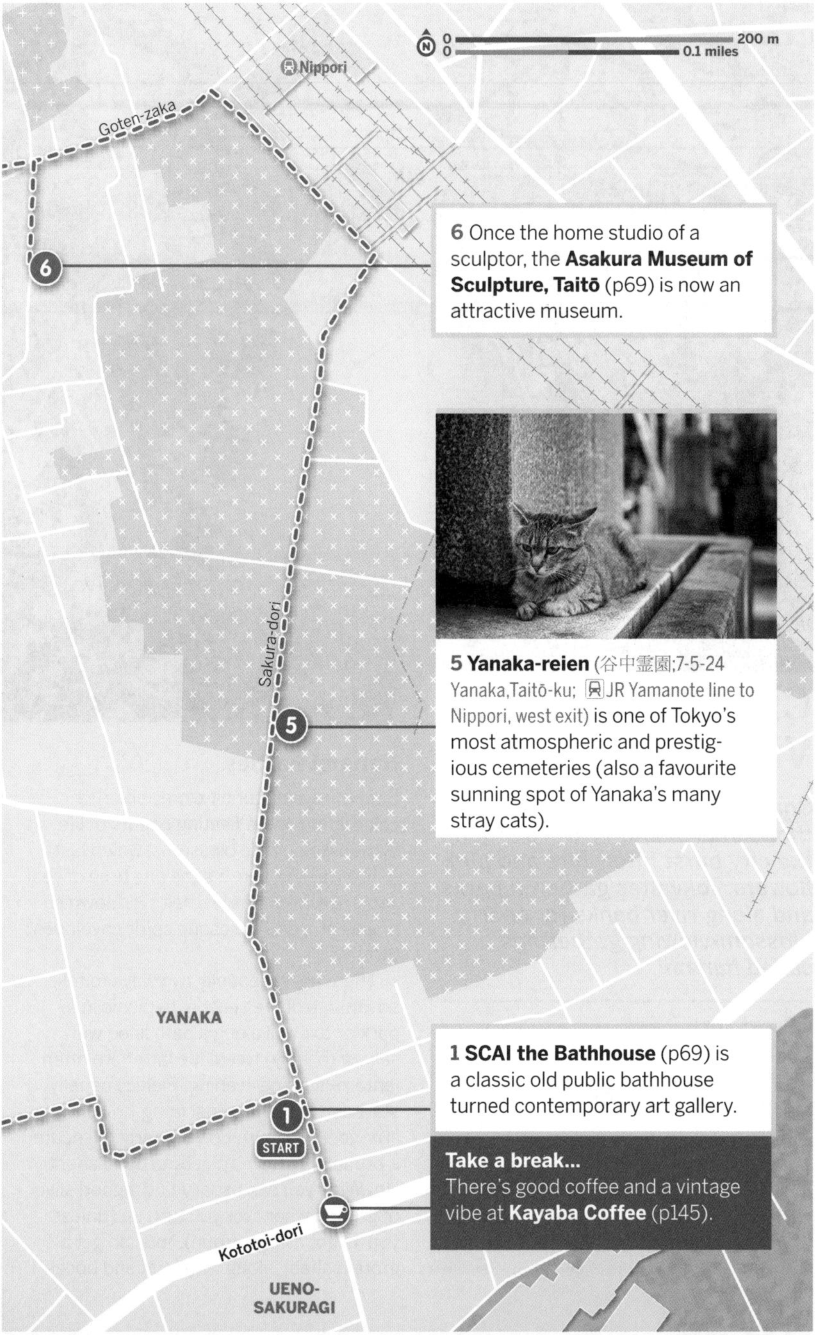

6 Once the home studio of a sculptor, the **Asakura Museum of Sculpture, Taitō** (p69) is now an attractive museum.

5 Yanaka-reien (谷中霊園;7-5-24 Yanaka,Taitō-ku; 🚃 JR Yamanote line to Nippori, west exit) is one of Tokyo's most atmospheric and prestigious cemeteries (also a favourite sunning spot of Yanaka's many stray cats).

1 SCAI the Bathhouse (p69) is a classic old public bathhouse turned contemporary art gallery.

Take a break...
There's good coffee and a vintage vibe at **Kayaba Coffee** (p145).

Goten-zaka

🚉 Nippori

Sakura-dori

YANAKA

START

Kototoi-dori

UENO-SAKURAGI

Sakura blossoms over Meguro-gawa canal

FILPHOTO / SHUTTERSTOCK ©

Cherry-Blossom Viewing

Come spring, thousands upon thousands of cherry trees around the city burst into white and pink flowers. Tokyoites gather in parks and along river banks for cherry-blossom-viewing gatherings called hanami.

Great For...

☑ Don't Miss

Yozakura – the cherry blossoms at night.

Hanami Parties

Hanami is a centuries-old tradition, a celebration of the fleeting beauty of life symbolised by the blossoms, which last only a week or two. It's the one time of year you'll see Tokyoites let their hair down *en masse* as a carnivalesque spirit envelopes the city.

There are essentially two ways to take advantage of the season: to picnic in a park or to stroll along a path lined with *sakura* (cherry) trees; the latter are often lantern-lit in the evening. Picnics usually start early and the most gung-ho *hanami*-goers will turn up very early to secure a prime spot with a plastic ground sheet. However, you can usually find a good sliver of ground whenever you turn up (unless you've got a large group). You can get a ground sheet, along with food and booze,

AODAODAODAOD / SHUTTERSTOCK ©

ⓘ Need to Know

Peak cherry-blossom season is hard to pin down, but usually occurs over the last week of March or the first week of April.

✕ Take a Break

Major spots have public toilets, but expect to queue (and keep tissues handy).

★ Top Tip

Pack a warm layer; it can still be surprisingly cold this time of year after the sun drops.

Shinjuku-gyoen (新宿御苑; ☎03-3350-0151; www.env.go.jp/garden/shinjukugyoen; 11 Naito-chō, Shinjuku-ku; adult/child ¥200/50; ⊙9am-4.30pm Tue-Sun; Ⓢ Marunouchi line to Shinjuku-gyoenmae, exit 1) is the best spot for families (or anyone seeking a more peaceful backdrop). The former imperial garden has a nicely manicured lawn, fixed opening hours, charges a small admission fee and – officially – doesn't allow alcohol, all of which encourages a less-debauched atmosphere.

Ueno-kōen (p68) is Tokyo's classic *hanami* spot. While some do go for spots under the trees here, this park is better for strolling as it doesn't have a lawn.

Another great strolling spot is Naka-Meguro's canal, **Meguro-gawa** (目黒川; Map p247; Ⓢ Hibiya line to Naka-Meguro, main exit). Local restaurants set up street stalls offering more upmarket food and drink than you'll find anywhere else.

There's also **Chidori-ga-fuchi** (千鳥ヶ淵; Map p250; Kudan-minami, Chiyoda-ku; Ⓢ Hanzōmon line to Hanzōmon, exit 5 or Kudanshita, exit 2), one of the moats around the Imperial Palace (p105), which is fringed with blossoms. You can also rent pedal boats here to view the blossoms from the water.

at a convenience store – or go upscale and stock up on picnic supplies at a *depachika* (department store food hall). It's common for *hanami* to last well into the evening, as public parks in Tokyo have no curfew.

Popular strolling spots usually draw food and drink vendors.

Top Spots

Grassy Yoyogi-kōen (p46) is a guaranteed good time. It's not the prettiest of parks but it has lots of *sakura* and sees the most spirited and elaborate bacchanals (some with barbecues and turntables). Inokashira-kōen (p93), which has a photogenic pond flanked with cherry trees, is also popular, especially with students.

ATTAPONG_THAILAND / SHUTTERSTOCK ©

Tokyo Sushi

Sushi – raw fish over rice seasoned with vinegar – comes in many forms: classic and nouveau, breathtakingly expensive and surprisingly good value. Whatever you go for (and we recommend it all), odds are it will taste better here than any you've had before.

Great For...

☑ Don't Miss

Splurging on *omakase* (the chef's tasting menu) at a top-class sushi restaurant.

Sushi Basics

Nowadays diners associate sushi (寿司 or 鮨) with super fresh seafood; however, the dish was originally designed to make fish last longer – the vinegar in the rice was a preserving agent. Older styles of sushi were designed to last for days, and have that heavy tang of fermentation.

The dish evolved dramatically in 19th- and early-20th-century Tokyo. Tokyo Bay provided a steady stream of fresh seafood, making preservation less crucial; more importantly, sanitation improved. Sushi became a sort of fast food: deft-handed chefs quickly formed bite-sized blocks of rice and pressed slivers of fish atop for hungry, harried urbanites. This style is called *nigiri-zushi*, which means hand-formed sushi. It's also known as *edo-mae-zushi* – sushi 'in the style of Edo', the old name for Tokyo.

order à la carte, by just pointing to the slabs of seafood usually displayed in refrigerated glass cases on the counter, though this is the least cost-efficient method.

In higher calibre shops you'll have the option of ordering *omakase*, which means 'up to you' – in this case, up to the chef. Usually there will be a set price *omakase* course (or a few different levels of courses) for which the chef will have selected the menu for that particular day, based on the season and what looked good at the market. Pieces are served one by one.

While the price for such a course – anywhere from ¥5000 to ¥20,000 per person for lunch and an absolute minimum of ¥10,000 per person for dinner (and two or three times that, before drinks) – might sting, this really is the most economical way to sample the best a restaurant has to offer.

The average, local *sushi-ya* (sushi restaurant), will likely offer *sushi no moriawase*, assortment platters with predetermined varieties of *nigiri-zushi* and *maki-zushi*. These typically cost between ¥1500 and ¥5000 per person and often come in three grades: *futsū* or *nami* (regular), *jō* (special) and *toku-jō* (extra-special). The price difference is determined more by the value of the ingredients than by volume. Many also offer *chirashi-zushi*, a bowl of vinegared rice topped with various *neta*, which is usually the cheapest option and particularly popular for lunch.

Common sushi toppings (called *neta*) include *ama-ebi* (sweet shrimp), *hamachi* (yellow tail), *ika* (squid), *katsuo* (bonito), *maguro* (tuna) and *toro* (fatty tuna belly meat). In truth not all *neta* are raw fish: you may encounter *anago* (conger eel) that has been grilled and lacquered in a sweet soy sauce glaze; *tako* (octopus) that has been boiled; or *hotate* (scallops) that have been seared – among others.

There are also many styles of sushi, such as *maki-zushi*, for which the rice and *neta* are rolled in *nori* (laver). Delicacies like *ikura* (salmon roe) and *uni* (sea urchin roe) are served as *gunkan-maki* ('battleship rolls'; it will make sense when you see it!).

Ordering & Costs

There are a few different ways to order and, fortunately, all of them are simple. You can

Kaiten-zushi

Of course the easiest way to experience Japan's sushi culture is with a visit to a *kaiten-zushi* (回転寿司), a restaurant where ready-made plates of sushi are sent around the counter on a conveyor belt. Just grab whatever looks good as it goes by; plates are colour-coded by price. If you don't see what you want, you can order off the menu.

Manners & Tips

All but the most extreme type-A chefs will say they'd rather have foreign visitors enjoy their meal than agonise over getting the etiquette right. Still, there's nothing that makes a Japanese chef grimace more than out-of-towners who over-season their food – a little soy sauce and wasabi go a long way. Many chefs serve *nigiri-zushi* pre-seasoned (you'll likely be instructed by the staff when to use soy sauce). You also might be surprised to learn that it is perfectly acceptable (nay, encouraged) to eat *nigiri-zushi* with your hands. The pickled ginger (called *gari*) served with sushi is to cleanse your palate between pieces.

Top Spots
Kyūbey   Sushi ¥¥¥

(久兵衛; Map p250; ☑03-3571-6523; www. kyubey.jp; 8-7-6 Ginza, Chūō-ku; lunch/dinner set from ¥4320/11,880; ⊙11.30am-2pm & 5-10pm Mon-Sat; ⊜⊕; ⑤Ginza line to Shimbashi, exit 3) Since 1935, Kyūbey's quality and presentation has won it a moneyed and celebrity clientele. Even so, this is a supremely open and relaxed restaurant. The friendly owner Imada-san speaks excellent English, as do some of his team of talented chefs, who will make and serve your sushi, piece by piece.

Sushi breakfast, Tsukiji (p36)

The ¥8000 lunchtime *omakase* (chef's selection) is great value.

Kizushi   Sushi ¥¥¥

(喜寿司; ☎03-3666-1682; 2-7-13 Nihombashi Ningyōchō, Chūō-ku; lunch/dinner course from ¥3500/10,000; ⊗11.45am-2.30pm Mon-Sat, 5-9.30pm Mon-Fri; ☻; ⑤Hibiya line to Ningyōchō, exit A3) While sushi has moved in the direction of faster and fresher, Kizushi, in business since 1923, is keeping it oldschool. Third-generation chef Yui Ryuichi uses traditional techniques, such as marinating the

> **★ Top Tip**
> If there is something you cannot or will not eat, tell staff when you book (or at a casual restaurant, when you order). Most places are accommodating and will replace the offending *neta* with something of equal value.

TODD FONG PHOTOGRAPHY / GETTY IMAGES ©

fish in salt or vinegar, from back when sushi was more about preservation than instant gratification. The shop is in a lovely old timber-frame house. Reservations required for dinner.

Numazukō   Sushi ¥

(沼津港; Map p253; ☎03-5361-8228; 3-34-16 Shinjuku, Shinjuku-ku; plates ¥100-550; ⊗11am-10.30pm; ☻ 🌐 👍; 🚃JR Yamanote line to Shinjuku, east exit) Shinjuku's best *kaiten-zushi* restaurant is pricier than many, but the quality is worth it. Its popularity means that few plates make it around the long, snaking belt without getting snatched up (you can also order off the menu, if you don't see what you want). This is a good choice if you don't want a full meal.

Courses

Learn the art of sushi making at **Tokyo Sushi Academy** (Map p250; ☎03-3362-2789; http://sushimaking.tokyo; 2nd fl, Tsukiji KY Bldg, 4-7-5 Tsukiji, Chūō-ku; adult/child ¥5400/2160; ⊗9am-3pm Sat; 👍; ⑤Hibiya line to Tsukiji, exit 1). English-speaking sushi chefs will give you a 30-minute crash course, after which you'll have an hour to make (and eat) as much of your favourite type of sushi as you like. Classes are held on Saturday (and sometimes Sunday).

> **☑ Don't Miss**
> While *kaiten-zushi* have a lowbrow image, some can be quite good – and they're a lot of fun.

Neon lights illuminate Akihabara

Akihabara Pop Culture

Akihabara – or 'Akiba', as it's known to locals – is the centre of Tokyo's otaku (geek) subculture. But you don't have to obsess about manga or anime to enjoy this quirky neighbourhood: with its neon-bright electronics stores, retro arcades, cosplay cafes – and now the chance to drive go-karts through the streets – it's equal parts sensory overload, cultural mind-bender and just plain fun.

Great For...

ℹ Need to Know

The JR Yamanote and Sōbu lines stop at Akihabara; Electric Town exit is the most convenient.

★ **Top Tip**

Stop in at **Akiba Info** (Map p254; ☏080-3413-4800; www.akiba-information.jp; 2nd fl, Akihabara UDX Bldg, 4-14-1 Soto-Kanda, Chiyoda-ku; ⊙11am-5.30pm Tue-Sun; 🛜; 🚉JR Yamanote line to Akihabara, Electric Town exit) for an English-language map of the neighbourhood.

MariCAR   Scenic Drive

(マリカー; Map p254; ☏080-8899-8899; https://maricar.com; 4-12-9 Soto-Kanda, Chiyoda-ku; per person from ¥8000; ⊙10am-10pm; ⑤Ginza line to Suehirochō, exit 1) We're not sure how this is legal, but at least at the time of writing it still is: go-karting on the streets of Tokyo dressed as your favourite Mario Kart character. It brings the idea of Tokyo as a real-life video game experience to a whole new level. You must, however, have a valid international (or Japanese) driver's licencse.

There's only a short tutorial on how to drive the go-karts, which can be tricky at first, before you're on the road with trucks and buses. Absolutely speak up if you're not comfortable; one of the English-speaking guides will hang back with you, or re-route the course. While daytime is best for snapping photos, the night course over the Rainbow Bridge across Tokyo Bay to Odaiba wins for sheer thrill.

MariCAR also has shops in Shibuya, Asakusa, Shinagawa and Shin-Kiba.

Mandarake Complex   Manga, Anime

(まんだらけコンプレックス; Map p254; www.mandarake.co.jp; 3-11-12 Soto-Kanda, Chiyoda-ku; ⊙noon-8pm; ◪JR Yamanote line to Akihabara, Electric Town exit) When *otaku* dream of heaven, it probably looks a lot like this giant go-to store for manga and anime. Eight storeys are piled high with comic books, action figures, cosplay accessories and cell art just for starters. The first floor has cases of some (very expensive) vintage toys.

@Home Cafe   Cafe

(@ほぉ〜むカフェ; Map p254; www.cafe-athome.com; 4th-7th fl, 1-11-4 Soto-Kanda,

Capsule toy vending machines

Chiyoda-ku; ⏱11am-10pm Mon-Fri, 10am-10pm Sat & Sun; 🚃JR Yamanote line to Akihabara, Electric Town exit) 'Maid cafes' with *kawaii* (cute) waitresses, dressed as saucy French or prim Victorian maids, are a stock-in-trade of Akiba. @Home is one of the more 'wholesome' of them. You'll be welcomed as *go-shujinsama* (master) or *o-jōsama* (miss) the minute you enter. Admission is ¥700 for one hour plus one drink order (from ¥570). The maids serve drinks and dishes, such as curried rice, topped with smiley faces. They'll also play games with customers, such as *moe moe jankan* (rock, paper, scissors). Photos with the maids cost extra.

☑ Don't Miss
Tokyo's latest craze: go-karting. Make sure to book ahead and have an international driver's licence.

JENNY JONES / GETTY IMAGES ©

It's a little titillating, perhaps, but this is no sex joint – just (more or less) innocent fun for Akiba's *otaku*.

Yodobashi Akiba　　　　Electronics
(ヨドバシカメラ Akiba; Map p254; www.yodobashi-akiba.com; 1-1 Kanda Hanaoka-chō, Chiyoda-ku; ⏱9.30am-10pm; 🚃JR Yamanote line to Akihabara, Shōwa-tōriguchi exit) This is the monster branch of Yodobashi Camera where many locals shop. It has eight floors not only of electronics, state-of-the-art camera and audio equipment, and household appliances but also toys, cosmetics and even food at competitive prices. Ask about export models and VAT-free purchases.

Super Potato Retro-kan　　Arcade
(スーパーポテトレトロ館; Map p254; www.superpotato.com; 1-11-2 Soto-kanda, Chiyoda-ku; ⏱11am-8pm Mon-Fri, from 10am Sat & Sun; 🚃JR Yamanote line to Akihabara, Electric Town exit) Are you a gamer keen to sample retro computer games? On the 5th floor of this store specialising in used video games, there's a retro video arcade where you can get your hands on some old-fashioned consoles at a bargain ¥100 per game.

What's Nearby?
3331 Arts Chiyoda　　　　Gallery
(Map p254; 📞03-6803 2441; www.3331.jp/en; 6-11-14 Soto-Kanda, Chiyoda-ku; ⏱groud floow 10am-9pm, exhibition space noon-7pm Wed-Mon; ♿; 🚃Ginza line to Suehirochō, exit 4) FREE A major exhibition space, smaller art galleries and creative studios now occupy this former high school, which has evolved into a forward-thinking arts hub for Akiba. It's a fascinating place to explore. On the main floor there's a good cafe and shop selling cute design items, as well as a play area for kids stocked with recycled toys and colourful giant dinosaurs made of old plastic toys.

✗ Take a Break
Walk over the Kanda-gawa for tasty noodles at Kanda Yabu Soba (p144).

Sumo wrestler prepares for a bout

Sumo at Ryōgoku Kokugikan

The purifying salt sails into the air; the two giants leap up and crash into each other; a flurry of slapping and heaving ensues: from the ancient rituals to the thrill of the quick bouts, sumo is a fascinating spectacle. Bashō (grand tournaments) are held in Tokyo three times a year, for 15 days each January, May and September, at Ryōgoku Kokugikan, the national sumo stadium.

Great For...

ℹ️ Need to Know

Ryōgoku Kokugikan (両国国技館; Map p255; ☎03-3623-5111; www.sumo.or.jp; 1-3-28 Yokoami, Sumida-ku; ¥2100-14,800; ☒JR Sōbu line to Ryōgoku, west exit)

★ Top Tip
Rent a radio (¥100 fee, plus ¥2000 deposit) to listen to commentary in English.

Tournaments

Tournaments are all-day events: doors open at 8am for the early matches that take place between junior wrestlers. The stakes (and pageantry) begin in earnest in the afternoon, when the *makuuchi* (top-tier) wrestlers enter the ring followed by the *yokozuna* (the top of the top), complete with sword-bearing attendants. Many spectators skip the morning, arriving around 2pm or 3pm. The final, most exciting, bouts of the day (featuring the *yokozuna*) finish around 6pm. Tournament ticket holders are allowed to exit and re-enter the stadium once, through the south gate only.

Getting Tickets

Tickets can be bought online five weeks prior to the start of the tournament from the official ticketing site, Ticket Oosumo (http://sumo.pia.jp/en). Note that there is a ¥1000 handling fee per ticket. You can also buy tickets directly from the box office in front of the stadium, though keep in mind that they do sell out, especially on the first and last few days of the tournament.

Around 200 general-admission tickets (the cheapest ticket available is ¥2100) are sold each day of the tournament on a first-come-first-served basis at the box office. You'll have to line up very early (say 6am) on the last couple of days of the tournament to snag one.

Sumo Basics

Japan's national sport is a ritualistic form of wrestling that developed out of ancient Shintō rites for a good harvest. Two large and amply muscled men, clothed only in *mawashi* (loin cloths) with their hair slicked back into a topknot, battle it out in a packed

Tokyo Grand Sumo Tournament

earth *dōyo* (ring) over which hangs a roof that resembles that of a shrine.

Before bouts, which typically last only seconds, the *rikishi* (wrestlers) rinse their mouths with water and toss salt into the ring – both purification rituals. They also perform the *shiko* movement, where they squat, clap their hands and alternately raise each leg as high as it can go before stamping it down – a show of strength and agility.

Size is important in sumo, but woe betide any *rikishi* who relies solely on bulk as, more often than not, it's *kimari-te* (wrestling techniques) that win the day. There are 82 official *kimari-te* a *rikishi* may

✕ Take a Break
The stadium's basement banquet hall serves *chanko-nabe* (the protein rich stew eaten by the wrestlers) for ¥300 a bowl. Or visit nearby Kappō Yoshiba (p140).

J. HENNING BUCHHOLZ / SHUTTERSTOCK ©

legitimately employ, including *oshidashi* (pushing an opponent's arms underneath or in the chest to force him out of the ring); *uwatenage* (grabbing an opponent's *mawashi* from outside the opponent's arms and throwing him to the ground); and *yorikiri* (lifting an opponent out of the ring by his *mawashi*).

Moves that will get a wrestler disqualified include punching with a closed fist, boxing ears, choking, grabbing an opponent in the crotch area and hair-pulling.

What's Nearby?

Edo-Tokyo Museum   Museum
(江戸東京博物館; Map p255; ☑03-3626-9974; www.edo-tokyo-museum.or.jp; 1-4-1 Yokoami, Sumi-da-ku; adult/child ¥600/free; ☺9.30am-5.30pm, to 7.30pm Sat, closed Mon; ⓇJR Sōbu line to Ryōgoku, west exit) Tokyo's history museum documents the city's transformation from tidal flatlands to feudal capital to modern metropolis via highly-detailed scale recreations of townscapes and artifacts. Newly reopened after a six-month renovation, the museum now also has interactive displays and multi-lingual touch screen panels and audio guides. Still, the best way to tour the museum is with one of the gracious English-speaking volunteer guides, who really bring the history to life.

Japanese Sword Museum Museum
(刀剣博物館; Tōken Hakubutsukan; Map p255; ☑03-6284-1000; www.touken.or.jp/museum; 1-12-9 Yokoami, Sumida-ku; adult/student/child ¥1000/500/free; ☺9.30am-5pm Tue-Sun; ⓇJR Sōbu line to Ryōgoku, west exit) For visitors with a keen interest in Japanese sword-making – an art that continues to this day – this new museum features exhibitions from contemporary craftspeople. There's good English information on the different styles and components (and more English-language references for sale in the small gift shop). Kids up to the age of 15 enter for free.

☑ Don't Miss
Not in town during a tournament? See sumo practice at Arashio Stable (p198).

Omoide-yokochō

URAIWONS / SHUTTERSTOCK ©

Tokyo's Eating & Drinking Alleys

Tokyo has not (yet!) completely erased all traces of an older city, the one of narrow alleyways and wooden buildings. Some of these alleys shelter small restaurants and bars; spending an evening in one is a must-do local experience.

Great For

☑ **Don't Miss**

If you like Tokyo's *yokochō*, you'll love Golden Gai, a collection of several alleyways and over 200 tiny bars and restaurants in Shinjuku.

Yokochō (literally 'side town') is the word used to describe Tokyo's commercial alleys, where eating, drinking and shopping happens away from the main streets. And while those main streets might just be one block over, *yokochō* feel worlds apart.

Nonbei-yokochō   Bar

(のんべえ横丁; Map p246; www.nonbei.tokyo; Shibuya 1-chōme, Shibuya-ku; ®JR Yamanote line to Shibuya, Hachikō exit) Nonbei-yokochō – literally 'Drunkard's Alley' – is one of Tokyo's anomalous (and endangered) strips of old wooden shanty bars, here in the shadow of the elevated JR tracks. There's a wonderfully eclectic assortment of teeny-tiny bars, though note that some have cover charges (usually ¥500 to ¥1000). Tight (p177) is one that doesn't.

Need to Know

Eating and drinking alleys are often found near train stations or even under elevated rail lines (*gādo-shita* means under the tracks).

☑ Don't Miss

Ueno's Ameya-yokochō (p69) is a huge open-air market with all kinds of vendors, one of the last of its kind in Tokyo.

★ Top Tip

It's common for these bars and restaurants to charge a small *o-tōshi* (cover charge) of a few hundred yen that also includes a small appetiser.

underneath the overhead JR tracks. Since most places are super-tiny, and the rail lines provide cover, there is often seating set outside, on folding tables or overturned beer carts. Some shops (indicated by a small sticker) have English menus.

Omoide-yokochō Yakitori ¥

(思い出横丁; Map p253; Nishi-Shinjuku 1-chōme, Shinjuku-ku; skewers from ¥150; ⊗varies by shop; 🖸; 🚃JR Yamanote line to Shinjuku, west exit) Since the postwar days, smoke has been billowing night and day from the rickety, wooden yakitori stalls that line this alley by the train tracks, literally translated as 'Memory Lane' (and less politely known as Shonben-yokochō, or 'Piss Alley'). Several stalls have English menus.

Kōenji Gādo-shita Street Food ¥

(高円寺ガード下; Kōenji, Suginami-ku; ⊗5pm-late; 🚃JR Sōbu line to Kōenji, north exit) This is Kōenji's signature eating and drinking strip, a collection of shabby (and cheap!) yakitori joints, spruced-up wine bars and more

Ebisu-yokochō Street Food ¥

(恵比寿横町; Map p246; www.ebisu-yokocho. com; 1-7-4 Ebisu, Shibuya-ku; dishes ¥500-1500; ⊗5pm-late; 🚃JR Yamanote line to Ebisu, east exit) Locals love this retro arcade chock-a-block with food stalls dishing up everything from humble *yaki soba* (fried buckwheat noodles) to decadent *hotate-yaki* (grilled scallops). Seating is on stools, while tables are fashioned from various items such as repurposed beer crates. It's a loud, lively (and smoky) place, especially on a Friday night; go early to get a table.

You won't find much English, but the adventurous can get away with pointing at their fellow diners' dishes (you'll be sitting cheek-to-jowl with them). Even if you don't stop to eat, it's worth strolling through. The entrance is marked with a rainbow-coloured sign.

Sensō-ji

Sensō-ji is the capital's oldest temple, far older than Tokyo itself. According to legend, in AD 628 two fishermen brothers pulled out a golden image of Kannon (the Bodhisattva of compassion) from the nearby Sumida-gawa. Sensō-ji was built to enshrine it. Today the temple stands out for its evocation of an older Japan, rarely visible in Tokyo today.

Great For...

🛈 Need to Know

Sensō-ji (浅草寺; Map p255; ☑03-3842-0181; www.senso-ji.jp; 2-3-1 Asakusa, Taitō-ku; ⊘24hr; ⑤Ginza line to Asakusa, exit 1) FREE

★ **Top Tip**

The minutes just before the sun sinks make for some of the best pictures of this photogenic sanctuary.

Consider the crowds part of the experience, as there doesn't seem to be a time during the day when Sensō-ji isn't packed. It does get much quieter in the evening, after the Nakamise-dōri shops close.

Kaminari-mon

The temple precinct begins at the majestic **Kaminari-mon** (雷門; Thunder Gate), which means Thunder Gate. An enormous *chōchin* (lantern), which weighs 670kg, hangs from the centre. On either side are a pair of ferocious protective deities: Fūjin, the god of wind, on the right; and Raijin, the god of thunder, on the left. Kaminari-mon has burnt down countless times over the centuries; the current gate dates to 1970.

Nakamise-dōri

Beyond Kaminari-mon is the shrine precinct's bustling shopping street, **Nakamise-dōri**. Along with the usual tourist swag (like t-shirts) you can find some true gems (artisan crafts, for example) and oddities (such as wigs done up in traditional hairstyles). There are also numerous snack vendors serving up traditional treats like crunchy *sembei* (rice crackers) and *age-man-ju* (deep-fried *anko* – bean-paste – buns).

At the end of Nakamise-dōri is **Hōzō-mon** (宝蔵門), another gate with fierce guardians. On the gate's back side are a pair of 2500kg, 4.5m-tall *waraji* (straw sandals) crafted by some 800 villagers in northern Yamagata Prefecture. These are meant to symbolise the Buddha's power, and it's believed that evil spirits will be scared off by the giant footwear.

Kaminari-mon Gate

Hondō (Main Hall)

The current Hondō, with its dramatic sloping roof, was constructed in 1958, replacing the one destroyed in WWII air raids. The style is similar to the previous one, though the roof tiles are made of titanium. The Kannon image (a tiny 6cm) is cloistered away from view deep inside (and admittedly may not exist at all). Nonetheless, a steady stream of worshippers visits the temple to cast coins, pray and bow in a gesture of respect.

In front is a large cauldron with smoking incense. The smoke is said to bestow health and you'll see people wafting it over their bodies. Off the courtyard stands a

> ☑ **Don't Miss**
> The tasty, traditional snack foods sold along Nakamise-dōri.

53m-high **Five-Storey Pagoda** (五重塔); the 1973 reconstruction of a pagoda built by Tokugawa Iemitsu; it is the second-highest pagoda in Japan.

Fortune Telling

One of the fun parts of a temple visit is drawing an *omikuji* (paper fortune). On either side of the approach to the Main Hall, there will be kiosks selling them. Drop ¥100 coin into the slot, grab a silver canister and shake it. Then extract a stick and note its number (in kanji). Find the matching drawer and withdraw your *omikuji* (there's English on the back) and return the stick to the canister. Fortunes can be shockingly bad, but if you get 大凶 (*dai-kyō*, Great Curse), don't fear: just tie the paper on the nearby rack, ask the gods for better luck, and try again!

Asakusa-jinja

On the east side of the temple complex is **Asakusa-jinja** (浅草神社; ☎03-3844-1575; www.asakusajinja.jp/english), built in honour of the brothers who discovered the Kannon statue that inspired the construction of Sensō-ji. The current building, painted a deep shade of red, dates to 1649 and is a rare example of early Edo architecture.

What's Nearby?
Super Dry Hall   Architecture
(フラムドール; Map p255; Flamme d'Or; 1-23-1 Azuma-bashi, Sumida-ku; ⑤Ginza line to Asakusa, exit 4) Also known as Asahi Beer Hall, the headquarters of the brewery was designed by Philippe Starck and completed in 1989 and remains one of the city's most distinctive buildings. The tower, with its golden glass facade and white top floors, is supposed to evoke a giant mug of beer, while the golden blob atop the lower jet-black building is the flame (locals, however, refer to it as the 'golden turd').

> ✖ **Take a Break**
> End the day with a beer at Asahi Sky Room (p117).

Ghibli Museum

Even those uninitiated in the magical world of master animator Miyazaki Hayao will find this museum dedicated to him and his works enchanting. Fans won't want to leave.

Great For...

☑ Don't Miss

The original animated shorts, which can only be seen here.

Master animator Miyazaki Hayao and his Studio Ghibli (pronounced 'jiburi') have been responsible for some of the best-loved films in Japan – and the world. Miyazaki designed this museum himself, and it's redolent of the dreamy, vaguely steampunk atmosphere that makes his animations so enchanting.

The building itself looks like an illustration from a European fairy tale. Inside, there is an imagined workshop filled with the kinds of books and artworks that inspired the creator, as well as vintage machines from animation's history.

This museum rewards curiosity and exploration; peer through a small window, for example, and you'll see little soot sprites (as seen in *Spirited Away*; 2001). A spiral staircase leads to a purposefully overgrown rooftop terrace with a 5m-tall statue of the

❶ Need to Know

Ghibli Museum (ジブリ美術館; www.
ghibli-museum.jp; 1-1-83 Shimo-Renjaku,
Mitaka-shi; adult ¥1000, child ¥100-700;
⊙10am-6pm, closed Tue; ℝJR Sōbu-Chūō
line to Mitaka, south exit)

✕ Take a Break

Takeaway tea spot Uni Stand (p126) is a
short walk from the museum.

★ Top Tip

Shuttle buses (round trip/one way
¥320/210; every 20 minutes) depart for
the museum from bus stop no 9 outside
the south exit of Mitaka Station.

Robot Soldier from *Laputa* (*Castle in the
Sky*; 1986). A highlight for children (sorry
grown-ups!) is a giant, plush replica of
the cat bus from the classic *My Neighbor
Totoro* (1988) that kids can climb on.

Inside the museum, Saturn Theatre
shows Ghibli short animations (you'll get
a ticket for this when you enter). The film
line-up changes regularly to keep fans
coming back.

Getting Tickets

Tickets must be purchased in advance, and
you must choose the exact time and date
you plan to visit. They are limited and go
fast (especially during the summer school
holiday). Overseas visitors can buy tickets
up to four months in advance from a travel
agent; this is the best option as you can reserve earlier. Otherwise you can get tickets

a month in advance from convenience
store Lawson's online ticket portal. Details
for both methods can be found on the
museum's website. Tickets are non-trans-
ferable; you may be asked to show an ID.

Inokashira-kōen

The Ghibli Museum is on the western edge
of **Inokashira-kōen** (井の頭公園; www.ken-
setsu.metro.tokyo.jp/seibuk/inokashira/index.
html; 1-18-31 Gotenyama, Musashino-shi; ℝJR
Sōbu-Chūō line to Kichijōji, Kōen exit), one of Tokyo's best parks. You can walk through the
park to or from the museum in about 30
minutes, using Kichijōji Station (one stop
before Mitaka on the JR Sōbu-Chūō line).
Inokashira-kōen has a big pond flanked
by woodsy strolling paths. Don't miss the
shrine here to the goddess Benzaiten, one
of Japan's eight lucky gods. There are a few
cafes and restaurants in the park, too.

SEAN PAVONE / SHUTTERSTOCK ©

Shibuya Crossing

This is the Tokyo you've dreamed about and seen in movies: the mind-boggling crowds, the glowing lights and the giant video screens beaming larger-than-life celebrities over the streets.

Rumoured to be the busiest intersection in the world (and definitely in Japan), Shibuya Crossing, also known as Shibuya Scramble, is like a giant beating heart, sending people in all directions with every pulsing light change. Perhaps nowhere else says 'Welcome to Tokyo' better than this.

Hundreds of people – and at peak times said to be over 1000 people – cross at a time, coming from all directions at once yet still managing to dodge each other with a practised, nonchalant agility. Then, in the time that it takes for the light to go from red to green again, all corners have replenished their stock of people – like a video on loop.

The intersection is most impressive after dark on a Friday or Saturday night, when the crowds pouring out of the station are at their thickest and neon-lit by the signs above. (Rainy days have their own visual

Great For...

☑ **Don't Miss**

The crossing at night, all lit up.

❶ Need to Know

Shibuya Crossing (渋谷スクランブル交
差点; Shibuya Scramble; 🚃JR Yamanote line
to Shibuya, Hachikō exit)

✕ Take a Break

Just up the road is craft-beer specialist,
Good Beer Faucets (p177).

★ Top Tip

There's a good view of the crossing from
above through the windows in Shibuya
train station, across from the Myth of
Tomorrow mural.

appeal, with all the colourful umbrellas).
The rhythms here are, however, tied to the
train station and after the last train pulls
out for the night, the intersection becomes
eerily quiet.

What's Nearby?

Shibuya Center-gai   Area
(渋谷センター街; Map p246; Shibuya Sentā-gai;
🚃JR Yamanote line to Shibuya, Hachikō exit)
Shibuya's main drag is closed to cars
and chock-a-block with fast-food joints
and high-street fashion shops. At night,
lit bright as day, with a dozen competing
soundtracks (coming from who knows
where), wares spilling onto the streets and
strutting teens, it feels like a block party –
or Tokyo's version of a classic Asian night
market.

Hachikō Statue   Statue
(ハチ公像; Map p246; Hachikō Plaza; 🚃JR
Yamanote line to Shibuya, Hachikō exit) Come
meet Tokyo's most famous pooch, Hachikō.
This Akita dog came to Shibuya Station
everyday to meet his master, a professor,
returning from work. After the professor
died in 1925, Hachikō continued to come to
the station daily until his own death nearly
10 years later. The story became legend
and a small statue was erected in the dog's
memory in front of Shibuya Station. The
surrounding plaza is Tokyo's most popular
rendezvous point and is always abuzz.

Myth of Tomorrow   Public Art
(明日の神話; Map p246; Asu no Shinwa; 🚃JR
Yamanote line to Shibuya, Hachikō exit) Okamoto
Tarō's mural, *Myth of Tomorrow* (1967),
was commissioned by a Mexican luxury
hotel but went missing two years later. It
finally turned up in 2003 and, in 2008, the
haunting 30m-long work, which depicts the
atomic bomb exploding over Hiroshima, was
installed inside Shibuya Station. It's on the
2nd floor, on the way to the Inokashira line.

Rotemburo (outdoor bath) in winter

DRYADPHOTOS / SHUTTERSTOCK ©

Onsen

Don't be shy! Many Japanese would argue that you couldn't possibly understand their culture without taking a dip in an onsen (natural hot-spring bath). The blissful relaxation that follows can turn a sceptic into a convert.

Great For...

☑ **Don't Miss**

A soak in a *rotemburo* (outdoor bath).

Highly volcanic Japan bubbles with natural hot springs. Don't let Tokyo's slick surface and countless diversions fool you; underneath the city it's pure, bubbling primordial pleasure. Natural hot spring water contains a number of minerals (unique to each spring); some are reputed to make one's skin *sube-sube* (smooth), or alleviate ailments such as high blood pressure and poor circulation. Onsen can be found in elaborate day spas or humble public bathhouses (called *sentō*), though not all *sentō* use natural spring water.

Bathing Basics

First of all, relax: really all you need to know to avoid causing alarm is to wash yourself before getting into the bath.

Upon entering a spa or bathhouse, the first thing you'll encounter is a row of

lockers in which to store your shoes. At the front desk you'll either pay your admission up front (always the case at *sentō*) or be given a wrist band (often the case at spas). The wrist band can be used to open and close your locker in the changing room and also to charge any food, drinks or additional services (like massage or facials) to your tab, which you'll settle upon checking out. Some places may keep your shoe locker key at the front desk as a deposit.

Inside the changing room there will be lockers or baskets for your clothes. Take everything off here, entering the bathing room with only a small towel. Park yourself on a stool in front of one of the taps and give yourself a thorough wash. Make sure you rinse off all the suds. When you're done, it's polite to rinse off the stool for the next person.

That little towel performs a variety of functions: you can use it to wash (but make sure to give it a good rinse afterwards) or to cover yourself as you walk around (somewhat; it won't cover much). It is not supposed to touch the water though, so leave it on the side of the bath or – as the locals do – folded on top of your head.

In the baths, keep splashing to a minimum and your head above the water. Keeping your heart above water can help prevent dizziness. Before heading back to the changing room, wipe yourself down with the towel to avoid dripping on the floor.

Day Spas

Day spas offer a variety of different baths and saunas. It's entirely possible to spend the better part of a day in one. Or night: they're usually open 24 hours and, for an extra fee, you can overnight here, sleeping on a reclining chair in the lounge (yes, this is a real thing people do). Day spas in central Tokyo are used to foreign visitors and usually have dos and don'ts posted in multiple languages. Towels and robes or pyjamas are provided; the washing and changing rooms have toiletries, disposable razors and combs, hair dryers and anything else you might need.

Ōedo Onsen Monogatari   Onsen

(大江戸温泉物語; www.ooedoonsen.jp; 2-6-3 Aomi, Kōtō-ku; adult/child ¥2610/1050, surcharge Sat & Sun ¥220; ⏰11am-9am, last entry 7am; Ⓡ Yurikamome line to Telecom Center, south exit or Rinkai line to Tokyo Teleport, exit B with free shuttle bus) Just to experience the truly Japanese phenomenon that is an amusement park centred on bathing is reason enough to visit. The baths here, which include gender-divided indoor tubs and outdoor *rotemburo*, are filled with real hot-spring water, pumped from 1400m below Tokyo Bay. Come after 6pm for a ¥500 discount. Visitors with tattoos will be denied admission.

There's a huge variety of baths here, including jet baths, pools of natural rock and, on the ladies' side, personal bucket-shaped baths made of cedar. Upon entering, visitors change their clothes for a choice of colourful *yukata* (light cotton kimonos) to wear while they stroll around the complex, which is a lantern-lit re-creation of an old Tokyo downtown area, with food stalls and carnival games.

Spa LaQua   Onsen

(スパ ラクーア; ☎03-5800-9999; www.laqua.jp; 5th-9th fl, Tokyo Dome City, 1-1-1 Kasuga, Bunkyō-ku; weekday/weekend ¥2850/3125; ⏰11am-9am; Ⓢ Marunouchi line to Kōrakuen, exit 2) One of Tokyo's few true onsen, this chic spa complex, renovated in 2017, relies on natural hot-spring water from 1700m below ground. There are indoor and outdoor baths, saunas and a bunch of add-on options, such as *akasuri* (Korean-style

Dinign area at Ōedo Onsen Monogatari

whole-body exfoliation). It's a fascinating introduction to Japanese health and beauty rituals.

Thermae-yu   Onsen
(テルマー湯; Map p253; ☑03-5285-1726; www. thermae-yu.jp; 1-1-2 Kabukichō, Shinjuku-ku; weekdays/weekends & holidays ¥2365/2690; ⊙11am-9am; ☒JR Yamanote line to Shinjuku, east exit) The best (and most literal) example to date that red-light district Kabukichō is cleaning up its act: the 2016 opening of this gleaming onsen complex. The tubs, which include several indoor and outdoor ones (sex-segregated), are filled with honest-to-goodness natural hot-spring water. There are several saunas, including a hot-stone sauna (*ganbanyoku*, ¥810 extra). Towels included. Sorry, no tattoos allowed.

Sentō

Sentō, mostly frequented by neighbourhood regulars, can be a little intimidating, but also a great local experience. Towels and toiletries (besides the communal bar of soap) aren't provided, though are available to purchase for a small fee.

Rokuryu Kōsen   Bathhouse
(六龍鉱泉; ☑03-3821-3826; 3-4-20 Ikenohata, Taitō-ku; ¥460; ⊙3.30-11pm Tue-Sun; ⑤Chiyoda line to Nezu, exit 2) Dating from 1931, this gem of a neighbourhood *sentō* has a beautiful mural of the wooden arched bridge Kintai-kyo in Iwasaki on the bathhouse wall. The amber-hued water is packed with minerals that are reputed to be excellent for your skin, if you can stand the water temperature – a scalding-hot 45°C in the cooler of the two pools!

Jakotsu-yu   Bathhouse
(蛇骨湯; ☑03-3841-8645; www.jakotsuyu.co.jp; 1-11-11 Asakusa, Taitō-ku; adult/child ¥460/180; ⊙1pm-midnight Wed-Mon; ⑤Ginza line to Tawaramachi, exit 3) Unlike at most *sentō*, the tubs here are filled with pure hot-spring water, naturally the colour of weak tea. Another treat is the lovely, lantern-lit, rock-framed *rotemburo*. Jakotsu-yu is a welcoming place; it has English signage and doesn't have a policy against tattoos. It's an extra ¥200 for the sauna, ¥100 for a small towel.

> ### ★ Top Tip
> See Tokyo Sentō (www.1010. or.jp/english) for more info on local bathhouses.

MARK BASSETT / ALAMY STOCK PHOTO ©

> ### ❶ Need to Know
> Day spas usually refuse entry to customers with tattoos because of the association of tattoos with the *yakuza* (Japanese mafia); *sentō* generally have no such restrictions.

Kabukiza Theatre

Kabukiza Theatre

Dramatic, intensely visual kabuki is Japan's most recognised art form. Kabuki developed in the Edo period (1603–1868), and an afternoon at the theatre has been a favourite local pastime ever since. Descendants of the great actors of the day still grace Tokyo stages, drawing devoted fans. Established in 1889 (and rebuilt in 2013), Kabukiza is Tokyo's dedicated kabuki theatre.

Great For...

ℹ Need to Know

Kabukiza (歌舞伎座; Map p250; ☏03-3545-6800; www.kabukiweb.net; 4-12-15 Ginza, Chūō-ku; tickets ¥3000-20,000, single-act tickets ¥800-2000; ℝHibiya line to Higashi-Ginza, exit 3)

★ **Top Tip**

Rent a captioning guide for explanations in English.

History

Kabuki got its start in Kyoto: around the year 1600, a charismatic shrine priestess led a troupe of female performers in a new type of dance people dubbed 'kabuki', a slang expression that meant 'cool' or 'in vogue' at the time. The dancing – rather ribald and performed on a dry riverbed for gathering crowds – was also a gateway to prostitution, which eventually led the shogunate to ban the female performers. Adolescent men took their place, though they too attracted amorous admirers. Finally, in 1653, the authorities mandated that only adult men with shorn forelocks could perform kabuki, which gave rise to one of kabuki's most fascinating elements, the *onnagata* (actors who specialise in portraying women).

When kabuki arrived in Edo (the old name for Tokyo), it developed hand in hand with the increasingly affluent merchant class, whose decadent tastes translated into the breathtaking costumes, dramatic music and elaborate stagecraft that have come to characterise the art form. It is this intensely visual nature that makes kabuki accessible to foreign audiences – you don't really have to know the story to enjoy the spectacle.

Understanding Kabuki

There is no pretence of reality in kabuki; it's ruled by aesthetics and plays to the senses rather than the intellect. Kabuki has been likened to a moving woodblock print (though really, it's the other way around), and when the actors pause in dramatic poses (called *mie*) the whole stage really does look fit to be framed.

The plays draw from a repertoire of popular themes, such as famous historical accounts, the conflict between love and loyalty and stories of star-crossed love ending in double suicide. But more than by plot, kabuki is driven by its actors, who train for the profession from childhood. The leading families of modern kabuki (such as Bandō and Ichikawa) go back many generations, as sons follow their fathers into the *yago* (kabuki acting house). The audience takes great interest in watching how different generations of one family perform the same part. At pivotal moments in a performance, enthusiastic fans shout out the actor's *yago* – an act called *kakegoe*.

Performances

Twice-daily performances are held 24 days out of the month at Kabukiza, with a new line-up of acts each month. A full kabuki performance comprises three or four acts – usually from different plays – over an afternoon or an evening (typically 11am to 3.30pm or 4.30pm to 9pm).

There are intervals of 15 to 30 minutes between acts; during the longest one, it is tradition to eat a *bentō* (boxed meal). Concessions stands selling *bentō* (around ¥1000), snacks and drinks can be found inside the theatre or in the basement entrance connected to the subway. As the break isn't that long, it's best to buy something before the show. It's OK to eat at your seat during intermissions.

If four-plus hours sounds too long, 90 sitting and 60 standing *makumi* (single act tickets; ¥500 to ¥1500, depending on the play) are sold on the day for each act. You'll be at the back of the auditorium, but the views are still good.

Captioning guides, which provide translations of the dialogue as well as points for understanding the significance of key scenes, are available for rent (full program/single act ¥1000/¥500; ID required as deposit).

Getting Tickets

Tickets go on sale from the 12th day of the preceding month and can be purchased online from the Kabukiza website. Single-act ticket sales begin an hour or two before each act; see the website for exact times (and other details). Some acts tend to be more popular than others, perhaps featuring a famous actor in a famous role, and may sell out quickly.

> ☑ **Don't Miss**
> The flamboyant costumes and outrageous make-up. (Tip: if you opt for the cheap seats, bring binoculars.)

ADAM HESTER / GETTY IMAGES ©

> ✕ **Take a Break**
> Offering a view of Kabukiza's roof garden is the tea salon Jugetsudo (p141).

GOLAIZOLA / GETTY IMAGES ©

Imperial Palace

Take a tour of the leafy grounds of the imperial family's residence, or content yourself to stroll along the ancient moat and climb an old castle keep in the garden.

Great For...

☑ Don't Miss

The view of the palace bridges and watchtower from Kōkyo-gaien Plaza.

In its heyday, Edo-jō was the largest fortress in the world. When the shogunate fell and the emperor moved to Tokyo, the castle became the imperial residence – Kōkyo. WWII air raids levelled most of the palace and the current ferro-concrete buildings were completed in the 1960s. The moats and imposing stone walls visible around the perimeter of the palace grounds belonged to the original castle.

Surrounding the palace is Kōkyo-gaien, a 115-hectare national garden, which includes public green spaces and cultural facilities; unlike the palace compound, it is open to the public with no restrictions.

Palace Tours

The only way to see the palace's inner compound is as part of an official tour organised by the Imperial Household Agency. Tours (lasting around 1¼ hours)

❶ Need to Know

Imperial Palace (皇居; Kōkyo; Map p250; ☎03-5223-8071; http://sankan.kunaicho. go.jp/english/guide/koukyo.html; 1 Chiyoda, Chiyoda-ku; ☉tours usually 10am & 1.30pm Tue-Sat; ⑤Chiyoda line to Ōtemachi, exit C13b or C10) **FREE**

✗ Take a Break

Wind down the day with a cocktail at Peter: the Bar (p116), which is adjacent to Kōkyo-gaien Plaza.

★ Top Tip

The Imperial Palace East Garden is closed on Mondays and Fridays, so don't come then if that's the part you wish to see.

run at 10am and 1.30pm usually on Tuesday through to Saturday, but not on public holidays nor afternoons from late July through to the end of August. They're also not held at all from 28 December to 4 January or when Imperial Court functions are scheduled.

Arrive no later than 10 minutes before the scheduled departure time at **Kikyō-mon** (桔梗門), the starting and ending point. You will need to show your passport.

Reservations are taken – via the website, phone or by post – up to one month in advance (and no later than four days in advance via the website). Alternatively, go to the office at Kikyō-mon from 8.30am (for the morning tour) or noon (for the afternoon tour) – if there is space available you'll be able to register.

The tour will give you a glimpse of the outside of the **Kyūden**, the building that

contains the throne room, Matsu-no-Ma (Pine Chamber), and a few other state-houses. Unfortunately, the tour doesn't enter any of the palace buildings.

You'll also have the opportunity for a close-up view of two watch towers, **Fujimi-yagura** and **Fushimi-yagura** (伏見 櫓), that date to the days of Edo-jō. Fush-imi-yagura, constructed in 1559, actually predates Edo-jō; it was dismantled and reassembled from the grounds of Kyoto's long-destroyed Fushimi Castle by the third Tokugawa shogun.

Explanations on palace tours are given only in Japanese; download the free app (www.kunaicho.go.jp/e-event/app.html) for explanations in English, Chinese, Korean, French or Spanish.

Imperial Palace East Garden

Once part of the original castle compound, the **Imperial Palace East Garden** (東御苑;

Kōkyo Higashi-gyoen ⏱9am-4pm Nov-Feb, to 4.30pm Mar–mid-Apr, Sep & Oct, to 5pm mid-Apr–Aug, closed Mon & Fri year-round) FREE is now a public garden. Here you can get up-close views of the massive stones used to build the castle walls, and even climb the ruins of one of the keeps, off the upper lawn. The large lawn is where the castle's **Honmaru** (main keep) was once located. Don't miss the **Ninomaru Grove**, a woodland area that is one of the prettiest parts of the garden, with a pond and the elegant teahouse, **Suwa-no-chaya**.

Entry is free, but the number of visitors at any one time is limited, so it never feels crowded. There are three gates: most people enter through Ōte-mon, the closest gate to Tokyo Station.

Free two-hour guided walking tours of the East Garden are offered on Wednesday, Saturday and Sunday; meet at the JNTO Tourist Information Center (p233) before 1pm.

Kōkyo-gaien Plaza

Kōkyo-gaien Plaza (皇居外苑広場; Kōkyo-gaien Hiroba; Map p250; 1 Chiyoda, Chiyoda-ku; Ⓢ Hibiya line to Hibiya, exit B6) is the grassy expanse southeast of the palace compound, planted with roughly 2000 immaculately maintained Japanese black pine trees. It is the closest you can get to the actual palace without taking the palace tour. There is a famous view from here, of two of the palace bridges, stone **Megane-bashi** (眼鏡橋) and iron **Nijū-bashi** (二重橋), with Fushimi-yagura (p105) rising behind them. Megane-bashi – 'Eyeglass Bridge' – is so nicknamed because its support arches reflected in the water create the appear-

Imperial Palace East Garden

ance of spectacles; both bridges date to the 1880s.

What's Nearby?

Intermediatheque   Museum

(インターメディアテク; Map p250; ☎03-5777-8600; www.intermediatheque.jp; 2nd & 3rd fl, JP Tower, 2-7-2 Marunouchi, Chiyoda-ku; ⊙11am-6pm, to 8pm Fri & Sat, usually closed on Sun & Mon; ℝJR Yamanote line to Tokyo, Marunouchi exit) **FREE** Dedicated to interdisciplinary experimentation, Intermediatheque cherry picks from the vast collection of the University of Tokyo (Tōdai) to craft a fascinating, contemporary museum experience. Go from viewing the best ornithological taxi-dermy collection in Japan to a giant pop-art print or the beautifully encased skeleton of a dinosaur. A handsome Tōdai lecture hall is reconstituted as a forum for events, including the playing of 1920s jazz recordings on a gramophone, or old movie screenings.

National Museum of
Modern Art (MOMAT)   Museum

(国立近代美術館; Kokuritsu Kindai Bijutsu-kan; ☎03-5777-8600; www.momat.go.jp; 3-1 Kitanomaru-kōen, Chiyoda-ku; adult/student ¥500/250, 1st Sun of the month free; ⊙10am-5pm Tue-Thu, Sun, to 8pm Fri & Sat; Ⓢ Tōzai line to Takebashi, exit 1b) Regularly changing displays from the museum's superb collection of more than 12,000 works, by both local and international artists, are shown over floors two to four; special exhibitions are mounted on the ground floor. All pieces date from the Meiji period onward and impart a sense of how modern Japan has developed through portraits, photography, contemporary sculptures and video works. The museum closes in-between exhibitions, so check the schedule online first.

Crafts Gallery   Museum

(東京国立近代美術館工芸館; Map p250; www.momat.go.jp; 1 Kitanomaru-kōen, Chiyoda-ku; adult/student ¥250/130, 1st Sun of the month free; ⊙10am-5pm Tue-Sun; Ⓢ Tōzai line to Takebashi, exit 1b) Housed in a vintage red-brick building, this annex of MOMAT stages excellent changing exhibitions of *mingei* (folk crafts): ceramics, lacquerware, bamboo, textiles, dolls and much more. Some exhibits feature works by contemporary artisans, including some by Japan's officially designated 'living national treasures'. The building was once the headquarters of the imperial guards, and was rebuilt after its destruction in WWII.

> ☑ **Don't Miss**
> MOMAT's 'Room with a View', which overlooks the Imperial Palace East Garden.

COLDBUSKETY / GETTY IMAGES ©

★ **Local Knowledge**
The 5km loop around the Imperial Palace's moats is a popular jogging course.

Autumn scenes in Rikugi-en

TAKASHI IMAGES / SHUTTERSTOCK ©

Rikugi-en

Considered by many to be Tokyo's most elegant garden, Rikugi-en was originally completed in 1702 at the behest of a feudal lord. It's hidden away in the city's sleepy north; rarely crowded, it's a blissful, timeless retreat.

Rikugi-en is a classic example of an Edo-era strolling garden, one of only three such gardens that remain in Tokyo. Strolling gardens are designed as a series of sensory encounters that unfold along a meandering path, usually around a central body of water. The encounters are typically visual, but they can be auditory, too – of rushing water, for example.

Great For...

☑ Don't Miss

Sipping tea while overlooking the garden's pond.

Famous Views

The garden has 88 viewpoints that evoke scenes from poetry and legend or recreate (in miniature) famous vistas found in Japan and China. An example of the former is the bridge, **Togetsukyō**, created from two huge stone slabs, that references a poem about a crane flying over a moonlit field. Another is the craggy rock in the garden's pond,

PHUONG D. NGUYEN / SHUTTERSTOCK ©

❶ Need to Know

Rikugi-en (六義園; ☎03-3941-2222; http://teien.tokyo-park.or.jp/en/rikugien; 6-16-3 Hon-Komagome, Bunkyō-ku; adult/senior/child ¥300/150/free; ⏰9am-5pm; 🚃JR Yamanote line to Komagome, south exit)

✕ Take a Break

There's a teahouse and a snack stand inside the park.

★ Top Tip

Pair a trip to Rikugi-en with one to the Tokyo National Museum in Ueno; it's just five stops away on the JR Yamanote line.

called **Hōrai-jima**, which represents the Taoist 'Isle of Immortals'.

The hill, **Fujishiro-tōge**, is named after a real one in Wakayama Prefecture; climb to the top for panoramic views over the garden.

Stone markers around the garden make note of some other scenic viewpoints (even the most erudite Japanese visitor wouldn't get them all); some are signposted with English explanations as well. Free, hour-long guided tours in English are offered at 11am and 2pm on the 1st and 3rd Sunday of the month.

Teahouses

Rikugi-en also has two vintage wooden teahouses: **Tsutsuji-chaya** dates to the Meiji period and is perfectly primed for viewing the maples in autumn. **Takimi-chaya** is perched on the edge of the stream where you can enjoy the view of a mini waterfall over rocks and giant koi (carp) swimming in the water.

Fukiage-chaya is not an antique but is attractive all the same – and it actually serves tea. Here you can sip *matcha* (powered green tea; ¥510) and enjoy a seasonal *wagashi* (sweet) alfresco on the edge of the pond.

Seasonal Blooms

The garden is most famous for its maple leaves, which turn bright red around late November and early December. During this time, the park stays open until 9pm and the trees are illuminated after sunset. In early spring you can catch plum blossoms, followed by the flowering of the magnificent weeping cherry tree near the entrance. In winter see the pruned pine trees strung with ropes to protect their branches from snowfall.

Temporary exhibition: *Port of Reflections* (2014), by Leandro Erlich. Photo courtesy: Mori Art Museum, Tokyo

Roppongi Hills

This postmodern mall covers more than 11 hectares and is home to a contemporary art museum, a sky-high observatory, shops galore, dozens of restaurants and even a formal Japanese garden.

Great For...

☑ **Don't Miss**

Catching an art exhibit and getting a view over the city at Mori Tower.

Roppongi Hills, which opened in 2005, set the standard for 21st-century real-estate developments in Tokyo. The complex was designed by Jerde, a California-based, global pioneer of postmodern mall design. It's imposing, upmarket and polarising – an architectural marvel, a grand vision realised or a crass shrine to conspicuous consumption? Explore this urban maze and decide for yourself.

Mori Tower

The centrepiece of the complex is the 54-storey Mori Tower. Atop it is the contemporary art exhibition space, **Mori Art Museum** (森美術館; www.mori.art.museum; 52nd fl, Mori Tower; adult/child/student/senior ¥1800/600/1200/1500; ⊙10am-10pm Wed-Mon, to 5pm Tue, inside Sky Deck 10am-10pm; ⑤Hibiya line to Roppongi, exit 1). Shows – there

❶ Need to Know

Roppongi Hills (六本木ヒルズ; Map p252; www.roppongihills.com; 6-chōme Roppongi, Minato-ku; ⊙11am-11pm; ⑤Hibiya line to Roppongi, exit 1)

✕ Take a Break

Catch a film at Toho Cinemas Roppongi Hills (p193), which is also here.

★ Top Tip

Unlike most museums, Mori Art Museum is open late – until 10pm every day except Tuesday.

Deck (additional fee adult/child ¥500/300; 11am to 8pm) for alfresco views.

Public Art & Garden

The open-air plaza near the street entrance is the lucky home of one of Louise Bourgeois' giant **Maman** spider sculptures. It has an amusing way of messing with the scale of the buildings, especially in photos. There are other sculptures, paintings and installations – including works by Miyajima Tatsuo and Cai Guo-Qiang – scattered around the complex, too.

Mohri Garden is the mall's recreation of an Edo-style strolling garden, complete with meandering paths and a central pond. When juxtaposed with the gleaming towers, the garden creates a fascinating study of luxury then and now.

is no permanent collection – take advantage of the galleries' high ceilings and broad views and feature superstars of the art world from both Japan and abroad. Every three years the museum stages a showcase of up-and-coming Japanese artists called Roppongi Crossing, the next of which will be held in 2019.

Admission to the museum is shared with the observatory, **Tokyo City View** (東京シティビュー; ☎03-6406-6652; www.roppongihills.com/tcv/en; 52nd fl, Mori Tower; adult/senior/student/child ¥1800/1500/1200/600; ⊙10am-11pm Mon-Thu & Sun, to 1am Fri & Sat), which wraps around the 52nd floor. From this 250m-high vantage point you can see 360-degree views of the seemingly never-ending city. Weather permitting, you can also pop out to the external rooftop Sky

Karaoke

Karaoke isn't just about singing: it's an excuse to let loose, a bonding ritual, a reason to keep the party going past the last train and a way to kill time until the first one starts in the morning.

Great For...

☑ **Don't Miss**

Finding your signature song and letting your inner diva shine.

Karaoke Basics

In Japan, karaoke (カラオケ; pronounced kah-rah-oh-kay) is usually sung in a private room among friends (though some bars have karaoke as well). Admission is typically charged per person per half-hour, with a minimum charge of one hour.

First up, go to the front desk to sign up for a room. Most places offer a variety of package deals that include a set number of singing hours with or without unlimited drinks; these can be good value. You can also just go in for the minimum one hour and decide later on if you wish to continue (be warned though: you probably will).

Most places in busy areas of Tokyo have at least one staff member who can communicate in basic English. You'll be able to choose from a wide range of English-language songs and the touch-screen devices

❶ Need to Know

Karaoke parlours can be found near any major train station – and especially in nightlife districts such as Shinjuku, Shibuya and Roppongi.

✕ Take a Break

Food and drinks can be ordered by the phone in the room and are brought to the door.

★ Top Tip

Karaoke rates fluctuate by day and time; the cheapest time to go is on a weekday afternoon.

used to search for songs by artist or title will have an English function too.

Each room has a telephone connected to the front desk; staff will ring when you have about 10 minutes remaining, giving you the chance to extend your singing session. They'll also ring to tell you when time is up, at which point head to the front desk to settle your bill.

Karaoke Parlours

Karaoke is dominated by a few major chains, which include: Karaoke-kan (カラオケ館), Pasela (パセラ), Big Echo (ビッグエコー) and Uta Hiroba (歌広場). They're always brightly lit and easy to spot. You can request a non-smoking room; larger parlours often have rooms designed for kids.

Karaoke-kan   Karaoke
(カラオケ館; Map p246; www.karaokekan.jp; 25-6 Udagawa-chō, Shibuya-ku; per 30min Mon-Thu ¥535, Fri-Sun ¥635; ⊙11am-6am; ➡; 🚇JR Yamanote Line to Shibuya, Hachikō exit) This branch of a generic national karaoke chain was immortalised as a location in the film *Lost in Translation*. Another draw: the rack of costumes in the lobby you can borrow for free. Sing all night from 11pm to 6am for just ¥1990 Monday to Thursday (or ¥2850 Friday to Sunday). Ask at the desk about all-you-can-drink (*nomihōdai*; 飲み放題) plans.

Pasela Resorts   Karaoke
(パセラ リゾーツ; Map p252; ☑0120-911-086; www.pasela.co.jp/shop/roppongi/pasela-rop-pongi; 5-16-3 Roppongi, Minato-ku; per hour per person Sun-Thu ¥1100, Fri & Sat ¥1300; ⊙noon-6am Sun-Thu, to 7am Fri & Sat; 📶; 🅂Hibiya line to Roppongi, exit 3) With decor that is a cut above the other yodelling parlours, Pasela offers six floors of karaoke rooms (including swanky VIP suites), an extensive selection of Western songs, and wine, champagne and sweets on the menu. The two-hour *nomihōdai* package (per person ¥3700, ¥4200 on Fridays; room rental included) is a good deal.

Tokyo skyline at night overlooking Tokyo Tower

Drinks with a View

By night, Tokyo appears truly beautiful, as if the sky were inverted and the glittering stars below. There's nothing quite like seeing the city from a couple of hundred metres in the air, cocktail glass in hand. Or stay closer to sea level, and see the skyline from Tokyo Bay.

Great For...

ⓘ Need to Know

Most of Tokyo's top-tier hotels have top-floor bars – you can take your pick, really.

★ Top Tip

Check for happy-hour deals, like the one at Peter: the Bar (p116).

MATT MUNRO / LONELY PLANET ©

New York Bar
Bar

(ニューヨークバー; Map p253; ☑03-5323-3458; http://restaurants.tokyo.park.hyatt.co.jp/en/nyb.html; 52nd fl, Park Hyatt, 3-7-1-2 Nishi-Shinjuku, Shinjuku-ku; ⏰5pm-midnight Sun-Wed, to 1am Thu-Sat; 🚇; 🚈Ōedo line to Tochōmae, exit A4) Head to the Park Hyatt's 52nd floor to swoon over the sweeping nightscape from the floor-to-ceiling windows at this bar (of *Lost in Translation* fame). There's a cover charge of ¥2700 if you visit or stay past 8pm (7pm Sunday); go earlier and watch the sky fade to black. Cocktails start at ¥2160. Note: dress code enforced and 15% service charge levied.

Two Rooms
Bar

(トゥールームス; Map p246; ☑03-3498-0002; www.tworooms.jp; 5th fl, AO bldg, 3-11-7 Kita-Aoyama, Minato-ku; ⏰11.30am-2am Mon-Sat, to 10pm Sun; 🚇; 🚈Ginza line to Omote-sandō, exit B2) Expect a crowd dressed like they don't care that wine by the glass starts at ¥1600. You can eat here too, but the real scene is at night by the bar. The terrace has sweeping views towards the Shinjuku skyline. Call ahead (staff speak English) on Friday or Saturday night to reserve a spot under the stars.

Peter: the Bar
Cocktail Bar

(Map p250; ☑03-6270-2763; http://tokyo.peninsula.com/en/fine-dining/peter-lounge-bar; 24th fl, 1-8-1 Yūrakuchō, Chiyoda-ku; ⏰noon-midnight, to 1am Fri & Sat; 🚈Hibiya line to Hibiya, exit A6 or A7) The Peninsula Tokyo hotel's 24th-floor bar has dress-circle views across the Imperial Palace, Hibiya Park and Ginza and a generous happy hour (5pm to 8pm Sunday to Thursday). happy-hour drinks – including the bar's signature 'Tokyo Joe' cocktail

Jicoo the Floating Bar

(gin, ume liqueur, Drambuie and cranberry juice) – and snacks are all ¥800. There's a 15% service charge, but no cover charge.

Jicoo the Floating Bar Cocktail Bar

(ジークザフローティングバー; ☑0120-049-490; www.jicoofloatingbar.com; cover from ¥2600; ⊗8-10.30pm Thu-Sat; ☒Yurikamome line to Hinode or Odaiba Kaihin-kōen, north exit) For a few nights a week, the futuristic cruise-boat *Himiko*, designed by manga and anime artist Leiji Matsumoto, morphs into this floating bar. Board on the hour at Hinode pier and the half-hour at Odaiba Kaihin-kōen. The evening-long 'floating pass' usually includes some sort of live music; check the

---

☑ Don't Miss

Sundown over the city. (Bonus: you're more likely to get a good seat at this time.)

PAOLO PATRIZI / ALAMY STOCK PHOTO ©

schedule online as sometimes events drive up the price.

Peak Bar Bar

(ピークバー; Map p253; ☑03-5323-3461; http://restaurants.tokyo.park.hyatt.co.jp/en/pbr. html; 41st fl, Park Hyatt, 3-7-1-2 Nishi-Shinjuku, Shinjuku-ku; ⊗5-11.30pm, ⊙; ⓈŌedo line to Tochōmae, exit A4) The views at the Park Hyatt's Peak Bar are arguably just as good as the ones from the hotel's more famous New York Bar. And for bargain hunters, there is the undeniable appeal of the bar's generous 'Twilight Time' all-you-can-drink deal (5pm to 8pm; ¥5000, unlimited canapes included). Otherwise, cocktails start at ¥2000; no cover charge.

(marunouchi) House Bar

(丸の内ハウス; Map p250; ☑03-5218-5100; www.marunouchi-house.com; 7th fl, Shin-Marunouchi Bldg, 1-5-1 Marunouchi, Chiyoda-ku; ⊗11am-4am Mon-Sat, to 11pm Sun; ⊙; ☒JR lines to Tokyo, Marunouchi north exit) On the 7th floor of the Shin-Maru Building, this collection of nine bars and pubs is a popular after-work gathering spot. There's a wrap-around terrace, so many spots have outdoor seating. The views aren't sky-high; instead you feel curiously suspended among the office towers, hovering over Tokyo Station below. The bars often come together to hold joint events.

Asahi Sky Room Bar

(アサヒスカイルーム; Map p255; ☑03-5608-5277; 22nd fl, Asahi Super Dry Bldg, 1-23-1 Azuma-bashi, Sumida-ku; beer ¥720; ⊗10am-10pm; ⊙; ⓈGinza line to Asakusa, exit 4) Spend the day at the religious sites and end at the Asahi altar, on the 22nd floor of the golden-tinged Asahi Super Dry Building. The venue itself isn't noteworthy, but the views over the Sumida River are spectacular, especially at sunset.

✕ Take a Break

Come down to earth with a bowl of ramen, Tokyo's favourite post-drinking meal.

DINING OUT

Opulent *kaiseki*, teahouses and *izakaya*

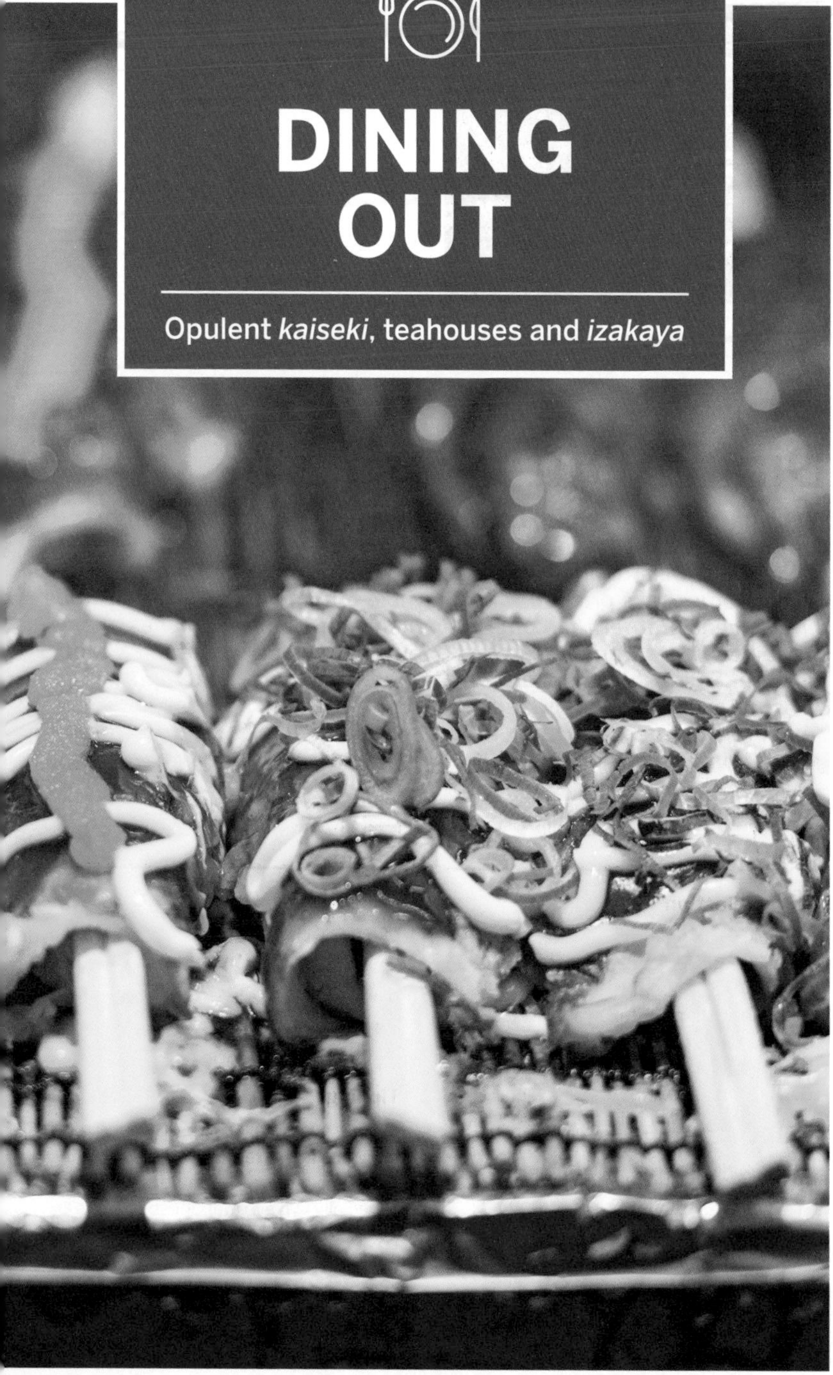

Dining Out

Tokyo has a vibrant and cosmopolitan dining scene and a strong culture of eating out – popular restaurants are packed most nights of the week. Best of all, you can get superlative meals on any budget. Tokyo foodies take pride in what they like to think of as their 'boutique' dining scene. Rather than offer long menus of elaborate dishes, many of the best restaurants make just a few things – and sometimes even just one! Sushi shops make sushi; tempura shops make tempura. A restaurant that does too much might be suspect: how can it compare to a speciality shop that has been honing its craft for three generations?

In This Section

Price Ranges

The following price ranges represent the cost of a meal for one person.

¥ less than ¥2000

¥¥ ¥2000 to ¥5000

¥¥¥ more than ¥5000

Tipping

It is not customary to tip. High-end restaurants and hotels usually add a 10% service fee to the bill. Some restaurants, especially *izakaya* (Japanese pub-eateries), may instead levy a kind of cover charge (usually a few hundred yen), which covers a small appetiser.

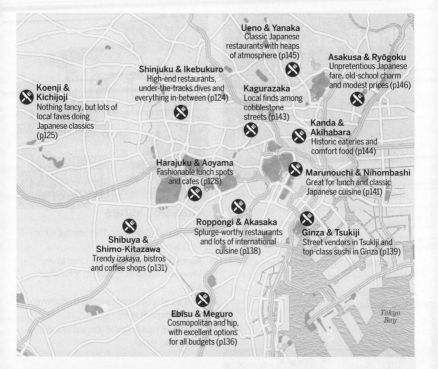

Ueno & Yanaka
Classic Japanese restaurants with heaps of atmosphere (p145)

Asakusa & Ryōgoku
Unpretentious Japanese fare, old-school charm and modest prices (p146)

Shinjuku & Ikebukuro
High-end restaurants, under-the-tracks dives and everything in-between (p124)

Kagurazaka
Local finds among cobblestone streets (p143)

Koenji & Kichijoji
Nothing fancy, but lots of local faves doing Japanese classics (p125)

Kanda & Akihabara
Historic eateries and comfort food (p144)

Harajuku & Aoyama
Fashionable lunch spots and cafes (p128)

Marunouchi & Nihombashi
Great for lunch and classic Japanese cuisine (p141)

Roppongi & Akasaka
Splurge-worthy restaurants and lots of international cuisine (p138)

Ginza & Tsukiji
Street vendors in Tsukiji and top-class sushi in Ginza (p139)

Shibuya & Shimo-Kitazawa
Trendy *izakaya*, bistros and coffee shops (p131)

Tokyo Bay

Ebisu & Meguro
Cosmopolitan and hip, with excellent options for all budgets (p136)

The Best...

Useful Phrases

I'd like to reserve a table for (two).	(2人)の予約を お願いします。 (fu·ta·ri) no yo·ya·ku o o·ne·gai shi·mas
That was delicious!	おいしかった。 oy·shi·kat·ta
Please bring the bill.	お勘定をください。 o·kan·jō o ku·da·sai

Classic Dishes

Soba Buckwheat noodles served hot in broth or at room temperature with sauce for dipping.

Okonomiyaki Savoury pancake, stuffed with pork, squid, cabbage, cheese – anything really.

Tempura Seafood and vegetables deep-fried in a fluffy, light batter.

Tonkatsu Tender pork cutlets battered and deep-fried, served with a side of grated cabbage.

Yakitori Chicken skewers (and veggies, too) grilled on hot coals.

The Best...

Experience Tokyo's best restaurants and cuisines

Japanese Cuisine

Kozue (p124) Exquisite Japanese dishes and stunning night views over Shinjuku.

Innsyoutei (p144) Lovely place to eat *kaiseki*-style (Japanese haute cuisine) in Ueno-kōen.

Tofuya-Ukai (p139) Handmade tofu becomes haute cuisine.

d47 Shokudō (p131) Regional specialities from around Japan.

Classic Dishes

Harajuku Gyōza-rō (p128) Addictive dumplings served all night.

Kanda Yabu Soba (p144; pictured above) Venerable Kanda shop making soba since 1880.

Bird Land (p140) Upscale *yakitori* from free-range, heirloom birds.

Sometarō (p147) Grill-it-yourself *okonomiyaki* in an old house.

Ramen

Kikanbō (p144) A match made in heaven for fans of ramen and spice.

Harukiya (p125) The definitive Tokyo ramen.

Afuri (p137) Light citrus-y broth and a cool industrial look.

Nagi (p124) Smoky *niboshi* (dried sardine) ramen in an old wooden shack.

Izakaya

Shinsuke (p145) Century-old *izakaya* adored by sake aficionados.

Shirube (p131) Loud, lively and hip, serving creative fusion dishes.

Donjaca (p124) Classic mid-20th-century vibe and home-style food.

Teahouses

Sakurai Japanese Tea Experience (p128) Stylish new interpretation of the classic Japanese tea ceremony.

Chashitsu Kaboku (p143) Sip paint-thick *matcha* (powdered green tea) from a famous Kyoto shop.

Uni Stand (p126) Single-origin teas and carefully crafted *matcha* lattes.

Old Tokyo Atmosphere

Omoide-yokochō (p87; pictured above) Atmospheric *yakitori* stalls near the train tracks.

Hantei (p145) Deep-fried skewers in a 100-year-old heritage house.

Komagata Dozeu (p147) Landmark restaurant serving *dojō-nabe* (loach hotpot) for 200 years.

Sweets

Ouca (p138) Ice cream in only-in-Japan flavours.

Higashiya Man (p129) Fresh-steamed, sweet bean dumplings.

Himitsu-dō (p145) Beloved *kakigōri* (shaved ice) vendor.

Suzukien (p147) Extreme *matcha* ice cream.

☆ Lonely Planet's Top Choices

Kyūbey (p76) Rarefied Ginza sushi at its finest.

Ginza Kagari (p139) Tokyo's current, favourite *ramen-ya* (ramen shop).

Tempura Kondō (p139) Magical, light-as-air tempura from a master chef.

Kikunoi (p138) Gorgeous *kaiseki* in the classic Kyoto style.

Tonki (p136) *Tonkatsu* raised to an art.

⊗ Shinjuku & Ikebukuro

Kozue
Japanese ¥¥¥

(梢; Map p253; ☎03-5323-3460; http://tokyo.
park.hyatt.jp/en/hotel/dining/Kozue.html; 40th
fl, Park Hyatt, 3-7-1-2 Nishi-Shinjuku, Shinjuku-
ku; lunch set menu ¥2850-12,400, dinner set
menu ¥12,400-27,300; ⊗11.30am-2.30pm &
5.30-9.30pm; Ⓢ Ōedo line to Tochōmae, exit A4)
It's hard to beat Kozue's combination of
well-executed, seasonal Japanese cuisine,
artisan crockery and soaring views over
Shinjuku from the floor-to-ceiling windows.
As the (kimono-clad) staff speak English
and the restaurant caters well to dietary
restrictions and personal preferences, this
is a good splurge spot for diners who don't
want to give up complete control. Reservations are essential.

Nagi
Ramen ¥

(凪; Map p253; www.n-nagi.com; 2nd fl, Golden
Gai G2, 1-1-10 Kabukichō, Shinjuku-ku; ramen from
¥850; ⊗24hr; Ⓡ JR Yamanote line to Shinjuku,
east exit) Nagi, once an upstart, has done well
and now has branches around the city – and
around Asia. This tiny shop, one of the originals, up a treacherous stairway in Golden
Gai, is still our favourite. (It's many people's
favourite and often has a line.) The house
speciality is *niboshi* ramen (egg noodles in a
broth flavoured with dried sardines).

Look for the sign with a red circle.

Donjaca
Izakaya ¥

(呑者家; Map p253; ☎03-3341-2497; 3-9-10
Shinjuku, Shinjuku-ku; dishes ¥350-850; ⊗5pm-
7am; Ⓢ Marunouchi line to Shinjuku-sanchōme,
exit C6) The platonic ideal of a Shōwa-era
(1926–89) *izakaya*, Donjaca, in business since 1979, has red leather stools,
paper-lantern lighting and hand-written
menus on the wall. The food is equal parts
classic (grilled fish and fried chicken) and
inventive: house specialities include *natto
gyoza* (dumplings stuffed with fermented
soy beans) and *mochi* gratin. Excellent sake
is served in convenient tasting sets.

Warning: Donjaca can get smoky. If the
main shop is full, staff will likely direct you
around the corner to the larger annex.

Croquettes

TMON / SHUTTERSTOCK ©

Nakajima — Kaiseki ¥

(中嶋; Map p253; ☑03-3356-4534; www.shin
jyuku-nakajima.com; basement fl, 3-32-5 Shinjuku, Shinjuku-ku; lunch/dinner from ¥800/8640;
☉11.30am-2pm & 5.30-9.30pm Mon-Sat;
Ⓢ Marunouchi line to Shinjuku-sanchōme, exit A1)
In the evening, Nakajima serves exquisite
kaiseki dinners. On weekdays it also serves
a set lunch of humble *iwashi* (sardines) for
one-tenth the price; in the hands of Nakajima's chefs they're divine. The line for lunch
starts to form shortly before the restaurant
opens at 11.30am. Look for the white sign
at the top of the stairs.

Gochisō Tonjiru — Japanese ¥

(ごちそうとん汁; ☑03-6883-9181; 1-33-2 Yoyogi, Shibuya-ku; meals from ¥840; ☉11.30am-mid-
night; Ⓡ JR Yamanote line to Yoyogi, west exit)
Tonjiru, a home-cooking classic, is a hearty
miso soup packed with root veggies (such
as burdock root, daikon, potato and carrot)
and chunks of pork. At this neighbourhood
hangout, styled more like a bar than a
restaurant, the pork comes in the form of
melting-off-the-bone barbecued spare ribs.
Choose between a Kyoto-style light miso or
a Tokyo-style dark miso.

Ohitotsuzen Tanbo — Japanese ¥

(おひつ膳田んぼ; ☑03-3320-0727; http://
tanbo.co.jp; 1-41-9 Yoyogi, Shibuya-ku; meals
¥1450-2050; ☉11am-11pm; Ⓡ JR Yamanote line
to Yoyogi, west exit) ✐ The speciality here is
the least glamorous part of the meal – the
rice, which comes from an organic farm
that the restaurant manages in Niigata
prefecture. There's nothing farm-to-table
trendy about Tanbo though, which serves
humble *ochazuke*, rice topped with meat
and fish over which hot tea is poured. English instructions explain how to eat it.

Berg — Cafe

(ベルグ; Map p253; www.berg.jp; basement fl,
Lumine Est, 3-38-1 Shinjuku, Shinjuku-ku; ☉7am-
11pm; Ⓡ JR Yamanote line to Shinjuku, east exit)
Berg is an unlikely throwback wedged
inside the super-trendy Lumine Est department store. It's cramped and popular with
chain-smoking pensioners. And yet, the

coffee shop – which charges just ¥216 for
a cup – has a certain cult status. The highly
recommended 'morning set' (*mōningu
setto;* ¥410), served until noon, includes
coffee, hard-boiled egg, potato salad and
toast.

It's inside the Shinjuku train station; look
for the 'Food Pocket' sign to the left of the
east exit ticket gates.

Tsunahachi — Tempura ¥¥

(つな八; Map p253; ☑03-3352-1012; www.
tunahachi.co.jp; 3-31-8 Shinjuku, Shinjuku-ku;
lunch/dinner from ¥1510/2485; ☉11am-
10.30pm; Ⓡ JR Yamanote line to Shinjuku, east
exit) Tsunahachi has been expertly frying
prawns and veggies for more than 90 years
and is an excellent place to get initiated in
the art of tempura. Locals know to come
for the inexpensive *hiruzen* (昼膳; ¥1510)
lunch special (which for reasons intentional
or not, isn't on the English menu). Indigo
noren (curtains) mark the entrance.

Tsunahachi has several outlets around
the city, often in department stores, and is
always a safe bet. This is the main shop.

⊗ Kōenji & Kichijōji

Tensuke — Tempura ¥

(天すけ; ☑03-3223-8505; 3-22-7 Kōenji-kita,
Suginami-ku; lunch/dinner from ¥1100/1600;
☉noon-2pm & 6-10pm Tue-Sun; Ⓡ JR Sōbu line
to Kōenji, north exit) An entirely legitimate
candidate for eighth wonder of the modern
world is Tensuke's *tamago* (egg) tempura.
We don't know how the chef (who is quite a
showman) does it, but the egg comes out
batter-crisp on the outside and runny in the
middle. It's served on rice with seafood and
vegetable tempura as part of the *tamago
tempura teishoku* (玉子天ぷら定食).

There's a blue and orange sign out front;
expect to queue.

Harukiya — Ramen ¥

(春木屋; www.haruki-ya.co.jp; 1-4-6 Kami-Ogi,
Suginami-ku; ramen ¥850-1350; ☉11am-9pm
Wed-Mon; Ⓡ JR Sōbu-Chūō line to Ogikubo, north
exit) Harukiya, open since 1949, is one of

🍽 Special Diets

Tokyo has a growing number of vegetarian restaurants or restaurants that have vegetarian dishes. Happy Cow (www.happycow.net) is a great resource. One note of caution: often dishes that look vegetarian are not (miso soup, for example) because they are prepared with *dashi* (fish stock).

Many chain restaurants and deli counters label their dishes with icons indicating potential allergens (such as dairy, eggs, peanuts, wheat and shellfish), but otherwise this can be tricky. You'll want to have a list of allergens written in Japanese on hand. Gluten-free is particularly challenging, as there is little awareness of coeliac disease in Japan and many kitchen staples, such as soy sauce, contain wheat (and even restaurant staff may not be aware of this). The Gluten-Free Expats Japan! Facebook group is a good resource.

Halal restaurants are on the rise. Halal Gourmet Japan (www.halalgourmet.jp) has a good list of certified restaurants.

Vegitarian nabe
MARINATAKANO / SHUTTERSTOCK ©

Tokyo's oldest ramen shops – so old that the menu here says 'chuka-soba' ('Chinese' soba, which the egg noodle dish was called when it was still an exotic import). The shop serves what has since come to be known as classic Tokyo-style ramen: a light chicken and fish stock seasoned with soy sauce.

Steak House Satou　　　　Steak ¥¥

(ステーキハウスさとう; 📞0422-21-6464; www.shop-satou.com; 1-1-8 Kichijōji Honchō, Mitaka-shi; lunch set ¥1200-10,000; dinner set ¥2600-10,000; ⏱11am-2.30pm & 5-8.30pm Mon-Fri, 11am-8.30pm Sat & Sun; 🚃JR Sōbu-Chūō line to Kichijōji, north exit) This is a classic Japanese-style steak house, where the meat is cooked at the counter on a *teppan* (iron hot plate), diced before serving and paired with rice, miso soup and pickles. It's also excellent value, considering the quality of the beef; even a 'splurge' on the chef's choice (lunch/dinner ¥4000/¥7000) is reasonable.

On the ground floor there's a counter selling *menchi-katsu* (メンチカツ; ¥220), deep-fried, minced-beef croquettes. You can spot the shop by the regular queue.

Tetchan　　　　Yakitori ¥

(てっちゃん; 📞0422-20-6811; 1-1-2 Kichijōji-Honchō, Musashino-shi; skewers & small dishes ¥110-540; ⏱3pm-midnight, from noon Sat & Sun; 🚃JR Sōbu-Chūō line to Kichijōji, north exit) Located inside the labyrinthine covered market Harmonica-yokochō, Tetchan has been drawing locals for years. But it's now become something of a tourist destination too, thanks to its new interior of acrylic 'ice' by architect Kuma Kengo (known for his more establishment works). There's no English menu, but safe bets include *tsukune* (chicken meatballs), *buta bara* (pork belly) and *motsu-ni* (stewed offal).

Uni Stand　　　　Teahouse ¥

(ユニスタンド; http://unistand.jp; 1-16-1 Shimorenjaku, Mitaka-shi; ⏱10am-7pm Wed-Mon; 🚃JR Sōbu-Chūō line to Mitaka, south exit) Taking a cue from the third-wave coffee movement, Uni Stand sells single-origin Japanese teas and carefully crafted *matcha* lattes (with high-grade powdered green tea from Uji, near Kyoto) from a little shop on the edge of Inokashira-kōen (drinks ¥380 to ¥560). It's a welcome addition: a good cup of tea is surprisingly hard to find on the go in Tokyo.

MAHATHIR MOHD YASIN / SHUTTERSTOCK ©; KUMACORE / GETTY IMAGES ©; PHILLIP MAGUIRE / SHUTTERSTOCK ©

☆ Best Tokyo Sweets

Ouca (p138)

Higashiya Man (p129

Himitsu-dō (p145)

Suzukien (p147)

Clockwise from top: wagashi (traditional sweets); cooking *dorayaki* (pancake filled with sweet adzuki paste); rabbit-themed icecream sundae

🍴 Street Food

Street-food stands, called *yatai* (屋台), don't have the same ubiquitous presence in Tokyo as they do in other Asian cities. However, you can find them in markets, including Tsukiji Outer Market (p36) or Ameya-yokochō (p69), heavily touristed areas, such as along Asakusa's Nakamise-dōri and in Ueno-kōen (p68), and always at festivals.

Typical *yatai* food includes *okonomiyaki* (お好み焼き; savoury pancakes), *yaki-soba* (焼きそば; stir-fried noodles) and *tai-yaki* (たい焼き; fish-shaped cakes stuffed with bean paste).

Food trucks are popular with the downtown office crowd, gathering daily around the Tokyo International Forum (p52) at lunchtime; they also make the rounds of weekend markets, including the Farmer's Market @UNU.

And keep an eye out for Tokyo's original food trucks: the *yaki-imo* (roasted whole sweet potato) carts that rove the city from October to March, crooning 'yaki-imohhhhh…!'.

Above: okonomiyaki
ARTRAN / GETTY IMAGES ©

⊗ Harajuku & Aoyama

Maisen   Tonkatsu ¥
(まい泉; Map p246; http://mai-sen.com; 4-8-5 Jingūmae, Shibuya-ku; lunch/dinner from ¥995/1680; ⊙11am-10pm; Ⓢ Ginza line to Omote-sandō, exit A2) You could order something else (maybe fried shrimp), but everyone else will be ordering the famous

tonkatsu (breaded, deep-fried pork cutlets). There are different grades of pork on the menu, including prized *kurobuta* (black pig), but even the cheapest is melt-in-your-mouth divine. The restaurant is housed in an old public bathhouse. A takeaway window (10am to 7pm) serves delicious *tonkatsu sando* (sandwiches).

Sakurai Japanese
Tea Experience   Teahouse ¥¥
(櫻井焙茶研究所; Map p246; ☑03-6451-1539; www.sakurai-tea.jp; 5th fl, Spiral bldg, 5-6-23 Minami-Aoyama, Minato-ku; tea from ¥800, course from ¥4800; ⊙11am-11pm; Ⓢ Ginza line to Omote-sandō. exit B1) Tea master (and former bartender) Sakurai Shinya's contemporary take on the tea ceremony is a must for anyone hoping to be better acquainted with Japan's signature brew. The course includes several varieties – you might be surprised how different tea can taste – paired with small bites, including some beautiful traditional sweets. Come in the evening for tea cocktails.

Harajuku Gyōza-rō   Dumplings ¥
(原宿餃子樓; Map p246; 6-4-2 Jingūmae, Shibuya-ku; 6 gyōza ¥290; ⊙11.30am-4.30am, to 10pm Sun; Ⓡ JR Yamanote line to Harajuku, Omote-sandō exit) *Gyōza* (dumplings) are the only thing on the menu here, but you won't hear any complaints from the regulars who queue up to get their fix. Have them *sui* (boiled) or *yaki* (pan-fried), with or without *niniku* (garlic) or *nira* (chives) – they're all delicious. Expect to wait on weekends or at lunchtime, but the line moves quickly.

Yanmo   Seafood ¥¥¥
(やんも; Map p246; ☑03-5466-0636; www.yanmo.co.jp/aoyama/index.html; basement fl, T Place bldg, 5-5-25 Minami-Aoyama, Minato-ku; lunch/dinner set menu from ¥1100/7000; ⊙11.30am-2pm & 6-10.30pm Mon-Sat; Ⓢ Ginza line to Omote-sandō, exit A5) Freshly caught seafood from the nearby Izu Peninsula is the speciality at this upscale yet unpretentious restaurant. If you're looking to splash out on a seafood dinner, this is a great place to do so. The reasonably priced set

menus include sashimi and steamed and grilled fish. Reservations are essential for dinner. Lunch is a bargain, but you might have to queue.

Commune 2nd   Market ¥

(Map p246; http://commune2nd.com; 3-13 Minami-Aoyama, Minato-ku; ⏰11am-10pm; 🏃; §Ginza line to Omote-sandō, exit A4) Commune 2nd is one of the rare alfresco dining spots in Tokyo. It's really more like a semi-permanent food-truck gathering (no one knows how long it will last; the land is incredibly valuable). There are a dozen or so vendors offering inexpensive curries, hotdogs, beer and the like. You can put together a meal for around ¥1000 to ¥1500, then grab a bench.

Higashiya Man   Sweets ¥

(ひがしや まん; Map p246; 📞03-5414-3881; www.higashiya.com/shop/man; 3-17-14 Minami-Aoyama, Minato-ku; sweets from ¥200; ⏰11am-7pm, to 8pm Jul & Aug; 🏃; §Ginza line to Omote-sandō, exit A4) *Manjū* (まんじゅう) – that's where the shop's name comes from; it's not just for men! – are hot buns stuffed with sweetened red-bean paste. They're steamed fresh at this take-away counter, a popular pit-stop for Aoyama shoppers. Inside the tiny shop, there's a greater selection of traditional Japanese sweets, many packaged beautifully as gifts.

Farmer's Market @UNU   Market ¥

(Map p246; www.farmersmarkets.jp; 5-53-7 Jingūmae, Shibuya-ku; ⏰10am-4pm Sat & Sun; §Ginza line to Omote-sandō, exit B2) On weekends a farmers' market, with colourful produce, pickles and preserves, sets up on the plaza in front of the United Nations University on Aoyama-dōri. There are usually at least half a dozen food trucks, too, serving up curry, noodles, coffee and the like. It's as much a social event as a shopping stop.

Events pop up, too, including the monthly flea market Raw Tokyo (p157).

Mominoki House   Japanese ¥¥

(もみの木ハウス; Map p246; www.mominoki-house.net; 2-18-5 Jingūmae, Shibuya-ku; lunch/dinner set menu from ¥980/4000; ⏰11am-3pm & 5-10pm Mon-Sat, to 9am Sun;

Omoide-yokochō (p87)

KASEM / SHUTTERSTOCK ©

🍽 Department Store Food Halls

The below-ground floors of Tokyo's department stores hold fantastic food halls called *depachika* (literally 'department store basement'). Dozens of vendors offer a staggering array of foodstuffs of the highest order; most are branches of famous restaurants, producers and confectioners. You can find prepared food, such as sushi and salads to take away, as well as sweets, *sembei* (rice crackers), tea and sake gorgeously packaged for presentation as gifts. Two *depachika* to try are Isetan (p154) in Shinjuku and Mitsukoshi (p161) in Ginza.

Sake tastings at Mitsukoshi department store (p161)
MATT MUNRO / LONELY PLANET ©

🗲; 🚃 JR Yamanote line to Harajuku, Takeshita exit) 🍃 Boho Tokyoites have been coming here for tasty macrobiotic fare since 1976. The casual dining room, which looks like a grown-up (indoor) tree fort and features several cosy, semi-private booths, has seen some famous visitors too, such as Paul McCartney. Chef Yamada's menu is heavily vegan, but also includes free-range chicken and *Ezo shika* (Hokkaidō venison, ¥4800).

Maru   Japanese ¥¥¥
(圖; Map p246; 📞03-6418-5572; www.maru-mayfont.jp; basement fl, 5-50-8 Jingū-mae, Shibuya-ku; dinner course from ¥6600; 🕙5.30pm–midnight Mon-Fri, 5pm–midnight Sat & Sun; ⑤Ginza line to Omote-sandō, exit B2) Maru's head chef trained at a Kyoto *kaiseki* restaurant and then decided he'd rather run a down-to-earth, accessible

restaurant. The seven-course meal (which changes monthly) is a good deal and Maru is deservedly popular; reservations are recommended.

The Ginza shop (p140) is open for lunch.

Koffee Mameya   Coffee ¥
(コーヒーマメヤ; Map p246; www.koffee-mameya.com; 4-15-3 Jingūmae, Shibuya-ku; coffee from ¥350; 🕙10am-6pm; ⑤Ginza line to Omote-sandō, exit A2) At any given time, Koffee Mameya (heir to the beloved Omotesando Koffee) has 15 to 20 different varieties of beans on rotation from indie roasters around Japan (and some from overseas) – single-origins and blends, on a spectrum from light-roasted Ethiopians to full-bodied Sumatrans. Pick your pleasure (English-speaking baristas can help). There's no seating but you can loiter at the counter.

Beans, in souvenir-appropriate packaging, are available, too.

Pariya   International ¥
(パリヤ; Map p246; 📞03-3409-8468; www.pariya.jp/shop/aoyama.html; 3-12-14 Kita-Aoyama, Minato-ku; meals from ¥1230; 🕙11.30am-11pm, to 10pm Sun; 🗲; ⑤Ginza line to Omote-sandō, exit B2) Pariya is the local cafeteria for the fashionable set. It's not cheap slop though; typical dishes include shrimp croquettes and curried potato salad. Grab a tray and choose one main, one salad and one side dish (or two salads and a side for vegetarians). There are colourful cupcakes and gelati for dessert.

Little Nap Coffee Stand   Cafe ¥
(リトルナップコーヒースタンド; Map p246; www.littlenap.jp; 5-65-4 Yoyogi, Shibuya-ku; 🕙9am-7pm Tue-Sun; ⑤Chiyoda line to Yoyogi-kōen, exit 3) Few people enter Yoyogi-kōen from the entrance near the subway stop of the same name, except those who live nearby. Odds are, on their way, they've stopped by Little Nap for a well-crafted latte (¥450). On Sundays, there's always a crowd loitering out front.

Street food stalls at Commune 2nd (p129)

Sakura-tei　　　　Okonomiyaki ¥

(さくら亭; Map p246; ☎03-3479-0039;
www.sakuratei.co.jp; 3-20-1 Jingūmae, Shibuya-
ku; okonomiyaki ¥1050-1800; ⏰11am-midnight;
🈂🈂; 🚉JR Yamanote line to Harajuku, Takeshita
exit) Grill your own *okonomiyaki* at this
funky place inside the gallery Design
Festa. In addition to classic options (with
pork, squid and cabbage), there are some
fusion-style ones (such as the 'Mexican
okonomiyaki' with taco fillings). There's
also a great value 90-minute all-you-can-
eat plan (¥2500).

Montoak　　　　　　　Cafe ¥

(モントーク; Map p246; 6-1-9 Jingūmae,
Shibuya-ku; ⏰11am-1.30am Sun-Thu, Fri & Sat
to 3am; 🚉JR Yamanote line to Harajuku, Omote-
sandō exit) This stylish, tinted-glass cube
is a calm, dimly lit retreat from the busy
streets. It's perfect for holing up with a pot
of tea or carafe of wine and watching the
crowds go by. Or, if the weather is
nice, score a seat on the terrace.
Drinks from ¥700.

☒ Shibuya & Shimo-Kitazawa

d47 Shokudō　　　　　Japanese ¥

(d47食堂; Map p246; www.hikarie8.com/
d47shokudo/about.shtml; 8th fl, Shibuya Hikarie,
2-21-1 Shibuya, Shibuya-ku; meals ¥1200-1780;
⏰11am-2.30pm & 6-10.30pm; 🚉JR Yamanote
line to Shibuya, east exit) There are 47 prefec-
tures in Japan and d47 serves a changing
line-up of *teishoku* (set meals) that evoke
the specialities of each, from the fermented tofu of Okinawa to the stuffed squid of
Hokkaido. A larger menu of small plates is
available in the evening. Picture windows
offer bird's-eye views over the trains coming and going at Shibuya Station.

Shirube　　　　　　　Izakaya ¥

(汁べゑ; ☎03-3413-3785; 2-18-2 Kitazawa,
Setagaya-ku; dishes ¥430-1060; ⏰5.30pm-
midnight; 🈂; 🚉Keiō Inokashira line to Shimo-
Kitazawa, south exit) It's a toss-up as to which
has the most character here: the inventive fusion dishes or the charismatic staff
who put on a show in the open kitchen.

Either way, Shirube is among Tokyo's most beloved *izakaya*. Don't miss the *aburi saba* (blow-torch grilled mackerel), the house speciality. Reservations recommended (and a must on weekends); cover charge ¥400 per person.

Heading down the hill from Shimo-Kitazawa Station's south exit, make a right in front of Mr Donuts and look for the white *noren* (doorway curtains) on your right.

Matsukiya — Hotpot ¥¥¥

(松木家; Map p246; ☑03-3461-2651; 6-8 Maruyama-chō, Shibuya-ku; meals from ¥5400; ☺5-11pm Mon-Sat; 圓JR Yamanote line to Shibuya, Hachikō exit) There are only two things on the menu at Matsukiya: *sukiyaki* (thinly sliced beef, simmered and then dipped in raw egg) and *shabu-shabu* (thinly sliced meat swished in hot broth and then dipped in a citrus and soy sauce or sesame sauce). Both use high-quality, finely marbled *wagyū* (Japanese beef) from Ōmi. Meals include veggies and noodles cooked in the broths.

There's a white sign out front and the entrance is up some stairs. Reservations are recommended.

Gyūkatsu Motomura — Tonkatsu ¥

(牛かつ もと村; Map p246; ☑03-3797-3735; www.gyukatsu-motomura.com; basement fl, 3-18-10 Shibuya, Shibuya-ku; set meal ¥1300-2200; ☺10am-10pm; 圓JR Yamanote line to Shibuya, east exit) You know *tonkatsu*, the deep-fried breaded pork cutlet that is a Japanese staple; meet *gyūkatsu*, the deep-fried breaded beef cutlet that is Tokyo's latest food craze. At Motomura, diners get a small individual grill to cook the meat to their liking. Set meals include cabbage, rice and soup. It's just off Meiji-dōri; look for signs on the main road.

Motomura is exceedingly popular, and queues are common. It has since opened other shops in Shibuya and around Tokyo to handle the overflow; check online for other locations.

☆ Best for Coffee

Cafe de l'Ambre (p140)

Glitch (p144)

Bear Pond (p135)

Onibus (p138)

Fuglen (p134)

From left: Fuglen (p134); Little Nap Coffee Stand (p130); Barista at Onibus (p138)

Narukiyo
Izakaya ¥¥¥

(なるきよ; Map p246; 📞03-5485-2223; 2-7-14 Shibuya, Shibuya-ku; dishes ¥700-4800; ⊘6pm-12.30am; 🚉JR Yamanote line to Shibuya, east exit) For evenings when you want to eat well and adventurously, head here. The menu, handwritten on a scroll, is undecipherable – which is fine, because you just want to have what the chef recommends anyway. Tell him how much you're willing to spend (say ¥5000 or ¥7000 per person) and say the magic word: *omakase* (I leave it up to you).

Odds are you'll get a platter of seasonal sashimi, *sumibiyaki* (charcoal-grilled) veggies and meat and a few surprises.

Just a warning: service here is about regular customers first – don't take it personally.

Fuglen Tokyo
Cafe ¥

(Map p246; www.fuglen.no; 1-16-11 Tomigaya, Shibuya-ku; ⊘8am-10pm Mon & Tue, to 1am Wed & Thu, to 2am Fri, 9am-2am Sat, 9am-midnight Sun; 📶; 🚇Chiyoda line to Yoyogi-kōen, exit 2) This Tokyo outpost of a long-running Oslo coffee shop serves Aeropress coffee by day (from ¥360) and some of the city's most creative cocktails (from ¥1250) by night. It's Tomigaya's principal gathering spot. Events featuring special food and drink or music take place most Wednesday evenings.

Camelback
Sandwiches ¥

(キャメルバック; Map p246; www.camelback.tokyo; 42-2 Kamiyama-chō, Shibuya-ku; sandwiches ¥410-900; ⊘8am-5pm Tue-Sun; 🖊; 🚇Chiyoda line to Yoyogi-kōen, exit 2) As Camelback demonstrates, when a sushi chef switches allegiance from rice to bread the result can be a beautiful thing. The speciality here is the *tamago-yaki* (the kind of rolled omelette that you get at sushi shops) sandwich, served on a fluffy roll with a hint of hot mustard. Good coffee, too. Seating is on a bench outside.

Sagatani
Soba ¥

(嵯峨谷; Map p246; 2-25-7 Dōgenzaka, Shibuya-ku; noodles from ¥320; ⊘24hr; 🚉JR Yamanote line to Shibuya, Hachikō exit) Proving that Tokyo is only expensive to those who don't know better, this all-night joint serves up bamboo steamers of delicious noodles

Wagyu display at Steak House Satou (p126)

for just ¥320. You won't regret 'splurging' on the *goma-dare soba* (ごまだれそば; buckwheat noodles with sesame dipping sauce) for ¥450. Look for the stone mill in the window and order from the vending machine.

Food Show   Supermarket ¥

(フードショー; Map p246; basement fl, 2-24-1 Shibuya, Shibuya-ku; ⏰10am-9pm; 🖉; 🚇JR Yamanote line to Shibuya, Hachikō exit) This takeaway paradise in the basement of Shibuya Station has steamers of dumplings, crisp *karaage* (Japanese-style fried chicken), artfully arranged *bentō*, sushi sets, heaps of salads and cakes almost too pretty to eat. There are some counters in one corner where you can stand and eat. Look for the green sign at Hachikō Plaza pointing downstairs.

Nagi Shokudō   Vegan ¥

(なぎ食堂; Map p246; 🖉03-3461-3280; http://nagishokudo.com; 15-10 Uguisudani-chō, Shibuya-ku; lunch/dinner set menu ¥1000/1500; ⏰noon-4pm daily, 6-11pm Mon-Sat; 🛜🖉; 🚇JR Yamanote line to Shibuya, west exit) A vegan haven in fast-food-laced Shibuya, Nagi serves up dishes like falafel and coconut curry. The most popular thing on the menu is a set meal with three small dishes you can choose, plus miso soup and rice. It's a low-key, homely place with mismatched furniture, cater-corner from a post office (and hidden behind a concrete wall; look for the red sign).

Bear Pond Espresso   Cafe ¥

(🖉03-5454-2486; www.bear-pond.com; 2-36-12 Kitazawa, Setagaya-ku; ⏰11am-5.30pm Wed-Mon; 🚇Keiō Inokashira line to Shimo-Kitazawa, north exit) Bear Pond is Tokyo's most haloed espresso stand and its most divisive: the thick syrupy 'angel stain' espresso is considered holy grail by many; others vow never to return because of the often testy service (rules include no photos without permission). Espresso shots are limited, served only until noon; lattes etc are served all day. Drinks ¥300 to ¥700.

🍽 Tokyo Speciality: Monjayaki

Monjayaki (もんじゃ焼き) is a Tokyo speciality. It's similar to the classic dish *okonomiyaki* (a thick savoury pancake stuffed with meat, seafood and cabbage), but the batter is runnier, making for a thin crêpe that crisps at the edges.

Tsukishima, a manmade island in Tokyo Bay near Tsukiji, is the birthplace of the dish and has a whole strip of specialists. **Monja Kondō** (もんじゃ近どう; 🖉03-3533-4555; 3-12-10 Tsukishima, Chūō-ku; monjayaki from ¥700-1500; ⏰5-10pm Mon-Fri, 11.30am-10pm Sat & Sun; 🚇Ōedo line to Tsukishima, exit 8), in business since 1950, is said to be the neighbourhood's oldest purveyor of the dish.

There are some 90 different toppings you can add to the basic mix, and the staff will help you to make it at your own table grill. Try the combination of mochi, cheese and *mentaiko* (spicy cod roe), a local favourite. There's okonomiyaki on the menu, too.

Monjayaki
GARY CONNER / GETTY IMAGES ©

Out   Italian ¥¥

(アウト; Map p246; www.out.restaurant; Vort Aoyama 103; 2-7-14 Shibuya, Shibuya-ku; pasta ¥2900; pasta & wine set ¥4000; ⏰6pm-2am Tue-Sun; 🖉; 🚇JR Yamanote line to Shibuya, east exit) Out serves only one dish – *tagliolini al tartufo* (egg noodles with truffles) – take it or leave it (we'll take it). The noodles are made from scratch in-house with flour imported from Italy; the truffles (rotated by season) are shaved on top of the pasta at the table; and the house wine is a boutique Australian red (also rotated).

Concept-wise, it's like a ramen restaurant: order from the vending machine and grab a seat at the counter. No reservations. Oh and there's one other quirk: Out only plays Led Zeppelin, on vinyl.

Ahiru Store Bistro ¥¥

(アヒルストア; Map p246; ☎03-5454-2146; 1-19-4 Tomigaya, Shibuya-ku; dishes ¥900-2800; ⏰6pm-midnight Mon-Fri, 3-9pm Sat; Ⓢ Chiyoda line to Yoyogi-kōen, exit 2) This tiny counter bistro, dishing up homemade sausages, fresh-baked bread and bio wines (¥1000 to ¥1200 per glass), has a huge local following. Reservations are accepted only for the first seating at 6pm on weekdays; otherwise join the queue (late, or during the middle of the week, is the best time to score a spot).

Kaikaya Seafood ¥¥

(開花屋; Map p246; ☎03-3770-0878; www.kaikaya.com; 23-7 Maruyama-chō, Shibuya-ku; lunch from ¥850, dishes ¥850-3680, set course from ¥3500; ⏰11.30am-2pm & 5.30-10.30pm Mon-Fri, 5.30-10.30pm Sat & Sun; 🚉JR Yamanote line to Shibuya, Hachikō exit) Traveller favourite Kaikaya serves seafood, much of which is caught in nearby Sagami Bay, in a variety of styles, from sashimi to steamed with herbs. It has a fun laidback vibe, with surfboards on the walls, though staff, who speak good English, can come across as pushy. Reservations recommended; there's a table charge of ¥400 per person.

From Dōgenzaka, turn right after the police box; the restaurant, with a red awning, will be on your right.

Ebisu & Meguro

Tonki Tonkatsu ¥

(とんき; ☎03-3491-9928; 1-2-1 Shimo-Meguro, Meguro-ku; meals ¥1900; ⏰4-10.45pm Wed-Mon, closed 3rd Mon of the month; 🚉JR Yamanote line to Meguro, west exit) Tonki is a Tokyo *tonkatsu* legend, deep-frying pork cutlets, recipe unchanged, for nearly 80 years. The seats at the counter – where you can watch the perfectly choreographed chefs – are the most coveted, though there is usually a queue. There are tables upstairs.

From the station, walk down Meguro-dōri, take a left at the first alley and look for a white sign and *noren* across the sliding doors.

Yakiniku Champion   Barbecue ¥¥

(焼肉チャンピオン; Map p246; ☎03-5768-6922; www.yakiniku-champion.com; 1-2-8 Ebisu, Shibuya-ku; dishes ¥780-3300, set course from ¥5600; ⏲5pm-midnight; 🚉JR Yamanote line to Ebisu, west exit) Champion's sprawling menu includes everything from sweetbreads to the choicest cuts of grade A5 *wagyū*, all cooked at a grill set on the table. The menu has a diagram of the cuts as well as descriptions. You can't go wrong with popular dishes such as *kalbi* (short ribs, ¥1180). It's very popular; best to reserve ahead.

Afuri   Ramen ¥

(あふり; Map p246; http://afuri.com; 1-1-7 Ebisu, Shibuya-ku; ramen from ¥880; ⏲11am-5am; 🚉JR Yamanote line to Ebisu, east exit) Afuri has been a major player in the local ramen scene, making a strong case for a light touch with its signature *yuzu-shio* (a light, salty broth flavoured with yuzu, a type of citrus) ramen. They've since opened branches around the city, but this industrial-chic Ebisu shop is the original. Order from the vending machine.

Higashi-Yama   Japanese ¥¥¥

(ヒガシヤマ; Map p246; ☎03-5720-1300; www.higashiyama-tokyo.jp; 1-21-25 Higashiyama, Meguro-ku; lunch/dinner from ¥1650/4950; ⏲11.30am-3pm Tue-Sat, 6pm-1am Mon-Sat; 🚇Hibiya line to Naka-Meguro, main exit) Higashi-Yama serves scrumptious modern Japanese cuisine paired with gorgeous crockery. The interior, a rustic take on minimalism, is stunning too. The restaurant is all but hidden, on a side street with little signage; see the website for a map. Tasting courses make ordering easy; the 'chef's recommendation' course (¥9020) is a worthwhile splurge. Best to book ahead.

Stay for an after-dinner drink in the stark, dimly lit basement lounge.

Ippo   Izakaya ¥

(一歩; Map p246; ☎03-3445-8418; www.sakanabar-ippo.com; 2nd fl, 1-22-10 Ebisu, Shibuya-ku; dishes ¥500-1500; ⏲6pm-3am; 🚉JR Yamanote line to Ebisu, east exit) This mellow little *izakaya* specialises in simple

Izakaya Ordering Tips

If you don't want alcohol it's fine to order a soft drink, but it would be strange to not order a drink. If you're unsure of what to order, you can say 'Omakase de onegaishimas[u]' ('I'll leave it up to you'). It's probably a good idea to set a price cap though!

From left: Casual ramen eatery; *takoyaki*; avocado appetizer

VICHAILAO / SHUTTERSTOCK ©

TOP PHOTO CORPORATION / SHUTTERSTOCK ©

🍽️ Convenience Stores

Konbini (コンビニ; convenience stores) are a way of life for many Tokyoites. Indeed, there seems to be a Lawson, 7-Eleven or Family Mart on just about every corner. In addition to *bentō* and sandwiches, *konbini* staples include *onigiri* (おにぎり), a triangle of rice and nori enveloping something savoury (tuna salad or marinated kelp, for example); *niku-man* (肉まん), steamed buns filled with pork, curry and more; and, in winter, *oden*, a dish of fish cakes, hard-boiled egg and vegetables in *dashi* (fish stock) broth that you'll find stewing at the counter.

Convenience store counter with *oden*
TUPUNGATO / SHUTTERSTOCK ©

pleasures: fish and sake (there's an English sign out front that says just that). The friendly chefs speak some English and can help you decide what to have grilled, steamed, simmered or fried (or if you can't decide, the ¥2500 set menu is great value). The entrance is up the wooden stairs.

Onibus Coffee   Coffee ¥

(オニバスコーヒー; ☏03-6412-8683; www.oni buscoffee.com; 2-14-1 Kami-Meguro, Meguro-ku; ⊗9am-6pm; ⓢHibiya line to Naka-Meguro, south exit) It takes a lot for a new coffee shop in Tokyo to get noticed these days. Sure, the single-origin beans roasted in-house and the shots pulled on the La Marzocco Linea PB are delicious. But it's Onibus' attention to detail in all areas that make it stand out:

from the location, in a lightly renovated old tofu shop, to the custom ceramic mugs.

Udon Yamachō   Udon ¥

(うどん山長; Map p246; 1-1-5 Ebisu, Shibuya-ku; udon ¥680-1180; ⊗11.30am-4pm & 5pm-4.30pm; ⓡJR Yamanote line to Ebisu, east exit) Go for bowls of perfectly *al dente* udon (thick white wheat noodles) in this stylish noodle joint alongside the Shibuya-gawa. In the evening you can tack on sides (such as seasonal veg tempura) and flasks of sake. The shop, with white curtains over the door, is next to a park with a slide shaped like an octopus.

Ouca   Ice Cream ¥

(櫻花; Map p246; www.ice-ouca.com; 1-6-6 Ebisu, Shibuya-ku; ice cream from ¥400; ⊗11am-11.30pm Mar-Oct, noon-11pm Nov-Feb; ⓡJR Yamanote line to Ebisu, east exit) Green tea isn't the only flavour Japan has contributed to the ice-cream playbook; other delicious innovations available (seasonally) at this famous Ebisu ice-cream stand include *kuro-goma* (black sesame), *kinako kurosato* (roasted soy-bean flour and black sugar), *beni imo* (purple sweet potato) and other seasonal concoctions.

⊗ Roppongi & Akasaka

Kikunoi   Kaiseki ¥¥¥

(菊乃井; Map p252; ☏03-3568-6055; http://kikunoi.jp; 6-13-8 Akasaka, Minato-ku; lunch/dinner set course from ¥11,900/19,000; ⊗noon-1pm Tue-Sat, 5-8pm Mon-Sat; ⓢChiyoda line to Akasaka, exit 7) Exquisitely prepared seasonal dishes are as beautiful as they are delicious at this Tokyo outpost of one of Kyoto's most acclaimed *kaiseki* restaurants. Kikunoi's third-generation chef, Murata Yoshihiro, has written a book translated into English on *kaiseki* that the staff helpfully use to explain the dishes you are served, if you don't speak Japanese. Reservations are necessary.

Tofuya-Ukai   Kaiseki ¥¥¥

(とうふ屋うかい; ☑03-3436-1028; www.ukai.
co.jp/english/shiba; 4-4-13 Shiba-kōen, Minato-
ku; lunch/dinner set menu from ¥6500/11,900;
⏱11am-10pm, last order 8pm; ☑; ⑤Ōedo line to
Akabanebashi, exit 8) One of Tokyo's most gracious restaurants is located in a former sake
brewery (moved from northern Japan), with
an exquisite traditional garden, in the shadow of Tokyo Tower. Seasonal preparations of
tofu and accompanying dishes are served in
the refined *kaiseki* style. Make reservations
well in advance. Vegetarians should tell the
staff when they book.

Sougo   Vegetarian ¥

(宗胡; Map p252; ☑03-5414-1133; www.sougo.
tokyo; 3rd fl, Roppongi Green Bldg, 6-1-8 Roppongi, Minato-ku; set lunch/dinner from ¥1500/6500;
⏱11.30am-3pm & 6-11pm Mon-Sat; ☑; ⑤Hibiya
line to Roppongi, exit 3) Sit at the long counter
beside the open kitchen or in booths and
watch the expert chefs prepare delicious
and beautifully presented *shōjin-ryōri*
(vegetarian cuisine as served at Buddhist
temples). Lunch is a bargain. Reserve at
least one day in advance if you want them
to prepare a vegan meal. Look for it in the
building opposite the APA Hotel.

Honmura-An   Soba ¥

(本むら庵; Map p252; ☑03-5772-6657;
www.honmuraantokyo.com; 7-14-18 Roppongi,
Minato-ku; noodles from ¥900; set lunch/dinner
¥1600/7400; ⏱noon-2.30pm & 5.30-10pm
Tue-Sun, closed 1st & 3rd Tue of the month; 📶;
⑤Hibiya line to Roppongi, exit 4) This fabled
soba shop, once located in Manhattan, now
serves its handmade buckwheat noodles at
this rustically contemporary noodle shop
on a Roppongi side street. The delicate
flavour of these noodles is best appreciated
when served on a bamboo mat, with tempura or with dainty slices of *kamo* (duck).

Jōmon   Izakaya ¥¥

(ジョウモン; Map p252; ☑03-3405-2585;
http://teyandei.com/?page_id=18; 5-9-17
Roppongi, Minato-ku; skewers ¥250-500, dishes
from ¥580; ⏱5.30pm-5am; ☑; ⑤Hibiya line
to Roppongi, exit 3) This wonderfully cosy

kitchen has bar seating, rows of ornate
shochu (potato liquor) jugs lining the wall
and hundreds of freshly prepared skewers
splayed in front of the patrons – don't miss
the heavenly *zabuton* beef stick. Jōmon is
almost directly across from the Family Mart
– look for the name in Japanese on the
door. Cover charge ¥300 per person.

Gogyō   Ramen ¥

(五行; Map p252; ☑03-5775-5566; www.
ramendining-gogyo.com; 1-4-36 Nishi-Azabu,
Minato-ku; ramen ¥890-1290; ⏱11.30am-4pm
& 5pm-3am, to midnight Sun; ⑤Hibiya line to
Roppongi, exit 2) Keep an eye on the open
kitchen: no, that's not your dinner going up
in flames but the cooking of *kogashi* (burnt)
ramen, which this dark and stylish *izakaya*
specialises in. It's the burnt lard that gives
the broth its dark and intense flavour. Try
the 'special kogashi miso-men'; there's lots
of other dishes on the menu, too.

⊗ Ginza & Tsukiji

Tempura Kondō   Tempura ¥¥¥

(てんぷら近藤; Map p250; ☑03-5568-0923;
Sakaguchi Bldg 9th fl, 5-5-13 Ginza, Chūō-ku;
lunch/dinner course from ¥7000/12,000;
⏱noon-3pm, 5-10pm Mon-Sat; ⑤Ginza line
to Ginza, exit B5) Nobody in Tokyo does
tempura vegetables like chef Kondo Fumiō.
The carrots are julienned to a fine floss; the
corn is pert, juicy; and the sweet potato is
comfort food at its finest. Courses include
seafood too, picked up that morning from
Tsukiji. Lunch service at noon or 1.30pm;
last dinner booking at 8.30pm. Reserve
ahead.

Ginza Kagari   Ramen ¥

(銀座篝; Map p250; ☑03-3561-0717; Basement,
Echika Fit, 4-1-2 Ginza, Chūō-ku; small/large
ramen ¥950/1050; ⏱11am-11pm; ⑤Ginza line
to Ginza, exit C1 or C2) Kagari, currently one
of Tokyo's most-obsessed-about ramen
shops, does a luscious *tori paitan* (fat-rich
chicken broth) topped with delicately
steamed seasonal vegetables – it will make
you rethink ramen. While the main shop

Tokyo Specialty: Chanko-nabe

Chanko-nabe is the protein-rich stew eaten daily by sumo wrestlers to put on weight. In reasonable-sized portions, this dish of meat and vegetables simmered in a light *dashi* broth is both belly-warming and actually rather healthy.

Try it at **Kappō Yoshiba** (割烹吉葉; ☎03-3623-4480; www.kapou-yoshiba.jp/english/index.html; 2-14-5 Yokoami, Sumida-ku; dishes ¥650-7800; ⊙11.30am-2pm & 5-10pm Mon-Sat; ⑤Ōedo line to Ryōgoku Station, exit 1), in a former sumo stable a short walk from Ryōgoku Kokugikan (p82). Seating is around the original *dōyō* (practice ring). At 7.30pm on Monday, Wednesday, Friday and Saturday, former wrestlers sing *sumo jinku* (a type of folk song associated with sumo) for 15 minutes here.

One stop east of Ryogoku on the JR Sōbu Line is **Koto-ga-ume** (琴ヶ梅; ☎03-3624-7887; www13.plala.or.jp/koto gaume; 3-4-4 Kinshi, Sumida-ku; chanko-nabe ¥3050; ⊙5-11pm Mon-Sat, closed irregularly; ℝJR Sōbu line to Kinshichō, north exit), run by the former sumo wrestler of the same name. His recipes are based on the ones from the stable where he trained. Get the *suishō-nabe* (水晶鍋), made with a rich chicken bone broth and stuffed with a dozen ingredients (including Koto-ga-ume's delicious chicken meatballs).

Chanko-nabe
NORIKKO / SHUTTERSTOCK ©

moves to a new location, visit this branch in the Echika Fit underground arcade in Ginza station. There are only eight seats so expect a queue.

Cafe de l'Ambre   Cafe ¥

(カフェ・ド・ランブル; Map p250; ☎03-3571-1551; www.h6.dion.ne.jp/~lambre; 8-10-15 Ginza, Chūō-ku; ⊙noon-10pm Mon-Sat, to 7pm Sun; ℝGinza line to Ginza, exit A4) The sign over the door here reads 'Coffee Only' but, oh, what a selection (coffee from ¥650). Sekiguchi Ichiro started the business in 1948 and – remarkably at the age of 100 – still runs it himself, sourcing and roasting aged beans from all over the world. It's dark, retro and classic Ginza.

Bird Land   Yakitori ¥¥¥

(バードランド; Map p250; ☎03-5250-1081; http://ginza-birdland.sakura.ne.jp; 4-2-15 Ginza, Chūō-ku; dishes ¥500-2000, set meals from ¥6480; ⊙5-9.30pm Tue-Sat; ⑤Ginza line to Ginza, exit C6) This is as suave as it gets for gourmet grilled chicken. Chefs in whites behind a U-shaped counter dispense *yaki-tori* in all shapes, sizes, colours and organs – don't pass up the dainty serves of liver pâté or the tiny cup of chicken soup. Pair it with wine from the extensive list. Enter beneath Suit Company; reservations are recommended.

Cha Ginza   Teahouse ¥

(茶・銀座; Map p250; ☎03-3571-1211; www.uogashi-meicha.co.jp/shop/ginza; 5-5-6 Ginza, Chūō-ku; ⊙teahouse noon-5pm Tue-Sat, shop 11am-6pm Tue-Sat; ⑤Ginza line to Ginza, exit B3) Take a pause for afternoon tea (¥700 to ¥1400) at this slick contemporary tea salon. The menu is seasonal, but will likely include a cup of perfectly prepared *matcha* (green tea) and a small sweet or two, or a choice of *sencha* (premium green tea). The ground floor shop sells top-quality teas from various growing regions in Japan.

Maru   Japanese ¥¥

(銀座圓; Map p250; ☎03-5537-7420; www.maru-mayfont.jp/ginza; 2nd fl, Ichigo Ginza 612 Bldg, 6-12-15 Ginza, Chūō-ku; lunch/dinner from ¥1100/4800; ⊙11.30am-2pm & 5.30-9pm

Mon-Sat; S Ginza line to Ginza, exit A3) In the evenings Maru offers a contemporary take on *kaiseki*. The chefs are young and inventive and the appealing space is dominated by a long, wooden, open kitchen counter across which you can watch them work. The good-value lunches offer a choice of *yaki-zakana* (grilled fish) dishes or *higawari teishoku* (the day's special).

Maru's Harajuku branch (p130) is only open for dinner.

Kagaya
Izakaya ¥¥

(加賀屋; Map p250; ☎03-3591-2347; http://ka gayayy.sakura.ne.jp; Basement fl, Hanasada Bldg, 2-15-12 Shimbashi, Minato-ku; meals ¥1080-4860; ☺7pm-midnight Mon-Sat; ℝ JR Yamanote line to Shimbashi, Shimbashi exit) It is safe to say that there is no other shop owner in Tokyo who can match Mark Kagaya for brilliant lunacy. His side-splitting antics are this humble *izakaya*'s star attraction although his mum's nourishing home cooking also hits the spot. Bookings are essential.

Nakajima no Ochaya
Teahouse ¥

(中島の御茶屋; 1-1 Hama-rikyū Onshi-teien, Chūō-ku; ☺9am-4.30pm; ℝ Ōedo line to Shiodome, exit A1) This beautiful teahouse from 1704 (and rebuilt in 1983) stands elegantly on an island in the central pond at Hama-rikyū Onshi-teien (p39), reached via a long cedar bridge. It's an ideal spot for a cup of *matcha* and a sweet (¥510 to ¥720) while contemplating the very faraway 21st century beyond the garden walls.

Jugetsudo
Teahouse ¥¥

(寿月堂; Map p250; ☎03-6278-7626; www. maruyamanori.com; 5th fl, Kabuki-za Tower, 4-12-15 Ginza, Chūō-ku; ☺10am-7pm; S Hibiya line to Higashi-Ginza, exit 3) This venerable tea seller's main branch is closer to Tsukiji, but this classy outlet in the Kabuki-za Tower has a Kengo Kuma–designed cafe where you can sample the various Japanese green teas, including *matcha*; sets, which include *wagashi* (Japanese sweets), cost ¥1100 to ¥2200. Book for its tea-tasting experience (¥3200; 11am to noon), which covers four different types of tea. Enter on Shōwa-dōri.

Trattoria Tsukiji Paradiso!
Italian ¥¥

(トラットリア・築地パラディーゾ; Map p250; ☎03-3545-5550; www.tsukiji-paradiso. com; 6-27-3 Tsukiji, Chūō-ku; mains ¥1500-3600; ☺11am-2pm & 6-10pm Thu-Tue; S Hibiya line to Tsukiji, exit 2) Paradise for food lovers, indeed. This charming, aqua-painted trattoria serves seafood pasta dishes that will make you want to lick the plate clean. Its signature linguine is packed with shellfish in a scrumptious tomato, chilli and garlic sauce. Lunch (from ¥980) is a bargain, but you'll need to queue; book for dinner. The menu is in Japanese and Italian.

Turret Coffee
Cafe ¥

(Map p250; http://ja-jp.facebook.com/tur retcoffee; 2-12-6 Tsukiji, Chūō-ku; ☺7am-6pm Mon-Sat, noon-6pm Sun; S Hibiya line to Tsukiji, exit 2) Kawasaki Kiyoshi set up his plucky indie coffee shop next to Starbucks. It takes its name from the three-wheeled delivery trucks that beetle around **Tsukiji Market** – there's one on the premises. Ideal for an early-morning espresso en route to or from the outer market area. Drinks cost ¥360 to ¥560.

⊗ Marunouchi & Nihombashi

Hōnen Manpuku
Japanese ¥

(豊年萬福; Map p250; ☎03-3277-3330; www. hounenmanpuku.jp; 1-8-6 Nihombashi-Muroma-chi, Chūō-ku; dishes ¥530-1950; ☺11.30am-2.30pm & 5-11pm Mon-Sat, 5-10pm Sun; S Ginza line to Mitsukoshimae, exit A1) This restaurant is a showcase for Nihombashi's gourmet retailers, such as Ninben (maker of *katsuobushi*, or dried bonito flakes, since 1699) and Yamamoto (maker of *nori*, laver, since 1849), whose ingredients appear in the dishes. Lunchtime set menus (¥1000 to ¥1200) are great value, and there's a riverside terrace in the warmer months.

Chashitsu Kaboku
Teahouse

(茶室 嘉木; Map p250; ☎03-6212-0202; www. ippodo-tea.co.jp; 3-1-1 Marunouchi, Chiyoda-ku;

Tokyo on a Tray

The main dish is usually fish or pork.

Miso soup and *tsukemono* (pickles) are a must.

Some restaurants will give you another serving of rice for free.

Eat a little of this, a little of that – there's no set order.

Teishoku
A teishoku is considered a perfectly balanced meal.

Teishoku Essentials

A *teishoku* (定食) is a meal set made up of a main dish, a small bowl of rice, miso soup and pickled vegetables – all served at once on a tray. It's the closest you can get to home-cooking outside the house. Common mains include *yaki-zakana* (焼き魚; grilled fish) and *shōga-yaki* (生姜焼き; thin strips of stir-fried pork with ginger). A *shokudō* (casual, all-around eatery) is the obvious place to order a *teishoku*, but some upscale restaurants serve modestly priced ones at lunch.

Teishoku set with grilled *hokke*
NAQIMA / SHUTTERSTOCK ©

Top Five Teishoku

Yanmo (p128) Perfectly grilled fish.

d47 Shokudō (p131) Regional specialities from all over Japan.

Maru (p140) Good value lunch at an upscale spot.

Kado (p143) Classic home cooking.

Nihonbashi Dashi Bar Hanare (p143) Healthy sets made from humble ingredients.

tea set ¥1080-2600; ⏱11am-7pm; 🚊JR Yamanote line to Yurakuchō, Tokyo International Forum exit) Run by famed Kyoto tea producer Ippōdō – which celebrated 300 years of business in 2017 – this teahouse is a fantastic place to experience the myriad pleasures of *ocha*, Japanese green tea. It's also one of the few places that serves *koicha*, 'thick tea', which is even thicker than ordinary *matcha*. Sets are accompanied by a pretty, seasonal *wagashi*.

If you sit at the counter, the staff will show you how to make the tea in the proper Japanese fashion. Packaged teas and tea utensils are sold in the small, attached shop.

Nihonbashi Dashi Bar Hanare
Japanese ¥

(日本橋だし場はなれ; Map p250; 📞03-5205-8704; www.ninben.co.jp/hanare; 1st fl, Coredo Muromachi 2, 2-3-1 Nihombashi-Muromachi, Chūō-ku; lunch set ¥1025-1950, dinner dishes ¥650-1300; ⏱11am-2pm, 5-11pm; ⓢGinza line to Mitsukoshimae, exit A6) This casual restaurant from longtime producer (300+ years!) of *katsuobushi*, Ninben, naturally serves dishes that make use of the umami-rich ingredient. Lunch, with dishes such as hearty miso soups and *dashi takikokomi gohan* (rice steamed in stock), is good value, and healthy to boot.

To sample just *dashi* (stock) made from *katsuobushi*, visit the Nihonbashi Dashi Bar on the ground floor of Coredo Muromachi 1.

Taimeiken
Japanese ¥¥

(たいめいけん; Map p250; 📞03-3271-2463; www.taimeiken.co.jp; 1-12-10 Nihonbashi, Chūō-ku; mains ¥750-3680; ⏱11am-8.30pm Mon-Sat, to 8pm Sun; ⓢGinza line to Nihombashi, exit C5) This classic restaurant, open since 1931, specialises in *yōshoku* – Western cuisine adapted to the Japanese palate. Its signature dish is *omuraisu* (an omelette stuffed with ketchup-flavoured fried rice), to which you can add a side of borscht and coleslaw for the very retro price of ¥50 each. The *tampopo omuraisu* was created for Itami Jūzō's cult movie.

It's easier to get a seat on the second floor, where the prices are higher, but the old-school atmosphere on the first floor is worth the wait if there's a queue.

Tokyo Rāmen Street
Ramen ¥

(東京ラーメンストリート; Map p250; www.tokyoeki-1bangai.co.jp/ramenstreet; B1 First Avenue Tokyo Station, 1-9-1 Marunouchi, Chiyoda-ku; ramen from ¥800; ⏱7.30am-11.30pm; 🚊JR lines to Tokyo Station, Yaesu south exit) Eight hand-picked *rāmen-ya* operate branches in this basement arcade on the Yaesu side of **Tokyo Station**. All the major styles are covered – from *shōyu* (soy-sauce base) to *tsukemen* (cold noodles served on the side). Long lines form outside the most popular shops, but they tend to move quickly.

Nihonbashi Dashi Bar
Japanese ¥

(日本橋だし場; Map p250; 📞03-5205-8704; www.ninben.co.jp; 1st fl, Coredo Muromachi 1, 2-3-1 Nihombashi-Muromachi, Chūō-ku; ⏱10am-7pm; ⓢGinza line to Mitsukoshimae, exit A4) A key ingredient of the stock *dashi* is flakes of *katsuobushi*, which the Nihombashi-based Ninben has been making and selling since 1699. The counter here serves cups of stock (¥100) as well as *tamago-yaki* (rolled omelette seasoned with *dashi*; ¥150) and, between 11am and 2pm, rice dishes topped with *katsuobushi*.

⊗ Kagurazaka

Kado
Japanese ¥¥

(カド; 📞03-3268-2410; http://kagurazaka-kado.com; 1-32 Akagi-Motomachi, Shinjuku-ku; lunch set meal ¥800-3000, dinner set menus from ¥3250-5400; ⏱11.30am-2.30pm & 5-11pm; 🚊Tōzai line to Kagurazaka, exit 1) Set in an old wooden house with a white lantern out front, Kado specialises in *katei-ryōri* (home-cooking). Dinner is a set course of seasonal dishes (such as grilled quail or fresh tofu). At lunch there's no English menu, so your best bet is the *kado teishoku* (カド定食; ¥850), the daily house special. Bookings are required for the dinner course.

In the entrance is a *tachinomi-ya* (standing bar), where you can order small dishes (around ¥300) à la carte, paired with sake in the evenings.

Mugimaru 2   Cafe ¥
(ムギマル 2 ; ☎03-5228-6393; www.mugi maru2.com; 5-20 Kagurazaka, Shinjuku-ku; coffee ¥550; ⏰noon-8pm Thu-Tue; Ⓢ Tozai line to Kagurazaka, exit 1) This old house, completely covered in ivy, is a charmer with a welcoming owner and two of Tokyo's most famous shop cats. Seating is on floor cushions; warm, squishy *manjū* (steamed buns) are the house speciality. It's in a tangle of alleys just off Ōkubo-dōri; you'll know it when you see it.

Sadly, the building is slated to be torn down sometime in 2018 or 2019 to make room for a road expansion.

⊗ Kanda & Akihabara

Kikanbō   Ramen ¥
(鬼金棒; http://karashibi.com; 2-10-8 Kaji-chō, Chiyoda-ku; ramen from ¥800; ⏰11am-9.30pm Mon-Sat, to 4pm Sun; Ⓡ JR Yamanote line to Kanda, north exit) The *karashibi* (カラシビ) spicy miso ramen here has a cult following. Choose your level of *kara* (spice) and *shibi* (a strange mouth-numbing sensation created by Japanese *sanshō* pepper). We recommend *futsu-futsu* (regular for both) for first-timers; *oni* (devil) level costs an extra ¥100. Look for the black door curtains.

The sister shop next door, with red curtains, specialises in *tsukemen* (noodles with condensed soup on the side for dipping).

Kanda Yabu Soba   Soba ¥
(神田やぶそば; Map p254; ☎03-3251-0287; www.yabusoba.net; 2-10 Kanda-Awajichō, Chiyoda-ku; noodles ¥670-1910; ⏰11.30am-8.30pm Thu-Tue; Ⓢ Marunouchi line to Awajichō, exit A3) Totally rebuilt following a fire in 2013, this is one of Tokyo's most venerable buckwheat noodle shops, in business since 1880. Come here for classic handmade noodles and accompaniments such as *ten-seiro soba* (shrimp tempura) or *kamo-nanban soba* (slices of duck).

Glitch Coffee & Roasters   Coffee ¥
(グリッチコーヒー・ロースターズ; ☎03-5244-5458; http://glitchcoffee.com; 3-16 Kanda Nishiki-chō, Chiyoda-ku; ⏰7.30am-8pm Mon-Fri, 9am-7pm Sat & Sun; Ⓢ Hanzōmon line to Jimbōchō, exit 7) In a sign that Tokyo's third-wave coffee scene is seeping into new territory, one of the most talked-about new shops of late opened not in Shibuya or Harajuku but in the old student haunt of Jimbōchō. The speciality here is single-origin beans, roasted very lightly in-house. Try the Ethiopia Alaka Washed, with notes of bergamot and honey.

Sabōru   Cafe ¥
(さぼうる; Map p254; ☎03-3291-8404; 1-11 Kanda-Jimbōchō, Chiyoda-ku; coffee from ¥450; ⏰9am-11pm Mon-Sat; Ⓢ Hanzōmon line to Jimbōchō, exit A7) Sabōru checks all the boxes of a classic mid-20th-century *kissaten* (coffee shop): dim-lighting, low tables, lots of dark wood and strong, dark *burendo kōhī* ('blend' coffee) to match. And then it adds a few of its own: totem poles, a Robinson Crusoe–vibe and copious potted plants. Come before 11am for the good-value morning set (coffee, hard-boiled egg, and two rolls for ¥500).

⊗ Ueno & Yanaka

Innsyoutei   Japanese ¥
(韻松亭; Map p254; ☎03-3821-8126; www.inn syoutei.jp; 4-59 Ueno-kōen, Taitō-ku; lunch/dinner from ¥1680/5500; ⏰restaurant 11am-3pm & 5-9.30pm, tearoom 11am-5pm; Ⓡ JR lines to Ueno, Ueno-kōen exit) In a gorgeous wooden building dating back to 1875, Innsyoutei (pronounced 'inshotei' and meaning 'rhyme of the pine cottage') has long been a favourite spot for fancy *kaiseki*-style meals while visiting Ueno-kōen. Without a booking (essential for dinner) you'll have a long wait but it's worth it. Lunchtime *bentō* offer beautifully presented morsels and are great value.

There's an attached rustic teahouse serving *matcha* and traditional desserts from ¥600.

Shinsuke — Izakaya ¥¥

(シンスケ; Map p254;☑03-3832-0469; 3-31-5 Yushima, Bunkyō-ku; dishes ¥500-2500, cover charge ¥300; ◷5-9.30pm Mon-Fri, to 9pm Sat; SChiyoda line to Yushima, exit 3) In business since 1925, Shinsuke has honed the concept of an ideal *izakaya* to perfection: long cedar counter, 'master' in *happi* (traditional short coat) and *hachimaki* (traditional headband), and smooth-as-silk *daiginjō* (premium-grade sake). The menu, updated monthly, includes house specialities (such as *kitsune raclette* – deep-fried tofu stuffed with raclette cheese) and seasonal dishes. Reservations recommended.

Also, unlike other storied *izakaya* that can be intimidating to foreigners, the staff here are friendly and go out of their way to explain the menu in English.

Kamachiku — Udon ¥

(釜竹; Map p254;☑03-5815-4675; http:// kamachiku.com/top_en; 2-14-18 Nezu, Bunkyō-ku; noodles from ¥850, small dishes ¥350-950; ◷11.30am-2pm Tue-Sun, 5.30-9pm Tue-Sat; SChiyoda line to Nezu, exit 1) Udon made fresh daily is the speciality at this popular restaurant, in a beautifully restored brick warehouse from 1910 with a garden view. In addition to noodles, the menu includes lots of *izakaya*-style small dishes (such as grilled fish and veggies). Expect to queue on weekends.

Sasa-no-Yuki — Tofu ¥¥

(笹乃雪; Map p254;☑03-3873-1145; 2-15-10 Negishi, Taitō-ku; dishes ¥400-700, lunch/dinner course from ¥2200/5000; ◷11.30am-8.30pm Tue-Sun; ; ℝJR Yamanote line to Uguisudani, north exit) ☞ Sasa-no-Yuki opened its doors in the Edo period, and continues to serve its signature dishes with tofu made fresh every morning using water from the shop's own well. Some treats to expect: *ankake-dofu* (tofu in a thick, sweet sauce) and *goma-dofu* (sesame tofu). Vegetarians should not assume everything is purely veggie – ask before ordering. There is bamboo out front.

The best-value lunch set (¥2200) is served 11.30am to 2pm Tuesday to Friday.

Kayaba Coffee — Cafe ¥

(カヤバ珈琲; Map p254;☑03-3823-3545; http://kayaba-coffee.com; 6-1-29 Yanaka, Taitō-ku; ◷8am-11pm Mon-Sat, to 6pm Sun; SChiyoda line to Nezu, exit 1) This vintage 1930s coffee shop (the building is actually from the '20s) in Yanaka is a hang-out for local students and artists (coffee ¥450). Come early for the 'morning set' (coffee and a sandwich for ¥800, served 8am to 11am). In the evenings, Kayaba morphs into a bar.

Himitsu-dō — Sweets ¥

(ひみつ堂; Map p254;☑03-3824-4132; http://himitsudo.com; 3-11-18 Yanaka, Taitō-ku; ◷10am-6pm, closed Mon Jun-Jul & Sep, closed Mon & Tue Oct-May; ; ℝJR Yamanote line to Nippori, north exit) Summer in Japan is synonymous with *kakigōri*, shaved ice topped with colourful syrups and sweetened condensed milk. So popular is Himitsu-dō, however, that a queue can form even in the dead of winter. One of the secrets to its success is natural ice harvested from frozen-over waters in Tochigi prefecture; another is its rotating selection of over 100 flavours.

Hantei — Japanese ¥¥

(はん亭; Map p254;☑03-3828-1440; http://hantei.co.jp; 2-12-15 Nezu, Bunkyō-ku; meals from ¥3240; ◷noon-3pm & 5-10pm Tue-Sun; SChiyoda line to Nezu, exit 2) Housed in a beautifully maintained, century-old traditional wooden building, Hantei is a local landmark. Delectable skewers of seasonal *kushiage* (fried meat, fish and vegetables) are served with small, refreshing side dishes. Lunch includes eight or 12 sticks and dinner starts with six, after which you can order additional rounds (three/six skewers ¥800/¥1400).

Torindō — Teahouse ¥

(桃林堂; Map p254; 1-5-7 Ueno-Sakuragi, Taitō-ku; ◷9.30am-5pm Tue-Sun; SChiyoda line to Nezu, exit 1) Sample a cup of paint-thick *matcha* (¥450) at this tiny teahouse on the edge of Ueno-kōen. Tradition dictates that the bitter tea be paired with something sweet, so choose from the artful desserts (¥280 to ¥435) in the glass counter, then pull up a stool at the communal table. It's a white building on a corner.

⊗ Asakusa & Ryōgoku

Asakusa Imahan   Japanese ¥¥¥

(浅草今半; Map p254; ☎03-3841-1114; www. asakusaimahan.co.jp; 3-1-12 Nishi-Asakusa, Taitō-ku; lunch/dinner set menu from ¥4000/10,000; ⊙11.30am-9.30pm; ⛾Tsukuba Express to Asakusa, exit 4) For a meal to remember, swing by this famous beef restaurant, in business since 1895. Choose between courses of su-kiyaki (sauteed beef dipped in raw egg) and *shabu-shabu* (beef blanched in broth); prices rise according to the grade of meat. For diners on a budget, Imahan sells a limited number of cheaper lunch sets (from ¥1620).

Onigiri Yadoroku   Japanese ¥

(おにぎり浅草宿六; Map p254; ☎03-3874-1615; http://onigiriyadoroku.com; 3-9-10 Asakusa, Taitō-ku; set lunch ¥660 & ¥900, onigiri ¥200-600; ⊙11.30am-5pm Mon-Sat, 6pm-2am Thu-Tue; ⛾Tsukuba Express to Asakusa, exit 1) *Onigiri* (rice-ball snacks), usually wrapped in crispy sheets of *nori*, are a great Japanese culinary invention. And they're not just convenience-store snacks: try them fresh at Tokyo's oldest *onigiri* shop, which feels more like a sushi counter. The set lunches are a great deal; at night there's a large range of flavours to choose from, along with alcohol.

Hosokawa   Soba ¥

(ほそ川; Map p254; ☎03-3626-1125; www. edosoba-hosokawa.jp; 1-6-5 Kamezawa, Sumida-ku; soba ¥1080-2650; ⊙11.45am-2.30pm, 5.30-8.30pm Tue-Sun, closed 3rd Tue of the month; ⛾JR Sōbu line to Ryōgoku, east exit) Chef Hosokawa Takashi grinds buckwheat fresh daily for the soba he kneads and cuts by hand. Get them in hot broth (*kake-soba*) or at room temperature on a bamboo tray (*seiro*) – and definitely with a side of crisp, seasonal tempura. With ochre walls and wildflowers on the table, Hosokawa brings a touch of country to the city.

No reservations and no small children.

Innsyoutei (p144)

WORLD DISCOVERY / ALAMY STOCK PHOTO ©

Suzukien   Ice Cream ¥

(壽々喜園; Map p254; ☎03-3873-0311; http://tocha.co.jp; 3-4-3 Asakusa, Taitō-ku; ice cream from ¥370; ◈10am-5pm, closed 3rd Tue of the month; ☒Tsukuba Express to Asakusa, exit 1) Suzukien boasts of having the most matcha-ful *matcha* ice cream around, and the deep moss-green Premium No. 7 does not disappoint. In addition to the seven levels of *matcha*, you can try ice cream in *hōjicha* (roasted green tea), *genmaicha* (brown rice tea) and *kōcha* (black tea) flavours.

Sometarō   Okonomiyaki ¥

(染太郎; Map p254; ☎03-3844-9502; 2-2-2 Nishi-Asakusa, Taitō-ku; mains from ¥700; ◈noon-10pm; ⓢGinza line to Tawaramachi, exit 3) Sometarō is a fun and funky place to try *okonomiyaki*. This historic, vine-covered house is a friendly spot where the menu includes a how-to guide for novice cooks. Tatami seating; cash only.

Daikokuya   Tempura ¥

(大黒家; Map p254; ☎03-3844-1111; www.tempura.co.jp/english/index.html; 1-38-10 Asakusa, Taitō-ku; meals ¥1550-2100; ◈11am-8.30pm Sun-Fri, to 9pm Sat; ⓢGinza line to Asakusa, exit 1) Near Nakamise-dōri, this is the place to get old-fashioned tempura fried in pure sesame oil, an Asakusa speciality. It's in a white building with a tile roof. If there's a queue (and there often is), you can try your luck at the annex one block over – it also serves set-course meals.

Komagata Dozeu   Japanese ¥

(駒形どぜう; ☎03-3842-4001; www.dozeu.com/en; 1-7-12 Komagata, Taitō-ku; hotpot ¥1750; ◈11am-9pm; ⓢGinza line to Asakusa, exits A2 & A4) Since 1801 Komagata Dozeu has been simmering and stewing *dojō* (Japanese loach, which looks something like a miniature eel). *Dojō-nabe*, served here on individual *hibachi* (charcoal stoves), was a common dish in the days of Edo, but few restaurants serve it today. The open seating around wide, wooden planks heightens the traditional flavour. There are lanterns out front.

Hoppy-dōri   Izakaya ¥

(ホッピー通り; 2-5 Asakusa, Taitō-ku; dishes ¥500-700; ◈noon until late, varies by shop; ☒Tsukuba Express to Asakusa, exit 4) Along either side of the street popularly known as Hoppy-dōri – 'hoppy' is a cheap malt beverage – are rows of *izakaya* with outdoor seating. As the name suggests, there's nothing fancy going on here (think rickety stools and plastic tarps for awnings). Many shops have picture menus. Try the *gyū-suji nikomi* (stewed beef tendons), a speciality of this strip.

TREASURE HUNT

Begin your shopping adventure

Treasure Hunt

Since the Edo era, when courtesans set the day's trends in towering geta (traditional wooden sandals), Tokyoites have lusted after both the novel and the outstanding. The city remains the trendsetter for the rest of Japan and its residents shop – economy be damned – with an infectious enthusiasm.

Shopping highlights include the grand department stores of Ginza and Nihombashi; the fashionable boutiques in Harajuku and Ebisu; the traditional craft shops in Ueno and Asakusa; and the flea markets (good for used kimono) that pop up around the city.

In This Section

Useful Phrases

I'd like to buy ...	…をください。 ... o ku·da·sai
How much is it?	おいくらですか? o·i·ku·ra des ka
Can I try it on?	試着できますか? shi·cha·ku de·ki·mas ka
Can I look at it?	それを見てもいいですか? so·re o mi·te mo ī des ka

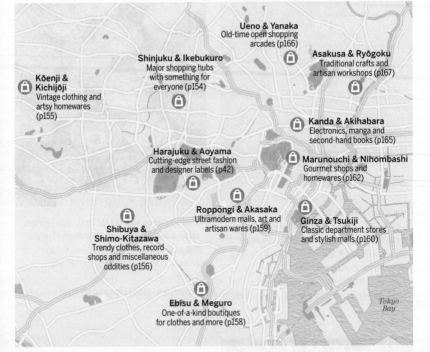

Caption

Opening Hours

Department stores open from 10am to 8pm. Boutiques get a late start, opening at 11am or noon and closing around 8pm. Most shops are open on Sundays, but may close an hour earlier; boutiques close one or two days a week, often during the middle of the week.

Duty Free

Department stores and electronics emporiums offer duty-free shopping. Increasingly so do smaller-scale shops; look for window stickers that say 'tax-free shop'. To qualify, you must show your passport and spend over ¥5000 in any one shop. For details, see http://enjoy.taxfree.jp. Otherwise, sales tax is 8%.

The Best...

Fashion

Dover Street Market Ginza (p161) Comme des Garçons and other avant-garde labels.

Kapital (p158) Denim woven on vintage looms and lush, hand-dyed textiles.

Beams Japan (p154) Trend-setting boutique.

Sou-Sou (p43) Traditional Japanese clothing with contemporary panache.

Laforet (p43) Harajuku department store stocked with kooky and cutting-edge brands.

Antiques & Vintage

Ōedo Antique Market (p53) Quality vendors twice a month at Tokyo International Forum.

Tokyo Hotarudo (p167) Treasure trove of early-20th-century accessories and homewares.

PukuPuku (p155) Hundred-year-old ceramics.

Food & Drink

Chabara (p165; pictured above) Miso, soy sauce and more from top regional producers.

Isego Honten (p166) Centuries-old sake specialist.

Tsuruya Yoshinobu (p162) Edible works of art.

Arts & Crafts

Takumi (p161) One-stop shop for earthy crafts from all over Japan.

Japan Traditional Crafts Aoyama Square (p159) Collection of high-end Japanese artisan work.

Tolman Collection (p160) Gallery specialising in contemporary print artists.

Books

Daikanyama T-Site (p158) Designer digs for art and travel tomes.

Books Kinokuniya (p155) The city's best selection of books on Japan in English.

Shibuya Publishing Booksellers (p157) Late-night hang-out with some good titles on Tokyo in English.

Character Goods

KiddyLand (p44) Toy emporium stocked with all your favourites from Sanrio and Studio Ghibli.

Pokémon Center Mega Tokyo (p154) The gang's all here.

Home & Kitchen

Yanaka Matsunoya (p166) Handmade household staples like brooms and baskets.

Tsukiji Hitachiya (p39) Hand-forged knives and other kitchen tools.

Kappabashi-dōri (p162; pictured above) Tokyo's kitchenware shopping strip, favoured by pros.

Muji (p162) Minimalist, utilitarian and indispensable homewares at reasonable prices.

☆ Lonely Planet's Top Choices

Tokyu Hands (p156) Fascinating emporium of miscellaneous oddities.

Akomeya (p160) Beautifully packaged, traditional gourmet foodstuffs.

Isetan (p154) Trendy Japanese fashion labels and a great basement food hall.

Itōya (p160) Ginza institution for stationery and art supplies.

Mandarake Complex (p80) Home sweet home for anime and manga fans.

🔵 Shinjuku & Ikebukuro

Isetan
Department Store

(伊勢丹; Map p253; www.isetan.co.jp; 3-14-1 Shinjuku, Shinjuku-ku; ⏰10.30am-8pm; §Marunouchi line to Shinjuku-sanchōme, exit B3, B4 or B5) Most department stores play to conservative tastes, but this one doesn't. For an always changing line-up of up-and-coming Japanese womenswear designers, check out the Tokyo Closet (2nd floor) and Re-Style (3rd floor) boutiques. Men get a whole building of their own (connected by a passageway). Don't miss the basement food hall, featuring famous purveyors of sweet and savoury goodies.

Beams Japan
Fashion & Accessories

(ビームス・ジャパン; Map p253; www.beams. co.jp; 3-32-6 Shinjuku, Shinjuku-ku; ⏰11am-8pm; ◉JR Yamanote line to Shinjuku, east exit) Beams, a national chain of boutiques, is a Japanese cultural institution. This multi-storey Shinjuku shop is particularly good for the latest Japanese streetwear labels and work from designers giving traditional looks a modern twist (including men's, women's and unisex fashion). Also sometimes available: crafts, housewares and original artwork (the line-up is always changing).

Pokémon Center Mega Tokyo
Toys

(ポケモンセンターメガトウキョー; ☎03-5927-9290; www.pokemon.co.jp/gp/ pokecen/english/megatokyo_access.html; 2nd fl, Sunshine City, 3-1-2 Higashi-Ikebukuro, Toshima-ku; ⏰10am-8pm; §Yūrakuchō line to Higashi-Ikebukuro, exit 2) Japan's largest Pokémon centre sells every piece of the series' merchandise, with goods geared to kids and grown-ups alike. You can also pose with several large statues around the store, including the one that is the store's mascot: Pikachu riding on the back of a Mega Charizard Y.

Tokyu Hands
Department Store

(東急ハンズ; Map p253; Takashimaya Times Sq, 5-24-2 Sendagaya, Shibuya-ku; ⏰10am-9pm; ◉JR Yamanote line to Shinjuku, new south exit) Ostensibly a do-it-yourself store, Tōkyū Hands stocks a wide variety of totally

Disk Union, Shinjuku

random (but oddly enticing) household goods. Though not quite as big as the Shibuya store (p156), this outlet in Takashimaya Times Sq is easier to navigate and less crowded.

NEWoMan
Mall

(www.newoman.jp; Map p253; 4-1-6 Shinjuku, Shinjuku-ku; ⊙11am-9.30pm, food hall 8am-10pm; ☒ JR Yamanote line to Shinjuku, new south exit) Awkward name and unlikely location (within the Shinjuku Bus Terminal complex) aside, this new mall is one of Tokyo's swankiest places to shop. There's a branch of the excellent food- and kitchen-stuffs shop Akomeya in the basement and a line-up of posh takeaway vendors on the 2nd-floor terrace.

Disk Union Shinjuku
Music

(ディスクユニオン新宿; Map p253; 3-31-4 Shinjuku, Shinjuku-ku; ⊙11am-9pm; ☒ JR Yamanote line to Shinjuku, east exit) Scruffy Disk Union is known by local audiophiles as Tokyo's best used CD and vinyl store. This eight-storey branch carries a variety of musical styles; if you still can't find what you're looking for there are several other branches in Shinjuku that stock more obscure genres, such as Shōwa-era (1926–1989) rock.

Books Kinokuniya
Books

(紀伊國屋書店; Map p253; www.kinokuniya.co.jp; Takashimaya Times Sq, 5-24-2 Sendagaya, Shibuya-ku; ⊙10am-8.30pm; ☒ JR Yamanote line to Shinjuku, south exit) A longtime lifeline for Tokyo expats, Kinokuniya stocks a broad selection of foreign-language books and magazines, including many titles on Japan, and English-teaching texts.

🔒 Kōenji & Kichijōji

Outbound
Homewares

(アウトバウンド; http://outbound.to; 2-7-4-101 Kichijōji-honchō, Musashino-shi; ⊙11am-7pm Wed-Mon; ☒ JR Sōbu-Chūō line to Kichijōji, north exit) Outbound stocks beautiful homewares and objets d'art for your bohemian dream house. Works are earthy, made by

Fashion on the Edge

Harajuku is synonymous in Tokyo (and the world!) with trendsetting street fashion. But if you want see stuff that is so cutting edge as to have possibly gone too far, pay a visit to Kōenji's **Kita-Kore Building** (キタコレビル; 3-4-11 Kōenji-kita, Suginami-ku; ⊙1-8pm; ☒ JR Sōbu line to Kōenji, north exit). This dilapidated shack of a structure houses a handful of seriously outré shops. Really, it's more art installation than shopping destination, though we do know of at least one person who's actually bought stuff here – Lady Gaga.

See Shopping in Harajuku (p42) for more on Harajuku's fashion.

contemporary artisans and displayed in gallery-like exhibitions.

PukuPuku
Antiques

(ぷくぷく; http://pukupukukichi.blogspot.jp; 2-26-2 Kichijōji-honchō, Musashino-shi; ⊙11.30am-7.30pm; ☒ JR Sōbu-Chūō line to Kichijōji, north exit) This cluttered little antiques shop stocks ceramics from the early Shōwa (昭和; 1926–89) period, through Taishō (大正; 1912–26) and Meiji (明治; 1868–1912) and all the way back to old Edo (江戸; 1603–1868). Flip the dishes over for a sticker that indicates the period. Hundred-year-old saucers can be had for as little as a few hundred yen.

Sokkyō
Vintage

(即興; www.sokkyou.net; 102 Nakanishi Apt Bldg, 3-59-14 Kōenji-minami, Suginami-ku; ⊙1-9pm, holidays irregular; ☒ JR Sōbu line to Kōenji, south exit) As far as vintage shops go, Sokkyō is more like a gallery of cool. The stock is impeccably edited down to a look that is both dreamy and modern. That said, we may have sent you on an impossible mission: the shop, in an ordinary house down a tiny alley, is marked only by a dressmakers' dummy next to the door.

KAMETARO / SHUTTERSTOCK ©

Ginza Six (p161)

🅐 Shibuya & Shimo-Kitazawa

Tokyu Hands Department Store

(東急ハンズ; Map p246; http://shibuya.tokyu-hands.co.jp; 12-18 Udagawa-chō, Shibuya-ku; ⏰10am-9pm; 🚃JR Yamanote line to Shibuya, Hachikō exit) This DIY and *zakka* (miscellaneous goods) store has eight fascinating floors of everything you didn't know you needed, including reflexology slippers, bee-venom face masks and cartoon-character-shaped rice-ball moulds. Most stuff is inexpensive, making it perfect for souvenir- and gift-hunting. Warning: you could lose hours in here.

There's another branch in Shinjuku (p154).

d47 design travel store Design

(📞03-6427-2301; Map p246; 8th fl, Shibuya Hikarie, 2-21-1 Shibuya, Shibuya-ku; ⏰11am-8pm; 🚃JR Yamanote line to Shibuya, east exit) The folks behind the D&D Department lifestyle brand and magazine are expert scavengers, searching Japan's nooks and crannies for outstanding examples of craftsmanship – be it ceramics from Ishikawa-ken or linens from Fukui-ken. An ever-changing selection of finds are on sale in this small store.

Loft Department Store

(ロフト; Map p246; 📞03-3462-3807; www.loft.co.jp; 18-2 Udagawa-chō, Shibuya-ku; ⏰10am-9pm; 🚃JR Yamanote line to Shibuya, Hachikō exit) This emporium of homewares, stationery and accessories specialises in all that is cute and covetable. The 1st floor, which stocks seasonal stuff and gifts, is particularly ripe for souvenir-hunting.

Tsukikageya Fashion & Accessories

(月影屋; Map p246; www.tsukikageya.com; 1-9-19 Tomigaya, Shibuya-ku; ⏰noon-8pm Thu-Sun; Ⓢ Chiyoda line to Yoyogi-kōen, exit 2) Forget cute. Natsuki Shigeta designs *yukata* (cotton kimonos) for men, women and babies with a punk-rock slant that pair with wild accessories. The shop is all but hidden in the back of an apartment complex; enter from the alley behind, and look for the jewellery vending machine out front.

Mega Donki   Variety

(MEGAドンキ; Map p246; ☏03-5428-4086;
28-6 Udagawa-chō, Shibuya-ku; ⏰24hrs; 🚃JR
Yamanote line to Shibuya, Hachikō exit) You
could show up in Tokyo completely empty-
handed and this huge, new outpost of all-
night, bargain retailer 'Don Quijote' would
have you covered. There are groceries,
toiletries, electronics and clothes – along
with all sorts of random stuff, including the
best selection of unusual-flavoured Kit-Kat
chocolates we've seen. Don't miss the giant
moray eel in the tank at the entrance.

Shibuya Publishing
Booksellers   Books

(SPBS; Map p246; ☏03-5465-0588; www.
shibuyabooks.co.jp; 17-3 Kamiyamachō,
Shibuya-ku; ⏰11am-11pm Mon-Sat, to 10pm Sun;
🚃JR Yamanote line to Shibuya, Hachikō exit)
Leading the wave of hipster bookshops,
SPBS is a high-brow alternative to the bars
along Shibuya's Kamiyamachō *shōtengai*
(market street). There's a decent offering
of English-language books and a fine
collection of artsy, photo-heavy Japanese
magazines.

Shibuya 109   Fashion & Accessories

(渋谷109; Map p246; Ichimarukyū; www.
shibuya109.jp; 2-29-1 Dōgenzaka, Shibuya-ku;
⏰10am-9pm; 🚃JR Yamanote line to Shibuya,
Hachikō exit) Nicknamed *marukyū,* this
cylindrical tower is a trend factory and
teen institution. Inside are dozens of small
boutiques, each with its own carefully
styled look (and competing soundtrack).
Pose for photos with giant, pastel-coloured
cupcakes and donuts in the top floor studio
Moreru Mignon.

Shibuya Hikarie   Mall

(渋谷ヒカリエ; Map p246; www.hikarie.jp;
2-21-1 Shibuya, Shibuya-ku; ⏰10am-9pm; 🚃JR
Yamanote line to Shibuya, east exit) The first five
floors of this glass skyscraper are filled with
fashionable boutiques from international
and domestic brands. In the basement
levels are dozens of gourmet takeaway
counters.

     Antique & Flea Markets

Tokyo's best-known outdoor market is
the long-running Ōedo Antique Market
(p53), held twice a month in the courtyard of the Tokyo International Forum.
With hundreds of dealers, this is a good
place to hunt for retro and antique Japanese goods, from old ceramics to kitsch
plastic figurines.

Held over one weekend a month, **Raw
Tokyo** (www.rawtokyo.jp; 5-53-7 Jingūmae,
Shibuya-ku; ⏰11am-6pm, 1st Sat & Sun of
the month; Ⓢ Ginza line to Omote-sandō,
exit B2) is a contemporary-style flea
market – the kind that has a DJ booth,
live painting and food trucks. Among the
vendors are young designers hoping for
a break.

Pretty much every weekend there is
a flea market, large or small, happening
somewhere. Oddly enough, many are
held on the grounds of Shintō shrines.
For an updated schedule of all the
city's flea markets, see www.frma.jp (in
Japanese).

Though bargaining is permitted, it is
considered bad form to drive too hard
a bargain.

Ōedo Antique Market (p53)
SÉRGIO NOGUEIRA / ALAMY STOCK PHOTO ©

Tower Records   Music

(タワーレコード; Map p246; ☏03-3496-3661;
http://tower.jp/store/Shibuya; 1-22-14 Jinnan,
Shibuya-ku; ⏰10am-11pm; 🚃JR Yamanote line
to Shibuya, Hachikō exit) Yes, Tower lives – in
Japan at least! This eight-storey temple of

☆ **Top 5 Malls**

Coredo Muromachi (p162)

Tokyo Midtown (p160)

KITTE (p162)

Ginza Six (p161)

Shibuya Hikarie (p157)

From left: Shopping in Ginza Six (p161); KITTE (p162); Anime figurine store, Akihabara

music has a deep collection of Japanese and world music. Even if you're not into buying, it can be a great place to browse and discover local artists. There are lots of listening stations.

🔒 Ebisu & Meguro

Okura
Fashion & Accessories

(オクラ; Map p246; www.hrm.co.jp/okura; 20-11 Sarugaku-chō, Shibuya-ku; ⏰11.30am-8pm Mon-Fri, 11am-8.30pm Sat & Sun; 🚉Tōkyū Tōyoko line to Daikanyama) Almost everything in this enchanting shop is dyed a deep indigo blue – from contemporary tees and sweatshirts to classic work shirts. There are some beautiful, original items (though unfortunately most aren't cheap). The shop itself looks like a rural house, with worn, wooden floorboards and whitewashed walls. Note: there's no sign out the front, but the building stands out.

Kapital
Fashion & Accessories

(キャピタル; Map p246; 📞03-5725-3923; http://kapital.jp; 2-20-2 Ebisu-Minami, Shibuya-ku; ⏰11am-8pm; 🚉JR Yamanote line to Ebisu, west

exit) Cult brand Kapital is hard to pin down, but perhaps a deconstructed mash-up of the American West and the centuries-old Japanese aesthetic of *boro* (tatty) chic comes close. Almost no two items are alike; most are unisex. The shop itself is like an art installation. The staff, not snobby at all, can point you towards the other two shops nearby.

Daikanyama T-Site
Books

(代官山T-SITE; Map p246; 📞03-3770-2525; http://real.tsite.jp/daikanyama; 17-5 Sarugaku-chō, Shibuya-ku; ⏰7am-2am; 🚉Tōkyū Tōyoko line to Daikanyama) Locals love this stylish shrine to the printed word, which has a fantastic collection of books on travel, art, design and food, including many books in English on Japan. The best part is that you can sit at the in-house Starbucks and read all afternoon – if you can get a seat that is.

Isego Naka-Meguro
Alcohol

(伊勢五中目黒店; Map p246; 📞03-5784-4584; www.isego.net; 1-20-2 Aobadai, Meguro-ku; ⏰11am-9pm Wed-Mon; 🚇Hibiya line to Naka-Meguro, main exit) This outpost of 300-year-old Sendagi *sake-ya* (liquor store), Isego

VASSAMON ANANSUKKASEM / SHUTTERSTOCK ©

(p166), has a counter bar where you can order *nihonshu* (sake) by the glass (about ¥500). There's usually an English-speaking clerk around who can help you select the right bottle for a *hanami* (cherry-blossom viewing) picnic or to bring home.

Vase Fashion & Accessories
(Map p246; http://vasenakameguro.com; 1-7-7 Kami-Meguro, Meguro-ku; ☺noon-8pm; ⓢHibi-ya line to Naka-Meguro) A perfect example of one of Naka-Meguro's tiny, impeccably cu-rated boutiques, Vase stocks avant-garde designers and vintage pieces (for men and women, but with a strong unisex bent), also hosting the occasional trunk show. It's in a little white house set back from the Meguro-gawa (with the name on the post box).

85 Food & Drinks
(ハチゴウ; Hachigō; ☎03-6452-3385; http://85life.jp; Nakame Gallery Street, 2-45-12 Kami-Meguro,, Meguro-ku; ☺11am-9pm; ⓢHibiya line to Naka-Meguro, south exit) What separates this small lifestyle goods and gourmet shop from the rest is its emphasis on fermented

foods. There's a selection of artisanal *shōyu* (soy sauce) and *tamari-jōyu* (soy sauce made without wheat, suitable for a gluten-free diet) and a deli counter where you can sample different kinds of miso. It's towards the end of the new development under the train tracks.

⑥ Roppongi & Akasaka & Around

Japan Traditional Crafts Aoyama Square
Arts & Crafts
(伝統工芸 青山スクエア; ☎03-5785-1301; http://kougeihin.jp; 8-1-22 Akasaka, Minato-ku; ☺11am-7pm; ⓢGinza line to Aoyama-itchōme, exit 4) Supported by the Japanese Ministry of Economy, Trade and Industry, this is as much a showroom as a shop, exhibiting a broad range of traditional crafts from around Japan, including lacquerwork boxes, woodwork, cut glass, textiles and pottery. There are some exquisite heirloom pieces here, but also beautiful things at reasonable prices.

Tokyo Midtown   Mall

(東京ミッドタウン; Map p252; www.
tokyo-midtown.com; 9-7 Akasaka, Minato-ku;
⊙11am-9pm; ⑤Ōedo line to Roppongi, exit
8) This sleek complex, where escalators
ascend alongside waterfalls of rock and
glass, brims with sophisticated shops. Most
notable is the selection of homewares and
lifestyle boutiques, which carry works by
Japanese designers and artisans, on the
3rd floor of the Galleria section.

Tolman Collection   Arts & Crafts

(トールマンコレクション; ☎03-3434-1300;
www.tolmantokyo.com; 2-2-18 Shiba-Daimon,
Minato-ku; ⊙11am-7pm Wed-Sun; ⑤Ōedo line to
Daimon, exit A3) Expat Norman Tolman has
been collecting modern and contemporary
Japanese print art for 50 years and has
authored many books on the subject. His
gallery, in a traditional wooden building,
represents nearly 50 leading Japanese
artists of printing, lithography, etching,
woodblock and more. Prints start at around
¥10,000 and rise steeply from there; international shipping available.

⑥ Ginza & Tsukiji

Akomeya   Food

(アコメヤ; Map p250; ☎03-6758-0271; www.
akomeya.jp; 2-2-6 Ginza, Chūō-ku; ⊙shop 11am-
8pm, restaurant 11.30am-10pm; ⑤Yūrakuchō
line to Ginza-itchōme, exit 4) Rice is at the core
of Japanese cuisine and drink. This stylish
store sells not only many types of the grain
but also products made from it (such as
sake), a vast range of quality cooking ingredients and a choice collection of kitchen,
home and bath items.

Itōya   Arts & Crafts

(伊東屋; Map p250; www.ito-ya.co.jp; 2-7-15
Ginza, Chūō-ku; ⊙10.30am-8pm Mon-Sat, to 7pm
Sun; ⑤Ginza line to Ginza, exit A13) Nine floors
(plus several more in the nearby annex) of
stationery-shop love await at this famed,
century-old Ginza establishment. There
are everyday items (such as notebooks
and greeting cards) and luxuries (such as
fountain pens and Italian leather agen-
das). You'll also find *washi* (fine Japanese
handmade paper), *tenugui* (beautifully

Uniqlo window display

hand-dyed thin cotton towels) and *furoshiki* (wrapping cloths).

Takumi
Arts & Crafts

(たくみ; Map p250; ☑03-3571-2017; www.ginza-takumi.co.jp; 8-4-2 Ginza, Chūō-ku; ⏰11am-7pm Mon-Sat; Ⓢ Ginza line to Shimbashi, exit 5) You're unlikely to find a more elegant selection of traditional folk crafts, including toys, textiles and ceramics from around Japan. Ever thoughtful, this shop also encloses information detailing the origin and background of the pieces if you make a purchase.

Dover Street Market Ginza
Fashion & Accessories

(DSM; Map p250; ☑03-6228-5080; http://ginza.doverstreetmarket.com; 6-9-5 Ginza, Chūō-ku; ⏰11am-8pm; Ⓢ Ginza line to Ginza, exit A2) A department store as envisioned by Kawakubo Rei (of Comme des Garçons), DSM has seven floors of avant-garde brands, including several Japanese labels and everything in the Comme des Garçons line-up. The quirky art installations alone make it worth the visit.

Mitsukoshi
Department Store

(三越; Map p250; http://mitsukoshi.mistore.jp/store/ginza; 4-6-16 Ginza, Chūō-ku; ⏰10.30am-8pm; Ⓢ Ginza line to Ginza, exits A7 & A11) One of Ginza's grande dames, Mitsukoshi embodies the essence of the Tokyo department store. Don't miss the basement food hall. The homewares selection on the 7th floor is good for ceramics and other artisan pieces.

Uniqlo
Fashion & Accessories

(ユニクロ; Map p250; www.uniqlo.com; 5-7-7 Ginza, Chūō-ku; ⏰11am-9pm; Ⓢ Ginza line to Ginza, exit A2) This now-global brand has made its name by sticking to the basics and tweaking them with style. Offering inexpensive, quality clothing, this is the Tokyo flagship store with 11 floors and items you won't find elsewhere.

Ginza Six
Mall

(Map p250; http://ginza6.tokyo; 6-10-1 Ginza, Chūō-ku; ⏰10am-10pm; Ⓢ Ginza line to Ginza, exit A2) This splashy mall opened in 2017.

 Jimbōchō Book Town

This fascinating neighbourhood of more than 170 new and secondhand booksellers is proof that the printed word is alive and well in Tokyo. It's one of Tokyo's many 'towns' where like-minded shops gather. Amid the tottering stacks of volumes here, you can find everything from antique guidebooks of the Yoshiwara pleasure district to obscure sheet music from your favourite symphony. Shops to seek out include Komiyama Shoten (p166) and Ohya Shobō (p166).

As befitting a neighbourhood full of bookstores, Jimbōchō also has lots of cafes for holing up with a favourite book. Check out Sabōru (p144) or Glitch Coffee & Roasters (p144).

MMPAI / SHUTTERSTOCK ©

There are shops from top international and local brands, of course, but also a branch of artsy Tsutaya Books, a superior food hall, a 4000 sq metre rooftop garden and changing contemporary art installations. On the ground floor, tourist information centre **Terminal Ginza** can arrange shipping and luggage storage.

Ginza Tsutaya Books
Books

(銀座蔦屋書店; Map p250; ☑03-3575-7755; https://store.tsite.jp/ginza; 6th fl, Ginza Six, 6-10-1 Ginza, Chūō-ku; ⏰9am-11.30pm; Ⓢ Ginza line to Ginza, exit A2) This big, beautiful bookstore has a well-curated selection of art, architecture, design and travel books. English titles are mixed in with the Japanese ones, arranged by genre.

Kappabashi Kitchenware Town

Kappabashi-dōri (合羽橋通り; www.
kappabashi.or.jp; S Ginza line to Tawaramachi, exit 3) is the Tokyo's wholesale
restaurant-supply and kitchenware
district – the largest of its kind in Japan.
There are dozens of stores here selling
gourmet kitchen tools such as bamboo
steamer baskets and *takoyaki* (octopus
dumpling) moulds; serving ware such as
lacquer trays and crockery; and display
items, including neon signs and *chōchin*
(paper lanterns). Most shops are open
from 10am to 5pm Monday to Saturday.

This is also where restaurants can
order those freakishly realistic plastic
food models. Pop into **Ganso Shoku-
hin Sample-ya** (元祖食品サンプル屋;
☎0120-17-1839; www.ganso-sample.com;
3-7-6 Nishi-Asakusa, Taitō-ku; ☺10am-
5.30pm; S Ginza line to Tawaramachi, exit 3),
one maker's showroom, which also sells
souvenir key chains, fridge magnets and
kits for creating your own food models
(with English instructions).

Ceramics for sale in Kappabashi-dōri
GREG ELMS / GETTY IMAGES ©

🄐 Marunouchi & Nihombashi

Muji   Homewares
(無印良品; Map p250; ☎03-5208-8241; www.
muji.com/jp/flagship/yurakucho/en; 3-8-3
Marunouchi, Chiyoda-ku; ☺10am-9pm; 🚉 JR
Yamanote line to Yūrakuchō, Kyōbashi exit) The
flagship store of the famously understat-
ed brand sells elegant, simple clothing,

accessories and homewares. There are
scores of outlets across Tokyo, but the
Yūrakuchō store, renovated in 2017, is the
largest with the biggest range. It also offers
tax-free shopping, bicycle rental (¥1080 a
day from 10am to 8pm; passport required)
and a great cafeteria.

Coredo Muromachi   Mall
(コレド室町; Map p250; http://31urban.
jp/lng/eng/muromachi.html; 2-2-1
Nihombashi-Muromachi, Chūō-ku; ☺most shops
11am-7pm; S Ginza line to Mitsukoshimae, exit
A4) Spread over three buildings, this stylish
development houses many shops from
famous gourmet food purveyors. There are
also elegant fashion and homewares boutiques here, as well as reliable places to eat.

Tsuruya Yoshinobu   Food
(鶴屋吉信; Map p250; ☎03-3243-0551; www.
turuya.co.jp; 1st fl, Coredo Muromachi 3, 1-5-5
Nihombashi-Muromachi, Chūō-ku; ☺10.30am-
8pm; S Ginza line to Mitsukoshimae, exit A4) This
is the Tokyo outpost of one of Kyoto's more
esteemed creators of *wagashi*, traditional
Japanese sweets made of rice flour, bean
paste and sugar. While the ingredients may
be simple, the designs – of seasonal motifs,
such as flowers and leaves – are spectacular. Sit at the counter to watch the in-house
patissier make the sweet of your choice,
served with tea (¥1296).

Bic Camera   Electronics
(ビックカメラ; Map p250; ☎03-5221-1111; www.
biccamera.co.jp; 1-11-1 Yūrakuchō, Chiyoda-ku;
☺10am-10pm; 🚉 JR Yamanote line to Yūrakuchō,
Kokusai Center exit) Cameras are just the
start of the electronic items and much
more (toys, sake, medicine and cosmetics)
sold in this mammoth discount store occu-
pying a block. Shopping here is like being
inside a very noisy computer game, but it's
worth enduring for the discounts and the
tax-free deals available to tourists.

KITTE   Mall
(Map p250; http://jptower-kitte.jp; 2-7-2
Marunouchi, Chiyoda-ku; ☺11am-9pm Mon-Sat,
to 8pm Sun; 🚉 JR lines to Tokyo, Marunouchi
south exit) This well-designed shopping mall

From left: Yanaka Matsunoya (p166); Beams Japan, Shinjuku (p154); Shibuya 109 (p157)

Top Tokyo Souvenirs

Cool Clothes

Bring back some Tokyo style from ahead-of-the-curve shops, such as Isetan (p154) and Dover Street Market Ginza (p161).

Kitchenware

You saw that sushi chef work magic with that knife. Get one (and other useful kitchen items) for yourself at Tsukiji Hitachiya (p39).

Furoshiki

These colourful patterned cloths can be knotted into totes and reusable wrappings. Try Musubi (p44) and Itōya (p160).

Cute Characters

Shop for mascots of Japanese pop culture (such as Hello Kitty and Pikachu) at KiddyLand (p44) and Tokyo Character Street (p165).

Gourmet Goods

Pick up green tea, jars of seasoned miso paste and more at gourmet shops such as Akomeya (p160) and Chabara (p165).

at the foot of JP Tower incorporates the restored facade of the former Tokyo Central Post Office. It is notable for its atrium, around which is arrayed a quality selection of craft-oriented, Japanese-brand shops selling homewares, fashion, accessories and lifestyle goods.

Tokyo Character Street   Toys

(東京キャラクターストリート; Map p250; www.tokyoeki-1bangai.co.jp; B1 First Avenue Tokyo Station, 1-9-1 Marunouchi, Chiyoda-ku; ⏱10am-8.30pm; 🚃JR lines to Tokyo Station, Yae-su exit) From Doraemon to Hello Kitty and Pikachu, Japan knows *kawaii* (cute) and how to merchandise it. In the basement on the Yaesu side of Tokyo Station, some 15 Japanese TV networks and toy manufactur-ers operate stalls selling official plush toys, sweets and accessories.

🅖 Kanda & Akihabara

Y. & Sons   Fashion & Accessories

(Map p254; 📞03-5294-7521; www.yandsons. com; 2-17-2 Soto-Kanda, Chiyoda-ku; ⏱11am-8pm Thu-Tue; 🚃JR Chūō line to Ochanomizu, Ochanomizu-bashi exit) Every once in a while in Tokyo, you'll spot a gentleman in a silk-wool kimono and fedora, looking as if he's stepped out of the 1900s. Bespoke tailor Y. & Sons would like to see this more often. Custom kimono with obi start at around ¥65,000 and take two weeks to complete; international shipping is available.

Chabara   Food

(ちゃばら; Map p254; www.jrtk.jp/chabara; 8-2 Kanda Neribei-chō, Chiyoda-ku; ⏱11am-8pm; 🚃JR Yamanote line to Akihabara, Electric Town exit) This under-the-train-tracks shopping mall focuses on artisan food and drinks from across Japan, including premium sake, soy sauce, sweets, teas and crackers – all great souvenirs and presents.

2k540 Aki-Oka
Artisan   Arts & Crafts

(アキオカアルチザン; Map p254; www.jrtk. jp/2k540; 5-9-23 Ueno, Taitō-ku; ⏱11am-7pm Thu-Tue; 🚃Ginza line to Suehirochō, exit 2) This

  Kimono

Kimono simply means 'thing to wear', but in modern-day Tokyo very few people wear them, except on special occasions. Made of silk and often hand-dyed, new kimono can be prohibitively expensive: a full set can easily cost a million yen.

Second-hand kimono, on the other hand, can be found for as little as ¥1000 – though one in good shape will cost more like ¥10,000. Gallery Kawano (p45) has a beautiful selection.

It takes a lot of practice to get down the art of tying an obi (sash) properly, so it's a good idea to get shop staff to help you (though there's no reason you can't just wear one like a dressing gown and forgo the sash entirely).

Another option is a *yukata*, a light-weight, cotton kimono that's easier to wear. During the summer you can find these at department stores and even Uniqlo new for less than ¥10,000. For something truly original, check out Tsukikageya (p156).

Harajuku vintage shop Chicago (p46) has racks of low-priced, used kimono and *yukata* of varying quality. Flea mar-kets are also a good bet for bargains.

Vintage kimono for sale at Chicago (p46), Harajuku
EDU VISION / ALAMY STOCK PHOTO ©

ace arcade under the JR tracks (its name refers to the distance from Tokyo Station) offers an eclectic range of stores selling Japanese-made goods – everything from pottery and leatherwork to cute aliens, a nod to Akihabara from a mall that is more akin to Kyoto than Electric Town. The best for colourful crafts is **Nippon Hyakkuten** (日本百貨店; http://nippon-dept.jp).

Komiyama Shoten
Books

(小宮山書店; Map p254; 03-3291-0495; www.book-komiyama.co.jp; 1-7 Kanda-Jimbōchō, Chiyoda-ku; 11am-6.30pm Mon-Sat, to 5.30pm Sun; S Hanzōmon line to Jimbōchō, exit A7) Komiyama Shoten, in business since 1939, stocks an incredible selection of art and photography books, posters and prints with some very famous Japanese and international artists represented. Every spare inch of wall is given over to gallery space.

Ohya Shobō
Books

(大屋書房; Map p254; 03-3291-0062; www.ohya-shobo.com; 1-1 Kanda-Jimbōchō, Chiyoda-ku; 10am-6pm Mon-Sat; R Hanzōmon line to Jimbōchō, exit A7) This splendid, musty old bookshop specialises in *ukiyo-e* (woodblock prints), both old and newly printed (from ¥2000). There are antique books and maps, too. The staff are friendly and can help you with whatever you're looking for. All purchases are tagged with a small origami crane.

🔒 Ueno & Yanaka

Yanaka Matsunoya
Homewares

(谷中松野屋; Map p254; www.yanakamatsunoya.jp; 3-14-14 Nishi-Nippori, Arakawa-ku; 11am-7pm Mon & Wed-Fri, 10am-7pm Sat & Sun; R JR Yamanote line to Nippori, west exit) At the top of Yanaka Ginza (p69), Matsunoya sells household goods – baskets, brooms and canvas totes, for example – simple in beauty and form, and handmade by local artisans.

Isego Honten
Alcohol

(伊勢五本店; Map p254; 03-3821-4573; www.isego.net; 3-3-13 Sendagi, Bunkyō-ku; 10am-7pm Mon-Sat; S Chiyoda line to Sendagi, exit 2) This *sake-ya* (liquor shop), on a residential street in Sendagi, has been run by the same family for over 300 years. There's usually someone on hand who speaks some English, who can help you pick something

from the selection of craft *nihonshu* (sake) and *shōchū* (distilled liquor usually made from barley or sweet potato) and domestic wines. The Naka-Meguro shop (p158) has a counter bar where you can order *nihonshu* by the glass (around ¥500).

Mita Sneakers
Shoes

(ミタスニーカーズ; Map p254; 03-3832-8346; www.mita-sneakers.co.jp; 2nd fl, Ameyoko Center Bldg, 4-7-8 Ueno, Taitō-ku; 11am-7.30pm Mon-Fri, 10am-7.30pm Sat & Sun, closed 3rd Wed of the month; R JR Yamanote line to Ueno, central exit) Ameya-yokochō (p69) is widely known as the place to pick up bargain kicks; but among sneaker heads, it's better known as the home of Mita Sneakers, which sells limited-edition made-in-Japan shoes and exclusive collaboration items from the big brands (Adidas, Puma et al). It's inside the wedge-shaped Ameyoko Center Bldg.

Edokoro Allan West
Art

(絵処アランウエスト; Map p254; 03-3827-1907; www.allanwest.jp; 1-6-17 Yanaka, Taitō-ku; 1-5pm, from 3pm Sun, closed irregularly; S Chiyoda line to Nezu, exit 1) In this masterfully converted garage, long-time Yanaka resident Allan West paints gorgeous screens and scrolls in the traditional Japanese style, making his paints from scratch just as local artists have done for centuries. Smaller votive-shaped paintings start at ¥5000; the screens clock in at a cool ¥6 million.

Isetatsu
Arts & Crafts

(いせ辰; Map p254; 03-3823-1453; 2-18-9 Yanaka, Taitō-ku; 10am-6pm; S Chiyoda line to Sendagi, exit 1) Dating back to 1864, this venerable stationery shop specialises in *chiyogami* – gorgeous, colourful paper made using woodblocks – as well as papier-mâché figures and masks.

Ōkuma Shōkai
Fashion & Accessories

(大熊商会; Map p254; 03-3832-4466; www.yokosuka-jumper.com; 4-7-8 Ueno, Taitō-ku; 11am-7pm, closed 3rd Wed of the month; R JR Yamanote line to Ueno, central exit) *Sukajan* are silken bomber jackets boldly embroidered, usually with traditional motifs such as cherry blossoms or cranes. They were originally created as souvenirs for American GIs during the Allied Occupation. Several shops in Ameya-yokochō (p69) sell them, but Ōkuma Shōkai, whose jackets are made in Japan, is our pick. Look for the awning with 'Art Jaket Okuma' written in English.

Asakusa & Ryōgoku

Kakimori — Stationery

(カキモリ; Map p254; 03-3864-3898; www.kakimori.com; 4-20-12 Kuramae, Taitō-ku; noon-7pm Tue-Fri, 11am-7pm Sat & Sun; Asakusa line to Kuramae, exit 3) Stationery lovers flock from far and wide to this shop that allows you to custom build your own notebooks (from around ¥1000). Choose the paper, covers, binding and other bits and pieces to make a unique keepsake. At next door's **Inkstand**, custom blend your own ink to match.

Tokyo Hotarudo — Vintage

(東京蛍堂; Map p254; 03-3845-7563; http://tokyohotarudo.com; 1-41-8 Asakusa, Taitō-ku; 11am-8pm Wed-Sun; Tsukuba Express to Asakusa, exit 5) This curio shop is run by an eccentric young man who prefers to dress as if the 20th century hasn't come and gone already. If you think that sounds marvellous, then you'll want to check out his collection of vintage dresses and bags, antique lamps, watches and decorative

objets. The entrance is tricky: look for a vertical black sign with a pointing finger.

Fujiya — Arts & Crafts

(ふじ屋; Map p254; 03-3841-2283; 2-2-15 Asakusa, Taitō-ku; 10am-6pm Wed-Mon; Ginza line to Asakusa, exit 1) Fujiya specialises in *tenugui*: dyed cloths of thin cotton that can be used as tea towels, handkerchiefs, gift wrapping (the list goes on – they're surprisingly versatile). Here they come in traditional designs and humorous modern ones.

Kurodaya — Stationery

(黒田屋; Map p254; 03-3844-7511; 1-2-5 Asakusa, Taitō-ku; 11am-7pm Tue-Sun; Ginza line to Asakusa, exit 3) Since 1856 Kurodaya has been specialising in *washi* and products made from paper such as cards, kites and papier-mâché folk-art figures. It sells its own designs and many others from across Japan.

Bengara — Arts & Crafts

(べんがら; 03-3841-6613; www.bengara.com; 1-35-6 Asakusa, Taitō-ku; 10am-6pm Mon-Fri, to 7pm Sat & Sun, closed 3rd Thu of the month; Ginza line to Asakusa, exit 1) *Noren* are the curtains that hang in front of shop doors. This store sells beautiful ones, made of linen and coloured with natural dyes (such as indigo or persimmon) or decorated with ink-brush paintings. There are smaller items too, such as pouches and book covers, made of traditional textiles.

BAR OPEN

Sake bars, craft beer, international DJs
and Japanese whisky

Bar Open

Make like Lady Gaga in a karaoke box; sip sake with an increasingly rosy salaryman in a tiny postwar bar; or dance under the rays of the rising sun at an enormous bayside club: that's nightlife, Tokyo-style. Shinjuku, Shibuya and Roppongi are the biggest nightlife districts, but there are bars everywhere – such is the importance of that time-honoured social lubricant, alcohol, in this work-hard, play-hard city. Tokyo also holds its own with London and New York when it comes to dance parties; top international DJs and domestic artists do regular sets at venues with body-shaking sound systems.

In This Section

Opening Hours

Tokyo's nightspots open from around 6pm and stay open until well into the wee hours – there's no mandated closing time. Many bars are open all week, and many people are out all nights of the week, though some bars close on Sunday. Clubs really get going on Friday and Saturday after midnight; note that a picture ID is required for entry.

Ueno & Yanaka
Largely quiet but with some local gems (p183)

Asakusa & Ryōgoku
Some fun spots in this historic area (p183)

Shinjuku & Ikebukuro
Cocktail dens and eccentric bars, plus plenty of pubs and karaoke parlours (p174)

Kōenji & Kichijōji
Counter culture gathering spots (p175)

Harajuku & Aoyama
Wine bars and late-night cafes (p176)

Marunouchi & Nihombashi
After work hang-outs (p182)

Roppongi & Akasaka
One big all night party (p181)

Ginza & Tsukiji
A pricey place to drink, but there are some exceptions (p182)

Shibuya & Shimo-Kitazawa
Nightclubs and bohemian haunts (p176)

Tokyo Bay

Ebisu & Meguro
Cocktail bars and hidden lounges (p178)

Odaiba & Tokyo Bay
Dance until dawn with international DJs (p183)

Caption

Costs & Tipping

To avoid a nasty shock when the bill comes, check prices and cover charges before sitting down. If you are served a small snack (*o-tsumami*) with your first round, this implies a cover charge of a few hundred yen or more. Consider this in lieu of a tip (which is unnecessary in Tokyo). Most bars are reasonably priced; avoid ones that pressure you to purchase a bottle.

Best Blogs

Japan Sake (www.japansake.or.jp) The official site of the Japan Sake and Shōchū Makers Association is full of articles on videos to help you better understand (and appreciate!) sake and *shōchū* (Japanese distilled liquor).

Beer Tengoku (http://beertengoku. com) Lowdown on Japan's craft beer scene.

iFLYER (https://iflyer.tv/en-jp) Find out what events are happening at Tokyo's top clubs and purchase discounted advance tickets online.

The Best...

Only in Tokyo

Nakame Takkyū Lounge (p178) Hang-out for ping-pong-playing hipsters.

Tight (p177) One of Tokyo's classically teeny-tiny bars.

Samurai (p174) Jazz-filled home of 2500 *maneki-neko* (praying cats).

Cocktails

BenFiddich (p174; pictured above) Exotic concoctions made with herbs and freshly ground spices.

Bar Trench (p181) Ebisu-based pioneer in Tokyo's new cocktail scene.

Open Book (p174) Retro cocktails paired with second-hand books.

Craft Beer

Popeye (p183) Get very merry working your way through the most beers on tap in Tokyo.

Good Beer Faucets (p177) Fine choice of ales in Shibuya.

Harajuku Taproom (p176) Serves the beers of Baird Brewing.

Yanaka Beer Hall (p183) Microbrew ales in a charming complex of old wooden buildings.

Clubs

Womb (p177) Four levels of lasers and strobes at this Shibuya club fixture.

Contact (p176) Sign up online to get into Tokyo's coolest members-only club.

Ageha (p183) One of Asia's largest clubs, set on Tokyo Bay.

For Music Lovers

Bar Martha (p181) Moodily lit bar with top whisky list and record collection.

Beat Cafe (p177) After-hours hang-out spot for musicians and their fans.

Rhythm Cafe (p178) Run by a record label, with fun events.

Late Nights

Oath (p176) DJs spin past dawn at this cult-fave after-party spot.

Trouble Peach (p57) Engineered for smokey convos that last until dawn.

Manpuku Shokudō (p183) Cheap beers all day and all night.

☆ Lonely Planet's Top Choices

SuperDeluxe (p181) Tokyo's most interesting club with an eclectic line-up of events.

Zoetrope (p174) Sip rare whiskies at this Shinjuku hole-in-the-wall.

Another 8 (p178) New hotspot for craft beer and craft sake.

Date Night

New York Bar (p116; pictured above) Sophisticated lounge with jaw-dropping views.

Two Rooms (p116) Swank wine bar with a terrace.

These (p181) Decadent cocktails and cosy sofas.

🍸 Shinjuku & Ikebukuro

BenFiddich   Cocktail Bar
(ベンフィディック; Map p253; ☎03-6279-
4223; 9th fl, 1-13-7 Nishi-Shinjuku, Shinjuku-ku;
⊙6pm-3am Mon-Sat; 🚃JR Yamanote line to
Shinjuku, west exit) BenFiddich is dark and
tiny. Vials of infusions line the shelves,
while herbs hang drying from the ceiling.
The English-speaking barman, Kayama
Hiroyasu, in a white suit, moves like a
magician. There's no menu, but the original
cocktails, made with fresh ground spices
and herbs, run about ¥2000; service
charge is 10%. Try the gimlet with herbs.

There's no sign on the street, but it's the
building in between the karaoke parlour
and the curry shop. You'll see the wooden
door when you get out of the elevator.

Zoetrope   Bar
(ゾートロープ; Map p253; ☎03-3363-0162;
3rd fl, 7-10-14 Nishi-Shinjuku, Shinjuku-ku;
⊙7pm-midnight Mon-Sat; 🚃JR Yamanote line
to Shinjuku, west exit) A must-visit for whisky
fans, Zoetrope has some 300 varieties of
Japanese whisky behind its small counter
– including hard-to-find bottles from cult
favourite Chichibu Distillery. The owner
speaks English and can help you pick from
the daunting menu if you tell him what you
like. Cover charge ¥600; whisky by the
glass from ¥400 to ¥19,000, though most
are reasonable.

The Open Book   Bar
(Map p253; Golden Gai 5-ban-gai, 1-1-6 Kabukichō,
Shinjuku-ku; ⊙7pm-1.30am Mon-Sat; 🚃JR
Yamanote line to Shinjuku, east exit) Part of
the new generation of Golden Gai bars,
The Open Book is run by the grandson of
award-winning novelist Tanaka Komimasa.
Fittingly, well-loved books line the shelves.
The house special is an upgraded take on
an old classic, the 'lemon sour' (*shōchū*
distilled liquor, soda water and lemon juice;
¥700). Look for the sliding wooden door.
¥300 cover charge.

Samurai   Bar
(サムライ; Map p253; http://jazz-samurai.
seesaa.net; 5th fl, 3-35-5 Shinjuku, Shinjuku-ku;
⊙6pm-1am; 🚃JR Yamanote line to Shinjuku,

Whisky bottles, Zoetrope

southeast exit) Never mind the impressive record collection, this eccentric jazz *kissa* (cafe where jazz records are played) is worth a visit just for the owner's overwhelming collection of 2500 *maneki-neko*. It's on the alleyway alongside the highway, with a small sign on the front of the building. There's a ¥300 cover charge (¥500 after 9pm); drinks from ¥650.

Ren   Bar

(蓮; Map p253; ☑03-6723-9736; http://ren-shinjuku.com; 3rd fl, Shinjuku Robot Bldg, 1-7-1 Kabukichō, Shinjuku-ku; ☺10pm-5am; ℝJR Yamanote line to Shinjuku, east exit) An over-the-top lounge bar brought to you by the folks behind the equally over-the-top Robot Restaurant (p188). Robot Restaurant ticket holders can use the bar as a lounge before it opens to the public at 10pm. Enter from the back of the Robot Restaurant. Drinks start at ¥700.

🚻 Kōenji & Kichijōji

Nantoka Bar   Bar

(なんとかバー; www.shirouto.org/nantokabar; 3-4-12 Kōenji-kita, Suginami-ku; drinks from ¥400; ☺7pm-late; ℝJR Sōbu line to Kōenji, north exit) Part of the collective of spaces run by the Kōenji-based activist group Shirōto no Ran (Amateur Revolt), Nantoka Bar is about as uncommercial as a place selling drinks can get: there's no cover charge, drinks are generous and cheap and it's run on any given day by whoever feels like running it (which is sometimes no one at all).

Cocktail Shobō   Bar

(コクテイル書房; 3-8-13 Kōenji-kita, Suginami-ku; ☺11.30am-3pm Wed-Sun, 5pm-midnight Mon-Sun; ℝJR Sōbu line to Kōenji, north exit) It's a beautiful match: worn paperbacks, a vintage wooden house and cocktails come together at this Kōenji bar, where the wooden counter doubles as a bookshelf. Drinks and small dishes start at just ¥450. During lunch hours, curry and coffee are served.

⚤ LGBT Tokyo

Shinjuku-nichōme (nicknamed 'Ni-chōme') is Tokyo's gay and lesbian enclave, with hundreds of small bars and dance clubs within a few square blocks. While the rest of the city may seem closeted, Ni-chōme is most definitely out – and a lot of fun.

Many evenings start at **Aiiro Cafe** (アイイロ カフェ; Map p253; http://aliving. net/aiirocafe/; 2-18-1 Shinjuku, Shinjuku-ku; ☺6pm-2am Mon-Thu, 6pm-5am Fri & Sat, 6pm-midnight Sun; ⑤Marunouchi line to Shinjuku-sanchōme, exit C8), for two reasons: its all-you-can-drink beer happy-hour special ('beer blast' until 9pm; ¥1000) and its central, corner location. This is the place to see and be seen, meet up with friends and find out what else is going on that night. On a warm evening the scene here swells to block-party proportions.

Later in the evening, there's usually a crowd on the (admittedly small) dance floor at **Arty Farty** (アーティファーティ; Map p253; ☑03-5362-9720; www.arty-farty. net; 2nd fl, 2-11-7 Shinjuku, Shinjuku-ku; ☺8pm-4am Sun-Thu, 8pm-5am Fri & Sat; ⑤Marunouchi line to Shinjuku-sanchōme, exit C8), a fixture on Tokyo's gay scene for many a moon. Weekend events sometimes have a cover charge (¥1000 to ¥2000), which includes entrance to sister club, The Annex, around the corner. Check twitter (@artyfarty_annex).

Both Aiiro and Arty are welcoming to all.

Summer Beer Gardens

Summer beer gardens are a Tokyo tradition (typically running late May to early September). Many department stores set up tables and chairs on their rooftops. But two of the best take place on ground level, within the grounds of Meiji-jingū Gaien.

The classiest is **Beer Terrace Sekirei** (ビアテラス鶺鴒; ☎03-3746-7723; www.meijikinenkan.gr.jp/english/restaurant_sekirei.html; Meiji Kinenkan, 2-2-23 Moto-Akasaka, Minato-ku; ⏱5-10.30pm Mon-Fri; 🚃JR Sōbu line to Shinanomachi), which sets up on the neatly clipped lawn of the elegant Meiji Kinenkan (one of the city's most sought-after wedding venues). Traditional Japanese dance shows are performed each night around at 6.30pm, 7.30pm and 8.30pm. You can reserve a 'premium table' for ¥6000 that seats four, otherwise it's first come, first served for ordinary seating. Food and drink start from a (relatively) reasonable ¥1000.

More egalitarian is **Mori no Beer Garden** (森のビアガーデン; ☎03-5411-3715; www.rkfs.co.jp/brand/beer_garden_detail.html; 14-13 Kasumigaoka-chō, Shinjuku-ku; ⏱5-10pm Mon-Fri, noon-10pm Sat & Sun; 🚃JR Sōbu line to Shinanomachi), which hosts up to 1000 revellers for all-you-can-eat-and-drink spreads of beer and barbecue under a century-old tree. Reserve ahead (online) for two hours of all-you-can-eat-and-drink (men/women ¥4200/3900).

🚇 Harajuku & Aoyama

Oath   Bar
(Map p246; http://bar-oath.com; 4-5-9 Shibuya, Shibuya-ku; ⏱9pm-5am Mon-Thu, to 8am Fri & Sat, 5-11pm Sun; ⑤Ginza line to Omote-sandō, exit B1) A tiny space along a somewhat forlorn strip of highway, Oath is a favourite after-hours destination for clubbers – helped no doubt by the ¥500 drinks and the unusually late (early?) opening hours. DJs spin most nights, in which case there's a ¥500 cover charge.

Harajuku Taproom   Pub
(原宿タップルーム; Map p246; ☎03-6438-0450; http://bairdbeer.com/en/tap/harajuku.html; 2nd fl, 1-20-13 Jingūmae, Shibuya-ku; ⏱5pm-midnight Mon-Fri, noon-midnight Sat & Sun; 🚃JR Yamanote line to Harajuku, Takeshita exit) Baird's Brewery is one of Japan's most successful and consistently good craft breweries. This is one of its two Tokyo outposts, where you can sample more than a dozen of its beers on tap; try the top-selling Rising Sun Pale Ale (pints ¥1000). Japanese pub-style food is served as well.

🚇 Shibuya & Shimo-Kitazawa

Contact   Club
(コンタクト; Map p246; ☎03-6427-8107; www.contacttokyo.com; basement, 2-10-12 Dōgenzaka, Shibuya-ku; ⏱closed Thu; 🚃JR Yamanote line to Shibuya, Hachikō exit) This large – by Tokyo standards – basement club is the city's latest hotspot. Friday and Saturday nights (entry ¥3000 to ¥3500; ¥2000 for under 23s) see big international DJs and a young, fashionable crowd. It's 'members only' but anyone can sign up for membership on the website (do this before you go). ID required. Look for the entrance in the back of a parking lot.

Enter before 11pm on Friday or Saturday and get in for ¥1000. It's mostly local DJs Monday through Wednesday (entry ¥1500 for all). Sundays are a wildcard.

JEREMY SUTTON-HIBBERT / ALAMY STOCK PHOTO ©

Manpuku Shokudō (p183)

Tight   Bar

(タイト; Map p246; 2nd fl, 1-25-10 Shibuya,
Shibuya-ku; ⏰6pm-2am Mon-Sat, to midnight
Sun; 🚉JR Yamanote line to Shibuya, Hachikō
exit) This teeny-tiny bar is wedged among
the wooden shanties of Nonbei-yokochō,
a narrow nightlife strip along the elevated
JR tracks. Like the name suggests, it's a
tight fit, but the lack of seats doesn't keep
regulars away: on a busy night, they line the
stairs. Look for the big picture window. No
cover charge; drinks around ¥700.

Womb   Club

(ウーム; Map p246; 📞03-5459-0039, VIP
reservations 050-3188-9608; www.womb.co.jp;
2-16 Maruyama-chō, Shibuya-ku; ⏰11pm-4.30am
Fri & Sat, from 10pm Mon-Thu, varies Sun;
🚉JR Yamanote line to Shibuya, Hachikō exit) A
long-time (in club years, at least) club-
scene fixture, Womb gets a lot of big-name
international DJs playing mostly house
and techno on Friday and Saturday nights.
Frenetic lasers and strobes splash across
the heaving crowds. Weekdays are quieter,
with local DJs playing EDM mix and ladies

getting free entry (with flyer). Cover ¥1500
to ¥4000; ID required.

You can book the tables in the VIP rooms
on the 3rd and 4th floors online.

Good Beer Faucets   Craft Beer

(グッドビアフォウセッツ; Map p246; http://
shibuya.goodbeerfaucets.jp; 2nd fl, 1-29-1 Shōtō,
Shibuya-ku; pints from ¥800; ⏰4pm-midnight
Mon-Thu & Sat, to 1am Fri, 3-11pm Sun; 📶; 🚉JR
Yamanote line to Shibuya, Hachikō exit) With 40
shiny taps, Good Beer Faucets has one of
the city's best selections of Japanese craft
brews and regularly draws a full house of
locals and expats. The interior is chrome
and concrete (and not at all grungy). Come
for happy hour (until 8pm Sunday to Thursday) and get ¥200 off any pint.

Beat Cafe   Bar

(Map p246; www.facebook.com/beatcafe; basement fl, 2-13-5 Dōgenzaka, Shibuya-ku; ⏰8pm-
5am; 🚉JR Yamanote line to Shibuya, Hachikō exit)
Join an eclectic mix of local and international regulars at this comfortably shabby
bar among the nightclubs and love hotels
of Dōgenzaka. It's a known hang-out for

Golden Gai

Golden Gai, a warren of tiny alleys and narrow, two-storey wooden buildings, began as a black market following WWII. Now those same buildings are filled with more than a hundred closet-sized bars. Each is as unique and eccentric as the 'master' or 'mama' who runs it. That Golden Gai – prime real estate – has so far resisted the kind of development seen elsewhere in Shinjuku is a credit to these stubbornly bohemian characters.

The best way to experience Golden Gai is to stroll the lanes and pick a place that suits your mood. Bars here usually have a theme – from punk rock to photography – and draw customers with matching expertise and obsessions (many of whom work in the media and entertainment industries). Since regular customers are their bread and butter, some establishments are likely to give tourists a cool reception. Don't take it personally. Japanese visitors unaccompanied by a regular get the same treatment; this is Golden Gai's peculiar, invisible velvet rope.

There are also an increasing number of bars that expressly welcome tourists with English signs posted on their doors. Open Book (p174) is one such example (though you'll have to look closely for the sign!). Ramen shop Nagi (p124) is here, too.

Note that many bars have a cover charge (usually ¥500 to ¥1500).

musicians and music fans; check the website for info on parties (and after-parties). Look for Gateway Studio on the corner; the bar is in the basement. Drinks from ¥600.

Rhythm Cafe   Bar

(リズムカフェ; Map p246; ☑03-3770-0244; http://rhythmcafe.jp; 11-1 Udagawa-chō, Shibuya-ku; ◷6pm-2am; ☒JR Yamanote line to Shibuya, Hachikō exit) Run by a record label, chill spot Rhythm Cafe is known for having off-beat event nights (such as the retro Japanese-pop night on the fourth Thursday of the month). Drinks start at ¥700; when DJs spin, the cover is around ¥1000.

🄯 Ebisu & Meguro

Another 8   Bar

(☑03-6417-9158; http://sakahachi.jp; 1-2-18 Shimo-Meguro, Meguro-ku; ◷5pm-1am, closed irregularly; ☒JR Yamanote line to Meguro, west exit) Choose from a changing selection of eight craft beers (pints ¥1200) and sakes (around ¥800) at this popular new hangout in an old garage just south of Meguro Station. DJs spin here most Friday and Saturday evenings.

Nakame Takkyū Lounge   Lounge

(中目卓球ラウンジ; Map p246; ☑03-5722-3080; http://mfs11.com/brand/nakame-takkyu-lounge-nakameguro; 2nd fl, Lion House Naka-Meguro, 1-3-13 Kami-Meguro, Meguro-ku; ◷6pm-2am Sun-Thu, to 3am Fri & Sat; ⓢHibiya line to Naka-Meguro, main exit) *Takkyū* means table tennis and it's a serious sport in Japan. This hilarious bar looks like a university table-tennis clubhouse – right down to the tatty furniture and posters of star players on the wall. It's in an apartment building next to a parking garage (go all the way down the corridor past the bikes); ring the doorbell for entry. Cover before/after 10pm ¥500/¥800.

Gem by Moto   Bar

(ジェムバイモト; Map p246; ☑03-6455-6998; 1-30-9 Ebisu, Shibuya-ku; ◷5pm-midnight Tue-Fri, 1-9pm Sat & Sun; ☒JR Yamanote line to Ebisu, east exit) Gem, bright and smoke-free,

DIDIER ZYLBERYNG / ALAMY STOCK PHOTO © ; JEREMY SUTTON-HIBBERT / GETTY IMAGES © ; SHINARI / SHUTTERSTOCK ©

Clockwise from top: diners at a streetside izakaya; Suntory Hibiki whisky; sushi and sake

Tokyo in a Glass

Sake is the best pairing for
traditional Japanese cuisine.

Unpasteurised sake
is called nama-zake.

Sake can be sweet
(ama-kuchi) or dry (kara-kuchi)

On average the alcohol
content of sake is
around 15%

Premium sake is usually
served chilled (reishu).

Sake can also be served
nuru-kan (warm) or
atsu-kan (hot).

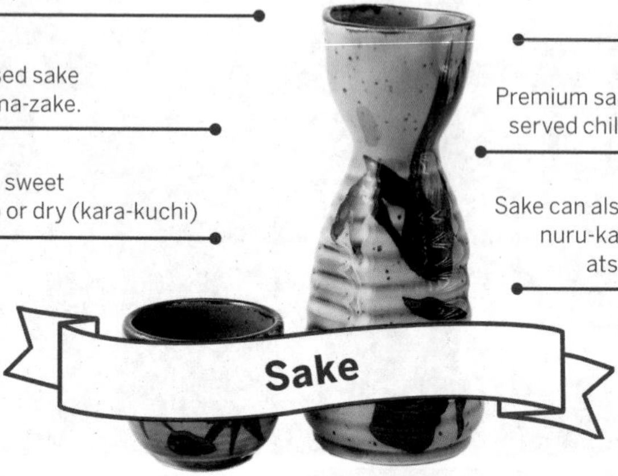

Sake

Get to Know Sake

In Japan 'sake' (which just means
alcohol) is called *nihonshu* (日本酒; 'the
drink of Japan'). It's made from rice,
water and a *kōji* (a kind of mould) and is
always brewed during the winter. Fresh,
young sake is ready by late autumn.

Sake is classed by the amount of rice
that is polished away before fermentation. Generally speaking, the more
polishing, the better the sake will be.
Premium grade *ginjō* is made from rice
that has been polished down to 60%;
ultra-premium *dai-ginjō* uses kernels
polished to less than 50%. The taste
of sake is often categorised as either
sweet (*ama-kuchi*) or dry (*kara-kuchi*).

When you order sake it will usually
come in a *tokkuri* (decanter) that holds
one or two *gō* (180ml) along with tiny
cups called *o-choko*.

☆ Top Spots for Sake

Another 8 (p178) Craft sake and cool
atmosphere.

**Japan Sake & Shōchū Information
Centre (p182)** For serious students.

Isego Naka-Meguro (p158) Shop and
bar all-in-one.

Gem by Moto (p178) New-wave sake
bar.

Toyama Bar (p182) Sake specialist
from Toyama prefecture.

may look more like a boutique than a sake bar but it has a seriously good selection of interesting sakes from ambitious brewers. The lack of English menu can be intimidating, but start with one of the Gem originals (brewed in collaboration with the bar) – or let owner Chiba-san select one for you. Cover charge ¥800.

Bar Trench
Cocktail Bar

(バートレンチ; Map p246; ☎03-3780-5291; http://small-axe.net/bar-trench/; 1-5-8 Ebisu-Nishi, Shibuya-ku; ⊗7pm-2am Mon-Sat, 6pm-1am Sun; ⊠JR Yamanote line to Ebisu, west exit) One of the pioneers in Tokyo's new cocktail scene, Trench (named for the trench-like alley in which it is nestled) is a tiny place with an air of old-world bohemianism. It has a short but sweet menu of ever-changing original tipples made with infusions, botanicals, herbs and spices. Drinks from ¥1500; cover ¥500.

If it's full, ask the staff for directions to sister bar Tram, one block over.

Bar Martha
Bar

(バー・マーサ; Map p246; www.martha-records.com; 1-22-23 Ebisu, Shibuya-ku; ⊗7pm-5am; ⊠JR Yamanote line to Ebisu, east exit) It's hard to say which is more impressive at this dim, moody bar: the nine-page whisky list or the collection of records. The latter are played on spot-lit turntables, amplified by 1m-tall vintage Tannoy speakers. The cocktails, especially the *nama shōga mosuko myūru* (生生姜モスコミュール; fresh ginger Moscow mule) are excellent, too. Cover includes bar snacks ¥800; drinks from ¥800. Quiet voices only, please.

Buri
Bar

(ぶり; Map p246; ☎03-3496-7744; 1-14-1 Ebisu-nishi, Shibuya-ku; ⊗5pm-3am; ⊠JR Yamanote line to Ebisu, west exit) Buri – the name means 'super' in Hiroshima dialect – is one of Ebisu's more popular *tachinomi-ya* (small, standing-only bars). Generous quantities of sake (more than 40 varieties; ¥830) are served semifrozen, like slushies, in colourful jars. Cover charge ¥260.

Urara
Beer Garden

(ウララ; Map p246; www.hrm.co.jp; 20-10 Sarugaku-chō, Shibuya-ku; ⊗11.30am-8pm; ⊠Tōkyū Tōyoko line to Daikanyama) The people behind the iconic Okura boutique (p158) next door have taken their folksy aesthetic and poured it into this new backyard-style beer garden. On the menu: organic draft beer from Karuizawa (¥800), *amazake* made in-house (sweet, non-alcoholic fermented rice beverage; ¥400) and additive-free juices (¥500). Closed for rain.

❹ Roppongi & Akasaka

These
Lounge

(テーゼ; Map p252; ☎03-5466-7331; www.these-jp.com; 2-15-12 Nishi-Azabu, Minato-ku; cover charge ¥500; ⊗7pm-4am, to 2am Sun; ⑤Hibiya line to Roppongi, exit 3) Pronounced '*teh*-zeh', this delightfully quirky, nook-ridden 'library lounge' overflows with armchairs, sofas, and books on the shelves and on the bar. Imbibe champagne by the glass, whiskies or seasonal-fruit cocktails. Bites include escargot garlic toast, which goes down very nicely with a drink in the secret room on the 2nd floor. Look for the flaming torches outside.

SuperDeluxe
Club

(スーパー・デラックス; Map p252; ☎03-5412-0515; www.super-deluxe.com; B1 fl, 3-1-25 Nishi-Azabu, Minato-ku; ⑤Hibiya line to Roppongi, exit 1B) This groovy basement performance space, also a cocktail lounge and club of sorts, stages everything from electronic music to literary evenings and creative presentations in the 20 x 20 PechaKucha (20 slides x 20 seconds) format. Check

Kamiya Bar

the website for event details. Sometimes events are free; some have a cover. It's in a brown-brick building by a shoe-repair shop.

Brewdog   Craft Beer

(Map p252; ☏03-6447-4160; www.brewdog. com/bars/worldwide/roppongi; 5-3-2 Roppongi, Minato-ku; ⊗5pm-midnight Mon-Fri, 3pm-midnight Sat & Sun; 🛜; 🅂Hibiya line to Roppongi, exit 3) This Scottish craft brewery's Tokyo outpost is nestled off the main drag. Apart from its own brews, there's a great selection of other beers, including Japanese ones on tap, mostly all served in small, regular or large (full pint) portions. Tasty food and computer and board games to while away the evening round out a class operation.

🕤 Ginza & Tsukiji

Japan Sake & Shōchū
Information Centre   Sake

(日本の酒情報館; Map p250; Nihon no Sake Jōhō-kan; ☏03-3501-0101; www.japansake.or.jp; 1-6-15 Nishi-Shimbashi, Minato-ku; ⊗10am-6pm

Mon-Fri; 🅂Ginza line to Toranomon, exit 9) This isn't a bar, but who cares when you can get 30mL thimbles of regionally brewed sake or *shōchū* for as little as ¥100 a shot? There are dozens from which to choose (and tasting sets of three glasses from ¥300 to ¥500 for those who can't make up their minds). It's an ideal place to get better acquainted with sake.

It's on the ground floor at the back of the Japan Sake Brewers Association Building (日本酒造会館).

🕤 Marunouchi & Nihombashi

Toyama Bar   Bar

(トヤマバー; Map p250; ☏03-6262-2723; http://toyamakan.jp; 1-2-6 Nihombashi-muromachi, Chūō-ku; ⊗11am-9pm; 🅂Ginza line to Mitsukoshimae, exit B5) This slick counter bar offers a selection of sakes from 17 different Toyama breweries. A set of three 30mL cups costs a bargain ¥700 (90mL cups from ¥700 each). English tasting notes are available. It's part of the Nihonbashi Toyama-kan (日本橋とやま館), which promotes goods produced in Japan's northern Toyama prefecture. Pick up a bottle of anything you like at the attached shop.

Manpuku Shokudō   Pub

(まんぷく食堂; Map p250; ☎03-3211-6001; www.manpukushokudo.com; 2-4-1 Yūrakuchō, Chiyoda-ku; cover charge ¥300; ⏰24hr Tue-Sun, until 11.30pm Mon; ⊞JR Yamanote line to Yūrakuchō, central exit) Down your beer or sake as trains rattle overhead on the tracks that span Harumi-dōri at Yūrakuchō. This convivial *izakaya* (Japanese pub-eatery), plastered with old movie posters, is open round the clock and has bags of atmosphere.

Happy hour, when beers are ¥280, runs from 11am to 8pm Monday to Friday and 3pm to 8pm Saturday and Sunday (otherwise, drinks and food start at ¥480).

🍺 Ueno & Yanaka

Yanaka Beer Hall   Craft Beer

(谷中ビアホール; Map p254; ☎03-5834-2381; www.facebook.com/yanakabeerhall; 2-15-6 Ueno-sakuragi, Taitō-ku; ⏰noon-8.30pm Tue-Fri, 11am-8.30pm Sat & Sun; ⑤Chiyoda line to Nezu, exit 1) Exploring Yanesen can be thirsty work so thank heavens for this craft-beer bar, a cosy place with some outdoor seating. It's part of a charming complex of old wooden buildings that also house a bakery-cafe, bistro and events space. It has several brews on tap, including a Yanaka lager (¥900) that's only available here.

🍺 Asakusa & Ryōgoku

Popeye   Pub

(ポパイ; Map p254; ☎03-3633-2120; www.70beersontap.com; 2-18-7 Ryōgoku, Sumida-ku; ⏰5-11.30pm Mon-Fri, 3-11.30pm Sat; ⊞JR Sōbu line to Ryōgoku, west exit) Popeye boasts an astounding 70 beers on tap, including the

world's largest selection of Japanese beers – from Echigo Weizen to Hitachino Nest Espresso Stout. The happy-hour deal (5pm to 8pm, from 3pm on Saturday) offers select brews with free plates of pizza, sausages and other munchables. It's extremely popular and fills up fast; get here early to grab a seat.

Kamiya Bar   Bar

(神谷バー; Map p254; ☎03-3841-5400; www.kamiya-bar.com; 1-1-1 Asakusa, Taitō-ku; ⏰11.30am-10pm Wed-Mon; ⑤Ginza line to Asakusa, exit 3) One of Tokyo's oldest Western-style bars, Kamiya opened in 1880 and is still hugely popular – though probably more so today for its enormous, cheap draught beer (¥1050 for a litre). Its real speciality, however, is Denki Bran (¥270), a herbal liquor that's been produced in-house for more than a century. Order at the counter, then give your tickets to the server.

'Cuzn Homeground   Bar

(カズンホームグラウンド; Map p254; ☎03-5246-4380; www.homeground.jpn.com; 2-17-9 Asakusa, Taitō-ku; beer ¥800; ⏰noon-5am; 🛜; ⑤Ginza line to Tawaramachi, exit 3) Run by a wild gang of local hippies, 'Cuzn is the kind of bar where anything can happen: a barbecue, a jam session or all-night karaoke, for example.

🍺 Odaiba & Tokyo Bay

Ageha   Club

(アゲハ; www.ageha.com; 2-2-10 Shin-Kiba, Kōtō-ku; cover ¥3000-5000; ⏰11pm-5am Fri & Sat; ⑤Yūrakuchō line to Shin-Kiba, main exit) This gigantic waterside club, the largest in Tokyo, rivals any you'd find in LA or Ibiza. Top international and Japanese DJs appear here. Free buses run between the club and a bus stop on the east side of Shibuya Station (on Roppongi-dōri) all night. Events vary widely; check the website for details and bring photo ID.

SHOWTIME

Kabuki, international acts, jazz clubs and traditonal dance theatre

Showtime

All styles of traditional performing arts can be seen on Tokyo stages, including dramatic, visually arresting kabuki – Japan's signature performing art – and austere, haunting nō (an even older form of dance-drama). Earphones or subtitles with an English translation of the plots and dialogue are usually provided; unfortunately, this isn't the case with contemporary theatre.

Tokyoites have a great appreciation for jazz and classical music and there are wonderful venues for both. If you'd prefer to catch an in-your-face noise performance in a smoky basement club, well Tokyo has that for you too.

In This Section

Tickets

Ticket Pia (http://t.pia.jp) kiosks, scattered across Tokyo, handle tickets for most shows; unfortunately, its online booking site is in Japanese only. See **Tokyo Gig Guide** (www.tokyogigguide.com) for more details on buying tickets.

Websites

Check out Tokyo Time Out (www.timeout.com/tokyo) and Tokyo Dross (www.tokyodross.blogspot.co.uk) for listings.

Traditional theatre performance

The Best...

Live Music

Unit (p192) Fashionable spot for both live gigs and DJ events.

Shinjuku Pit Inn (p188) Tokyo jazz-scene institution for decades.

WWW (p191) Shibuya live house with a solid line-up of indie acts.

Tokyo Bunka Kaikan (p193) Superb acoustics and interiors at this Ueno-kōen classical venue.

Theatre

National Theatre (p192) Top-notch *nō*, bunraku and other traditional performances in a grand setting.

Kabukiza (p100) The place for the visual and dramatic feast that is kabuki.

Setagaya Public Theatre (p191) Renowned for contemporary drama and dance.

From left: *Nō* performer; Tokyo Opera City Concert Hall; Robot Restaurant cabaret performance

⚙ Shinjuku & Ikebukuro

Tokyo Opera City Concert Hall   Classical Music
(東京オペラシティコンサートホール; ☎03-5353-9999; www.operacity.jp; 3rd fl, Tokyo Opera City, 3-20-2 Nishi-Shinjuku, Shinjuku-ku; ¥2500-7000; ℝKeiō New line to Hatsudai, east exit) This beautiful, oak-panelled, A-frame concert hall, with legendary acoustics, hosts the Tokyo Philharmonic Orchestra among other well-regarded ensembles, including the occasional *bugaku* (classical Japanese music) group. Free lunchtime organ performances take place monthly, usually on Fridays. Information and tickets can be acquired at the box office next to the entrance to the Tokyo Opera City Art Gallery.

Shinjuku Pit Inn   Jazz
(新宿ピットイン; Map p253; ☎03-3354-2024; www.pit-inn.com; basement, 2-12-4 Shinjuku, Shinjuku-ku; from ¥3000; ⊘matinee 2.30pm, evening show 7.30pm; ⑤Marunouchi line to Shinjuku-sanchōme, exit C5) This is not the kind of place you come to talk over the music. This small basement club, open for half a century now, is Tokyo's best jazz spot, drawing a mix of influential, avant-garde and up-and-coming musicians from Japan and abroad. Weekday matinees feature young artists and cost only ¥1300.

Robot Restaurant   Cabaret
(ロボットレストラン; Map p253; ☎03-3200-5500 ; www.shinjuku-robot.com; 1-7-1 Kabukichō, Shinjuku-ku; tickets ¥8000; ⊘shows at 5.55pm, 7.50pm & 9.45pm; ℝJR Yamanote line to Shinjuku, east exit) This Kabukichō spectacle has hit it big with its vision of 'wacky Japan': bikini-clad women ride around on giant robots against a backdrop of animated screens and enough neon to light all of Shinjuku. Reservations aren't necessary but are recommended: the show's popularity is evinced by the ever-creeping ticket price. Look for discount tickets at hotels around town.

If the price makes you think twice, you can still swing by for a photo-op with two

of the robots parked outside. You can also grab a drink (and a taste of Robot Restaurant's signature gilded plastic, game-show-set aesthetic) at Ren (p175), in the same building (entrance in the back).

New National Theatre
Performing Arts

(新国立劇場; Shin Kokuritsu Gekijō; ☎03-5351-3011; www.nntt.jac.go.jp/english/index.html; 1-1-1 Hon-machi, Shibuya-ku; 🚉Keiō New line to Hatsudai, theatre exit) This is Tokyo's premier public performing-arts centre. There's a playhouse and an opera house, both state-of-the-art venues with built-in flexibility to accommodate different styles of staging. Unfortunately for international visitors, the plays are in Japanese, while the operas are usually visiting international productions). Contemporary dance (including the avant-garde Japanese style known as *butō*) is sometimes performed here, which happily requires no language ability.

Tickets are easy to purchase in English through the website.

⭐ Kōenji & Kichijōji

Star Pine's Cafe
Live Music

(スターパインズカフェ; ☎0422-23-2251; www.mandala.gr.jp/spc.html; basement fl, 1-20-16 Kichi-jōji Honchō, Musashino-shi; tickets ¥2500-5000; 🚉JR Sōbu-Chūō line to Kichijōji, north exit) This is an attractive, intimate venue, sunk deep so the ceiling feels refreshingly high. The line-up is jazz, but that's a wide net, encompassing everything from standards to the quirky, avant-garde and experimental. The audience will likely be multi-generational and attentive. One drink minimum order (but the drinks are actually decent).

Ni Man Den Atsu
Live Music

(二万電圧; www.den-atsu.com; basement fl, 1-7-23 Kōenji-Minami, Suginami-ku; tickets ¥1800-4000; Ⓢ Marunouchi line to Higashi-Kōenji, exit 3) Kōenji's most well-known punk venue boasts of having 'the world's loudest sound system'. Oddly enough, it's in the basement of a large, nondescript apartment complex

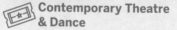

Contemporary Theatre & Dance

Theatre in Tokyo today doesn't have the same sway over audiences that it did in centuries past – much to the lament of those involved. The city has many theatres, but most show mainly Western works in translation (especially musicals) or unchallenging performances starring celebrities from film and television. There is an active fringe scene, one that has supported some compelling, introspective and daring playwrights, though this is difficult to access without some Japanese-language ability.

If you do want to experience contemporary theatre in Tokyo, the Setagaya Public Theatre (p191), a short train ride from Shibuya, has the most consistently interesting schedule of performances. Unless otherwise noted, though, performances are in Japanese.

Butō is Japan's unique and fascinating contribution to contemporary dance. It is raw, electrifying and often unsettling – and requires no language ability. Both the Setagaya Public Theatre and the New National Theatre (p189) occasionally show *butō*. Dairakudakan (www.dairakudakan.com) is one of the more active troupes today.

Tokyo annual theatre festival, **F/T** (http://www.festival-tokyo.jp/), takes place in autumn. Works, including those from playwrights from outside of Japan, are sometimes staged with subtitles. For the latest news from the theatre world, follow @JapanTheatre on Twitter.

New National Theatre (p189)
CHRISTINAYAN BY TAKAHIRO YANAI / GETTY IMAGES ©

(and must also have the world's best soundproofing). If you like your nights loud and unpredictable then this is the place. One drink (¥500) minimum order.

⊙ Harajuku & Aoyama

National Nō Theatre   Theatre

(国立能楽堂; Kokuritsu Nō-gakudō; ☏03-3423-1331; www.ntj.jac.go.jp/english; 4-18-1 Sendagaya, Shibuya-ku; adult ¥2700-4900, student ¥1900-2200; ☒JR Sōbu line to Sendagaya) The traditional music, poetry and dances that *nō* is famous for unfold here on an elegant cypress stage. Each seat has a small screen displaying an English translation of the dialogue. Shows take place only a few times a month and can sell out quickly; purchase tickets one month in advance through the Japan Arts Council website.

Crocodile   Live Music, Comedy

(クロコダイル; Map p246; www.crocodile-live.jp; basement fl, 6-18-8 Jingūmae, Shibuya-ku; ☺6pm-1am; ⑤Chiyoda line to Meiji-jingūmae, exit 1) Decked out in neon, mirrors and chrome, Crocodile is a classic dive. Live music of all sorts plays here nightly, but the most popular event is the English comedy night put on by Tokyo Comedy Store on the last Friday of the month (admission ¥1500, plus drink order). Advanced bookings are recommended; see www.tokyocomedy.com/improvazilla_main_stage_show.

Blue Note Tokyo   Jazz

(ブルーノート東京; Map p246; ☏03-5485-0088; www.bluenote.co.jp; 6-3-16 Minami-Aoyama, Minato-ku; ☺5.30pm-1am Mon-Sat, 5pm-12.30am Sun; ⑤Ginza line to Omotesandō, exit B3) This is the place to take in the likes of Maceo Parker, Herbie Hancock and Doctor John. Just like its sister acts in New York and Milan, the digs here are classily decorated with dark wood and deep velvet. Tickets typically run ¥6000 to ¥9800, plus a drink or food order.

Students can get in for 50% off with ID, but you have to reserve over the phone (or try your luck at the door).

✪ Shibuya & Shimo-Kitazawa

WWW
Live Music

(Map p246; http://www-shibuya.jp; 13-17 Udagawa-chō, Shibuya-ku; tickets ¥2000-5000; ☒JR Yamanote line to Shibuya, Hachikō exit) In a former arthouse cinema (with the tell-tale tiered floor still intact), this is one of those rare venues where you could turn up just about any night and hear something good. The line-up varies from indie pop to hip-hop to electronica. Upstairs is the newer WWW X, with more space.

Setagaya Public Theatre
Performing Arts

(世田谷パブリックシアター; ☒03-5432-1515; www.setagaya-pt.jp; 4-1-1 Taishidō, Setagaya-ku; tickets ¥5000-7500; ☒Tōkyū Den-en-toshi line to Sangenjaya, Carrot Tower exit) The best of Tokyo's public theatres, Setagaya Public Theatre puts on contemporary dramas as well as modern *nō* and sometimes *butō*. The smaller **Theatre Tram** shows more experimental works. Both are located inside the Carrot Tower building connected to Sangenjaya Station, a five-minute train ride from Shibuya.

Club Quattro
Live Music

(クラブクアトロ; Map p246; ☒03-3477-8750; www.club-quattro.com; 4th & 5th fl, 32-13-4 Udagawa-chō, Shibuya-ku; tickets ¥3000-4000; ☒JR Yamanote line to Shibuya, Hachikō exit) This small, intimate venue has the feel of a slick nightclub and attracts a more grown-up, artsy crowd than the club's location – near Center-gai – might lead you to expect. Though there's no explicit musical focus, emphasis is on rock and world music, with many an indie darling passing through.

Uplink
Cinema

(アップリンク; Map p246; ☒03-6825-5503; www.uplink.co.jp; 37-18 Udagawa-chō, Shibuya-ku; adult/student/senior ¥1800/1500/1100; ☒JR Yamanote line to Shibuya, Hachikō exit) Watching indies at Uplink feels a bit like hanging out in a friend's basement; with just 40 (comfy, mismatched) seats, it's officially Tokyo's smallest theatre. Artsy domestic and foreign films (subtitled in Japanese), including documentaries, are screened here. Uplink is also one of the few Tokyo cinemas that

Nippon Budōkan (p193)

 Nō

Nō is not drama in the usual sense; it seeks to express a poetic moment by symbolic and almost abstract means: glorious movements, sonorous chorus and music, and subtle expression. It's Japan's oldest existent performing art.

The stage is furnished with only a single pine tree. There are two principal characters: the *shite*, who is sometimes a living person but more often a demon or a ghost whose soul cannot rest; and the *waki*, who leads the main character towards the play's climactic moment.

Wooden masks are used to depict female or nonhuman characters; adult male characters are played without masks. These are works of art in their own right; some are on display at the Tokyo National Museum.

Providing light relief to the sometimes heavy drama of *nō* are the comic vignettes known as *kyōgen*. Using the colloquial language of the time and a cast of stock characters, *kyōgen* poke fun at such subjects as samurai, depraved priests and faithless women. Masks are not worn, and costumes tend to feature bold, colourful patterns.

Some visitors find *nō* rapturous and captivating; others (including most Japanese today) find its subtlety all too subtle. Decide for yourself with a performance at the National Nō Theatre (p190) or the National Theatre.

Nō performance
JACK VARTOOGIAN / GETTY IMAGES ©

screens films with a political bent. On weekdays students pay just ¥1100.

Shelter
Live Music

(シェルター; ☎03-3466-7430; www.loft-prj.co.jp/SHELTER; 2-6-10 Kitazawa, Setagaya-ku; tickets ¥2500-3500; ⓇKeiō Inokashira line to Shimo-Kitazawa, south exit) Of all the venues on the Shimo-Kitazawa circuit, this small basement club, going strong for more than 25 years now, has the most consistently solid line-up. It can be an excellent place to catch (and even meet) up-and-coming artists, usually of the rock persuasion.

✪ Ebisu & Meguro

Unit
Live Music

(ユニット; Map p246; ☎03-5459-8630; www.unit-tokyo.com; 1-34-17 Ebisu-nishi, Shibuya-ku; ¥2500-5000; ⓇTōkyū Tōyoko line to Daikanyama) This subterranean club stages live music and DJ-hosted events (sometimes on the same night). The solid line-up includes Japanese indie bands, veterans playing to a smaller crowd and overseas artists making their Japan debut. Unit is less grungy than other Tokyo live houses and, with high ceilings, doesn't get as smoky.

Liquid Room
Live Music

(リキッドルーム; Map p246; ☎03-5464-0800; www.liquidroom.net; 3-16-6 Higashi, Shibuya-ku; ⓇJR Yamanote line to Ebisu, west exit) When this storied concert hall moved to Ebisu from seedy Kabukichō, it cleaned up its act – but not its line-up. Liquid Room is still a great place to catch edgier performers (and some big names too). Both Japanese and international bands play here, and every once in a while there's an all-night gig. Tickets sell out fast.

✪ Roppongi & Akasaka

National Theatre
Theatre

(国立劇場, Kokuritsu Gekijō; ☎03-3265-7411, box office 03-3230-3000; www.ntj.jac.go.jp; 4-1 Hayabusa-chō, Chiyoda-ku; tickets ¥1800-12,500; ⓈHanzōmon line to Hanzōmon, exit 1) This is the capital's premier venue for traditional performing arts with a 1600-seat and a 590-seat auditorium. Performances include kabuki, *gagaku* (music of the imperial court) and bunraku (classic puppet theatre). Earphones with English translation are available for hire (¥700 plus ¥1000 deposit). Check the website for performance schedules.

Toho Cinemas Roppongi Hills
Cinema

(TOHOシネマズ 六本木ヒルズ; Map p252; ☑10am-9pm 050-6868-5024; https://toho theater.jp; Keyakizaka Complex, Roppongi Hills, 6-chōme Roppongi, Minato-ku; adult/student/senior/child ¥1800/1500/1100/1000; Ⓢ Hibiya line to Roppongi, exit 1c) Besides being one of Tokyo's nicest and biggest cinemas (it has nine screens, some with 3D and 4D capability), Toho's Roppongi Hills theatre has started screening some popular Japanese new releases with English subtitles. 3D and 4D screenings cost extra.

Billboard Live
Live Music

(ビルボードライブ東京; Map p252; ☑03-3405-1133; www.billboard-live.com; 4th fl, Tokyo Midtown, 9-7-4 Akasaka, Minato-ku; Ⓢ Hibiya or Ōedo line to Roppongi, exit 8) This glitzy amphitheatre-like space plays host to major foreign talent as well as Japanese jazz, soul and rock groups who all come in to shake the rafters. The service is excellent and the drinks are reasonably priced.

⊛ Kanda & Akihabara

Nippon Budōkan
Live Music

(日本武道館; ☑03-3216-5100; www.nippon budokan.or.jp; 2-3 Kitanomaru-kōen, Chiyoda-ku; Ⓢ Hanzōmon line to Kudanshita, exit 2) The 14,000-plus-seat Budōkan was originally built for the judo competition of the 1964 Olympics (*budō* means 'martial arts') and will be pressed into service again for the 2020 event. Martial-arts contests are still held here, but the Budōkan is better known

as a concert hall: lots of big names, from the Beatles to Beck, have played here.

Club Goodman
Live Music

(クラブグッドマン; Map p254; ☑03-3862-9010; http://clubgoodman.com; Basement fl, AS Bldg, 55 Kanda-Sakumagashi, Chiyoda-ku; cover ¥1000-5000; Ⓡ JR Yamanote line to Akihabara, Shōwa-dōri exit) In the basement of a building with a guitar shop and recording studios, it's no surprise that this live house is a favourite with Tokyo's indie-scene bands and their fans.

⊛ Ueno & Yanaka

Tokyo Bunka Kaikan
Classical Music

(東京文化会館; Map p254; www.t-bunka.jp; 5-45 Ueno-kōen, Taitō-ku; ⊙library 1-8pm Tue-Sat, to 5pm Sun, closed irregularly; Ⓡ JR lines to Ueno, Ueno-kōen exit) The Tokyo Metropolitan Symphony Orchestra and the Tokyo Ballet both make regular appearances at this concrete bunker of a building designed by Maekawa Kunio, an apprentice of Le Corbusier. Prices vary wildly; look out for monthly morning classical-music performances that cost only ¥500. The gorgeously decorated auditorium has superb acoustics.

⊛ Asakusa & Ryōgoku

Oiwake
Traditional Music

(追分; Map p254; ☑03-3844-6283; www.oiwake. info; 3-28-11 Nishi-Asakusa, Taitō-ku; ¥2000 plus 1 food item & 1 drink; ⊙5.30pm-midnight Tue-Sun; Ⓡ Tsukuba Express to Asakusa, exit 1) Oiwake is one of Tokyo's few *minyō izakaya*, pubs where traditional folk music is performed. It's a homely place, where the waitstaff and the musicians – who play *tsugaru-jamisen* (a banjo-like instrument), hand drums and bamboo flute – are one and the same. Sets start at 7pm and 9pm; children are welcome for the early show. Seating is on tatami.

ACTIVE
TOKYO

Baseball, sumo, amusement parks, cooking courses and traditional crafts

Active Tokyo

More and more courses in Tokyo – including traditional crafts workshops and cooking classes – are available in English. Not only do these courses offer a chance to engage with Japanese culture, they also get you talking to and getting to know the savvy locals who run them. Meanwhile, the city's latest trend, virtual-reality theme parks, offer a whole different experience.

Tokyo has never been a terribly sporty city, but the 2019 Rugby World Cup and the upcoming 2020 Summer Olympics are looking to change that – even if it just means more active spectators.

In This Section

What to Watch When

Sumo Tournaments are held in Tokyo in January, May and September; see a practice session year-round (except when tournaments take place).

Baseball The season runs March to October.

Rugby The 2019 Rugby World cup is happening 20 September to 2 November, with matches at stadiums in the Tokyo area and around Japan – and will be screened live at bars around the city.

MARINATAKANO / SHUTTERSTOCK ©

Ikebana arrangement

The Best...

Spectator Sports

Ryōgoku Kokugikan (p82) Location of the three annual Tokyo sumo *bashō* (tournaments).

Tokyo Dome (p198) Where the Yomiuri Giants, Japan's top baseball team, play.

Jingū Baseball Stadium (p198) Home to the city's number-two team, the Yakult Swallows.

Courses

Tsukiji Soba Academy (p198) Soba-making lessons from a seasoned pro.

Wanariya (p198) Indigo-dyeing and hand-loom weaving workshops.

Mokuhankan (p199) Make your own woodblock prints.

Ohara School of Ikebana (p199) Learn the Japanese art of flower arranging.

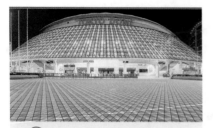

Baseball in Japan

Even if you don't follow baseball, it's worth catching a game in Tokyo just to experience the culture around it. Fans stage perfectly choreographed cheers – Swallows fans are famous for their 7th-inning stretch routine – and young women called *uriko* work the stands selling draft beer from the kegs strapped to their backs.

Within Tokyo, the Yomiuri Giants and the Yakult Swallows are cross-town rivals. While Giants tickets often sell out, same-day outfield tickets to see the Swallows cost just ¥1300 (¥500 for children) and are usually available – unless the they are playing the Giants, of course.

Tokyo Dome
KAI AYASE / SHUTTERSTOCK ©

🟠 Spectator Sports

Tokyo Dome   Baseball

(東京ドーム; www.tokyo-dome.co.jp/e; 1-3 Kōraku, Bunkyō-ku; tickets ¥1700-6200; 🚆 JR Chūō line to Suidōbashi, west exit) Tokyo Dome (aka 'Big Egg') is home to the Yomiuri Giants. Love 'em or hate 'em, they're the most consistently successful team in Japanese baseball. If you're looking to see the Giants in action, the baseball season runs from the end of March to the end of October. Tickets sell out in advance; get them early at www.giants.jp/en.

Jingū Baseball Stadium   Baseball

(神宮球場; Map p246; Jingū Kyūjo; 📞 0180-993-589; www.jingu-stadium.com; 3-1 Kasumigaoka-machi, Shinjuku-ku; tickets ¥1600-4600; ⑤ Ginza line to Gaienmae, exit 3) Jingū Baseball Stadium, built in 1926, is home to the Yakult Swallows, Tokyo's number-two team (but number one when it comes to fan loyalty). Night games start at 6pm; weekend games start at 1pm or 2pm. Get tickets from the booth next to Gate 9, which is open 11am to 5pm (or until 20 minutes after the game starts).

Same-day outfield tickets cost just ¥1300 (¥500 for children) and are usually available – unless the Swallows are playing crosstown rivals, the Yomiuri Giants.

Arashio Stable   Spectator Sport

(荒汐部屋, Arashio-beya; 📞 03-3666-7646; www.arashio.net/tour_e.html; 2-47-2 Hama-chō, Nihombashi, Chūō-ku; ⑤ Toei Shinjuku line to Hamachō, exit A2) **FREE** Catch morning sumo practice through the window between 7.30am and 10am at this friendly stable. Call the day before to double-check that practice (*keiko*) is on; more info is on the English website.

🟠 Courses

Tsukiji Soba Academy   Cooking

(築地そばアカデミー; Map p250; http://soba.specialist.co.jp; Hins Minato #004, 3-18-14 Minato, Chūō-ku; up to 3 people from ¥30,000, per additional person ¥10,000; ⑤ Yūrakuchō line to Shintomichō, exit 7) Genial English-speaking chef Inoue Akila is a master of soba – noodles made from nutty buckwheat flour. He's taught chefs who have gone on to win Michelin stars for their cooking how to make and eat this classic Tokyo dish. Classes are held in a compact kitchen overlooking the Sumida River.

Additional vegetarian and gluten-free menus available for an extra fee.

Wanariya   Traditional Craft

(和なり屋; 📞 03-5603-9169; www.wanariya.jp; 1-8-10 Senzoku, Taitō-ku; indigo dyeing/weaving from ¥1920/1980; ⏰ 10am-5pm Thu-Tue; ⑤ Hibiya line to Iriya, exit 1) A team of young and friendly Japanese runs this indigo

Kandagawa river

dyeing and traditional hand-loom weaving workshop. In under an hour you can learn to dye a t-shirt or tote bag or weave a pair of coasters. It's a fantastic opportunity to make your own souvenirs. Book at least three days in advance; solo travellers OK.

Mokuhankan   Traditional Craft

(木版館; ☎070-5011-1418; http://mokuhankan. com/parties; 2nd fl, 1-41-8 Asakusa, Taitō-ku; per person ¥2000; ⓢ10am-5.30pm Wed-Mon; Ⓡ Tsukuba Express to Asakusa, exit 5) Try your hand at making *ukiyo-e* (woodblock prints) at this studio run by expat David Bull. Hour-long 'print parties' are great fun and take place daily; sign up online. There's a shop here too, where you can see Bull's and Jed Henry's humorous *Ukiyo-e Heroes* series – prints featuring video-game characters in traditional settings.

Ohara School of Ikebana   Ikebana

(小原流いけばな; Map p246; ☎03-5774-5097; www.ohararyu.or.jp; 5-7-17 Minami-Aoyama, Minato-ku; per class ¥4000; ⓢ Ginza line to Omote-sandō, exit B1) Every Thursday, from 10.30am to 12.30pm, this well-regarded,

modern ikebana school teaches introductory flower-arrangement classes in English. Sign up via email by 3pm the Tuesday before (the earlier the better, as spaces are limited). The flowers are included in the lesson fee; take a lesson early in your trip and have them to decorate your hotel room or vacation rental.

Buddha Bellies   Cooking

(http://buddhabelliestokyo.jimdo.com; 2nd fl, Uekuri Bldg, 22-4-3 Kanda-Jimbōchō, Chiyoda-ku; courses ¥5500-9000; ⓢ Shinjuku line to Jimbōchō, exit A2) Professional sushi chef and sake sommelier Ayuko leads small hands-on classes in sushi, *bentō* (boxed lunch), udon and *wagashi* (Japanese sweets) making. Classes run most days from 11am, last 2½ hours and often book out early. Vegetarian, vegan and halal menus available.

Tokyo Kitchen   Cooking

(☎090-9104-4329; www.asakusa-tokyokitchen. com; 502 Ayumi Bldg, 1-11-1 Hanakawado, Taitō-ku; per person from ¥7560; ⓢ Ginza line to Asakusa, exit 4A) English-speaking Yoshimi is

🚲 Cycling

In Yanaka – a fun place to cycle around – bicycle manufacturer **Tokyobike** (📞03-5809-0980; https://tokyobikerentals.com/en/rental; 4-2-39 Yanaka, Taitō-ku; 1st day ¥3000, additional day ¥1500; ⊙10am-6.30pm Thu-Tue; 🚃JR Yamanote line to Nippori, west exit) rents single- and seven-speed city bikes. Book ahead online; helmet and locker rentals (¥500 each) are available, too. For more info on cycling in Tokyo see p235.

Bike path
SMILEIMAGE9 / SHUTTERSTOCK ©

an Asakusa-based cook who teaches small groups of visitors how to make a range of Japanese dishes. Her menu list is broad and includes mosaic sushi rolls, tempura, ramen and *gyōza*. Vegetarians and those with gluten intolerance are catered for too. Yoshimi will also meet you at the subway exit and guide you to her kitchen.

😊 Amusement Parks

Tokyo Disney Resort   Amusement Park

(東京ディズニーリゾート; 📞domestic calls 0570-00-8632, from overseas +81-45-330-5211; www.tokyodisneyresort.co.jp; 1-1 Maihama, Urayasu-shi, Chiba-ken; 1-day ticket for 1 park adult/child ¥7400/4800, after 6pm ¥4200; ⊙varies by season; 🚃JR Keiyō line to Maihama, south exit) Here you'll find not only Tokyo Disneyland, modelled after the one in California, but also Tokyo DisneySea, an original theme park with seven 'ports' evoking locales real and imagined (the

Mediterranean and 'Mermaid Lagoon', for example). DisneySea targets a more grown-up crowd, but still has many attractions for kids. Both resorts get extremely crowded, especially on weekends and during summer holidays; you'll have to be strategic with your fast passes. Book admission tickets online to save time.

Tokyo Joypolis   Amusement Park

(東京ジョイポリス; http://tokyo-joypolis.com; 3rd-5th fl, DECKS Tokyo Beach, 1-6-1 Daiba, Minato-ku; adult/child ¥800/500, all-rides passport ¥4300/3300, passport after 5pm ¥3300/2300; ⊙10am-10pm; 🚃Yurikamome line to Odaiba Kaihin-kōen, north exit) This indoor amusement park is stacked with virtual-reality attractions and adult thrill rides, such as the video-enhanced Halfpipe Tokyo; there are rides for little ones, too. Separate admission and individual ride tickets (¥500 to ¥800) are available, but if you plan to go on more than half a dozen attractions, the unlimited 'passport' makes sense.

VR Zone Shinjuku   Amusement Park

(Map p2; 📞03-3200-8076; http://vrzone-pic.com; 1-29-1 Kabukichō, Shinjuku-ku; adult/child ¥800/500, attractions ¥1000-1200; ⊙10am-10pm, last entry 9pm; 🚃JR Yamanote line to Shinjuku, east exit) Fancy playing virtual reality Mario Kart? Or schussing like a pro down steep alpine slopes? This limited-time-only game centre (until July 2019) has dozens of VR attractions; some are a bit clunky, but fun just the same. Basic English instructions are provided. A one-day pass (¥4400; reserve online) covers admission and four ride coupons.

Children must be 13 or over to ride virtual-reality attractions; see the website for other restrictions. Note that virtually crashing and falling can cause real-life dizziness.

Tokyo Dome City Attractions   Amusement Park

(東京ドームシティアトラクションズ; 📞03-5800-9999; www.tokyo-dome.co.jp/e/attractions; 1-3-61 Kōraku, Bunkyō-ku; day pass adult/teenager/child ¥3900/3400/2100; ⊙10am-

From left: *gyōza at Tokyo Kitchen (p199)*; Thunder Dolphin rollercoaster at Tokyo Dome City Attractions

9pm; ♿; ℝ JR Chūō line to Suidōbashi, west exit) The top attraction at this amusement park next to Tokyo Dome (p198) is the 'Thunder Dolphin' (¥1030), a roller coaster that cuts a heart-in-your-throat course in and around the tightly packed buildings of downtown. There are plenty of low-key, child-friendly rides as well. You can buy individual-ride tickets, day passes, night passes (valid from 5pm) and a five-ride pass (¥2600).

🅢 Tours

Nihombashi Cruise   Cruise
(日本橋クルーズ; Map p250; ☎03-5679-7311; http://ss3.jp/nihonbashi-cruise/; 1 Nihombashi, Chūō-ku; 45/60min cruises ¥1500/2000; ⓢ Ginza line to Mitsukoshimae, exit B5 or B6) For a unique perspective on Tokyo, hop aboard one of these daily river cruises. Lasting either 45 minutes or an hour, they proceed along the Nihombashi-gawa towards the Sumida-gawa, or make a loop around Nihombashi-gawa to Kanda-gawa. The landing stage is next to Nihombashi.

You'll get to see beneath many historic bridges as well as the expressway built above the river.

Gray Line   Bus
(☎03-5275-6525; www.jgl.co.jp/inbound/index. htm; half-day/full day per person from ¥4900-8800) Offers half-day and full-day tours with stops, covering key downtown sights and also day trips to Mt Fuji and Hakone (from ¥12,500 per person). Pick-up service from major hotels is available, otherwise most tours leave from in front of the Dai-Ichi Hotel in Shimbashi (near Ginza). Discounts for children under 12.

SkyBus   Bus
(Map p250; ☎03-3215-0008; www.skybus.jp; 2-5-2 Marunouchi, Chiyoda-ku; tours adult/child from ¥1600/700, Sky Hop Bus ¥3500/1700; ⊗ticket office 9am-6pm; ℝ JR Yamanote line to Tokyo, Marunouchi south exit) Open-top double-decker buses cruise through different neighbourhoods of the city (for roughly 50 to 80 minutes). The Sky Hop Bus plan allows you to hop on and off buses on any of the three routes. English-language guidance is provided via earphones on board.

REST YOUR HEAD

Top tips for the best accommodation

Rest Your Head

Tokyo is known for being expensive; however, more attractive budget and midrange options are popping up every year. Business hotels are an economic, if institutional, option. If it's luxury you're after, you can take your pick from Tokyo's vast array of top-tier hotels. For budget travellers, the best deals are on the east side of town, in neighbourhoods such as Ueno and Asakusa; increasingly, however, there are great guesthouses everywhere. For a truly local experience, stay in a ryokan (traditional inns with Japanese-style bedding). Levels of cleanliness and service are generally high everywhere.

In This Section

Prices

Hostels and ryokan have fixed rates and often charge per person; for hotels of all classes, rates vary tremendously, and discounts significantly below rack rates can be found online. Sales tax (8%) applies to hotel rates. There is also a city-wide 'accommodation tax' of ¥100 on rooms over ¥10,000 and ¥200 for rooms over ¥15,000 – these are per person, per night.

Capsule hotel

The Best...

Reservations

It's really best to reserve in advance; on many weekends Tokyo hotels are near full capacity and the best properties book out early. At smaller inns or ryokan, walk-ins can fluster staff (or staff might not be present); hostels are better prepared for this. The busiest periods include the first week of January, 'Golden Week' (29 April to 5 May), and August.

Useful Websites

Jalan (www.jalan.net) Popular local discount accommodation site.

Japanese Inn Group (www.japanese inngroup.com) Bookings for ryokan and other small inns.

Japanican (www.japanican.com) Accommodation site run by JTB, Japan's largest travel agency.

Lonely Planet (lonelyplanet.com/Japan/Tokyo/hotels) Reviews, recommendations and bookings.

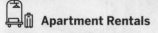

Apartment Rentals

Apartment rentals (called *minpaku* in Japanese) are a popular option in Tokyo. A studio can cost less than a double room in a business hotel (but with the added perks of a kitchen). Many hosts have portable wi-fi devices for guests to use – another money saver.

Japanese law allows the operation of *minpaku* but with numerous stipulations, and wards within Tokyo (not to mention homeowners associations!) may have their own regulations or restrictions. While some rentals are operated in full accordance with the law, note that a good number are not.

Traditional-style tatami room
PRINN CHANSINGTHONG / SHUTTERSTOCK ©

Accommodation Types

Business Hotels

Functional and economical, 'business hotels' are geared to the lone traveller on business. The compact rooms usually have semidouble beds (140cm across; roomy for one, a bit of a squeeze for two) and tiny en-suite bathrooms. They're famous for being deeply unfashionable, though many chains have updated their rooms in recent years. Expect to pay from ¥10,000 to ¥15,000 (or ¥14,000 to ¥19,000 for double occupancy). Credit cards accepted.

Capsule Hotels

Classic capsule hotels offer rooms the size of a single bed, with just enough headroom for you to sit up. Think of it like a bunk bed with more privacy (and a reading light, TV and alarm clock). Prices range from ¥3500 to ¥5000, which includes access to a large shared bath. They may be men-only or with gender-segregated floors and bar guests with visible tattoos. The newer breed of capsule hotels have roomier berths and usually no policy against tattoos (but will be gender-segregated and a little pricier).

Hostels

Tokyo hostels are clean and well-managed; many have staff fluent in English, who arrange cultural activities and social events for guests. Most have a mixture of dorms and private rooms, and cooking and laundry facilities. Expect to pay about ¥3000 for a dorm and ¥8000 for a private room (double occupancy).

Luxury Hotels

Tokyo's top-end hotels – mostly foreign brands, but there are some local options, too – have English-language concierge service and enough space to properly unwind. Many are in high-rise buildings and offer fantastic city views. They also offer direct airport access, via the Limousine Bus. Good deals can sometimes be found online.

Ryokan

Ryokan offer a traditional experience, with tatami (woven-mat) floors and futons (traditional quilt-like mattresses) on the floor instead of beds. Upscale ones can charge upwards of ¥25,000; however, there are several inexpensive ryokan in Tokyo, starting at around ¥8000 a night (for double occupancy). Most have 'family rooms' that can sleep four or five – an economical choice if you're travelling as a group or with kids. Some offer rooms with private baths, but one of the pleasures of staying in a traditional inn is the communal bath, which will be much nicer than what you'd find at a business hotel. At inns with frequent foreign guests, these communal baths can often be used privately.

Where to Stay

Neighbourhood	Atmosphere
Shinjuku & Ikebukuro	Superb transport, food and nightlife; very crowded, and cheaper options are clustered around the red-light district.
Kōenji & Kichijōji	Cheaper than central Tokyo and local vibe. Far from main sights; riding the crowded Chūō line everyday can be a drag.
Harajuku & Aoyama	Sights, restaurants and shops galore; limited sleeping options.
Shibuya & Shimo-Kitazawa	Shibuya is a major transport hub with plenty to entertain, but gets extremely crowded and is hardly relaxing.
Ebisu & Meguro	Good transit links, bars and restaurants, with fewer crowds; can feel removed from city centre.
Roppongi & Akasaka	Art museums by day; bar scene at night; noisy and hectic after dark with some seedy pockets.
Ginza & Tsukiji	Ginza's shops and restaurants at your doorstep; congested, and few inexpensive options compared to other districts.
Marunouchi & Nihombashi	Convenient for all sights and for travel out of the city; business district with sky-high prices and quiet weekends.
Kanda & Akihabara	Central, reasonable prices, and with good transit links. Can feel dead at night.
Ueno & Yanaka	Lots of greenery and museums and easy airport access; good ryokan tend to be isolated in residential neighbourhoods.
Asakusa & Ryōgoku	Atmospheric old-city feel, great budget options; quieter at night and far from central areas.
Odaiba & Tokyo Bay	Proximity to family-friendly attractions; otherwise inconvenient.

Sakura (cherry blossom) viewing

In Focus

STEPMOREM / SHUTTERSTOCK ©

Viewing deck, Tokyo Sky Tree tower

Tokyo Today

*Tokyo has reinvented itself countless times over its
400-year-long history. With the 2020 Summer Olympic
Games not far away, it hopes to do so again, with
plans for a greener, friendlier city. Following decades
of economic stagnation, a new era on the horizon and
a soon-to-be-shrinking workforce, the stakes are high.
Does Tokyo still have what it takes to pull off another
reincarnation?*

A New Era Begins

It caught everyone off guard when Emperor Akihito announced abruptly in 2016 – on TV
no less – that he wished to abdicate. No emperor had abdicated since 1817; the modern
constitution had no provision for what to do in this situation. For over a year, lawmakers
debated whether or not Akihito, Japan's 125th emperor (according to the Imperial House
Agency's record-keeping), should even be allowed to abdicate. Public opinion was on the
emperor's side; he's in his mid-80s after all. Finally, a bill was passed that would allow him
to retire. The date was set for 30 April 2019.

When Crown Prince Naruhito ascends the chrysanthemum throne, the Heisei era will
end and a new one will begin. Of course, the start and end of Japan's historic periods – in
modern times determined by the passing of emperors – are determined by natural causes;

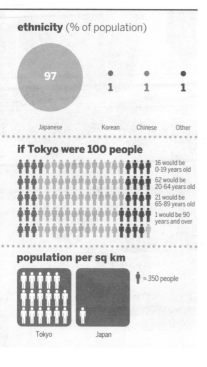

ethnicity (% of population)

97 | 1 | 1 | 1

Japanese | Korean | Chinese | Other

if Tokyo were 100 people

16 would be 0-19 years old
62 would be 20-64 years old
21 would be 65-89 years old
1 would be 90 years and over

population per sq km

≈ 350 people

Tokyo | Japan

and yet, they really do seem to effectively bracket the culture's shifting moods. The Heisei era began in 1989, as Japan's bubble economy was collapsing. A whole generation has now come of age in a Japan where lifelong employment is no longer a guarantee and where the country's place in the world seems increasingly uncertain. In the current, unstable global climate, everyone can't help but wonder, what changes will the new era bring?

Countdown to 2020

No doubt prime minister Abe Shinzō's appearance at the 2016 Rio Olympics closing ceremony dressed as Mario (from the iconic Nintendo video game, *Super Mario Bros*) got the world at least a little excited for the 2020 Tokyo Olympics. But while Tokyo may be playing it cool, it is impossible to understate just how much the games mean to the city, and the country. Tokyo first hosted the Summer Olympics in 1964. The first games to be held in Asia, they marked the city's big comeback after it was all but destroyed in WWII. The powers that be hope that the 2020 games will again be symbolic, reaffirming Tokyo's position in the pantheon of the world's great cities.

Much of the city's current infrastructure dates to the manic preparations leading up to the 1964 Games. Tokyo sold the International Olympic Committee on a compact Games that would use many existing structures, but that hasn't stopped the city from going on a building spree. In addition to a new stadium in Sendagaya, the Olympic Village and other facilities in bayside district Odaiba, developers are putting up dozens of new skyscrapers; the Yamanote line is getting a new station; and some streets will be cleared of unsightly (but-oh-so-Tokyo) utility wires.

The City of the Future

Tokyo has so far managed to stave off the population decline that began to haunt Japan in the 2000s, but it too is predicted to see numbers drop off, as early as 2025. The government has campaigned for more women to enter the workforce to bolster numbers (though gender discrimination remains pernicious) *and* for families to have more children. Tokyoites vocal on social media say they can't win: the combination of the city's high cost of living, long working hours and long waiting lists for daycare means something has to give.

Tokyo is seen as a forerunner – facing the kinds of problems that major modern cities around the world will face as their populations begin a similar tapering off. Included in the city's development plans are strategies to boost livability, including job centres for senior citizens, special economic zones for foreign companies and yes, more childcare facilities. If it works, Tokyo could become a model for cities of the future. For Tokyoites any progress can't come soon enough. And if it doesn't? Well, there are always robots.

Wooden carvings, Daienji, Yanaka

MANUEL ASCANIO / SHUTTERSTOCK ©

History

Tokyo is one of the world's great cities. In the four centuries since its founding the city has played many roles: samurai stronghold, imperial capital and modern metropolis. Its latest identity as a city of the future – as it is portrayed in manga (Japanese comics), anime (Japanese animation) and think pieces – is just another example of Tokyo's protean nature.

400 BC	**794**	**12th century**
Wet-rice farming cultures begin supplanting older neolithic hunter-gatherer cultures around Japan.	The capital is moved to Heian-kyō (later renamed Kyoto), which would be the centre of Japanese politics for a millennium.	Monks travel to China for study and return with Ch'an (Zen) Buddhism, which would have a huge cultural impact.

Statue of Saigo Takamori, Ueno-kōen (p68)

COWARDLION / SHUTTERSTOCK ©

Early History

For most of Japan's first thousand or so years, power was concentrated in the imperial capital, Kyoto. Here noble families vied for influence, upstart warriors challenged authority and Buddhist sects instigated cultural shifts. Tokyo, meanwhile, was a sleepy backwater. Then, and for most of its history, it was called Edo, meaning 'estuary' – which was fitting, given its location on the tidal flats at the mouth of the Sumida-gawa (Sumida River).

Early on, the imperial court was the ultimate authority. But as the young empire sought to expand its territory over the archipelago, it enlisted warriors to assert dominion over outlying territories. And eventually these warriors wanted power for themselves. In the 12th century a new arrangement emerged: one in which the emperor continued to rule in title but a new figure, the shogun (generalissimo), would have the real authority. The feudal era had begun.

In truth though, the shoguns struggled just as the emperors had. Provincial warlords (called *daimyō*) were still needed to carry out orders and keep the peace in areas far from

1543

Portuguese, the first Westerners, arrive by chance in Japan, bringing firearms and Christianity.

1603

Shogun Tokugawa Ieyasu establishes his government in Edo (present-day Tokyo).

1657

Great Meireki Fire devastates Edo, killing over 100,000 people and destroying two-thirds of the city.

The Great Kantō Earthquake

At noon on 1 September 1923, a magnitude 7.9 earthquake struck Japan just south of Tokyo in Sagami Bay. More damaging were the fires that spread through the city as a result, lasting some 40 hours and killing an estimated 142,000 people. Reconstruction began immediately in classic Tokyo style, though this meant that opportunities to improve infrastructure – widening streets, for example – were lost.

But the quake did succeed in changing the landscape of Tokyo. Until then, the population of Tokyo had been concentrated in what now appears to be the eastern edge of the city, in the old merchants' quarters around the Sumida-gawa. Many who lost their homes resettled in areas such as Shibuya and Shinjuku, which at the time were little more than small towns on the fringe of the metropolis.

the capital; and the more successful they became, the bigger threat to cohesion they posed. By the 15th century, the *daimyō* had carved Japan into a patchwork of fiefdoms. Castles and fortresses were erected around the country (including one by a warrior poet named Ōta Dōkan in Edo). A series of powerful *daimyō* contested (violently; guns were now in the picture) for rule of the land. Finally, after much bloodshed and betrayal, one emerged victorious: Tokugawa Ieyasu.

The Tokugawa Shoguns

Tokugawa Ieyasu (1543–1616) was the ambitious son of a minor warlord in what is present-day Aichi prefecture (near Nagoya). With his power base lying far to the east of the capital, he chose to establish his government seat not in Kyoto, but in a small provincial castle town – Edo. Within a half-century, Edo would become Japan's largest city; in another hundred years it would be the largest city in the world.

Like previous shoguns, Ieyasu left the emperor alone; but unlike his predecessors, he established a dynasty that would manage to rule Japan with a fairly consistent iron fist for the next 250 years. They required *daimyō* and their retainers to spend every second year in Edo, where their families were kept permanently as hostages – an edict known as *sankin kōtai*. This dislocating policy also bankrupted many a fiefdom as the processions to and from the provinces required expensive pageantry (which in turn bolstered Edo's economy). Society was made rigidly hierarchical, comprising (in descending order of importance): *shi* (samurai), *nō* (farmers), *kō* (artisans) and *shō* (merchants). Class dress, living quarters and even speech were strictly codified; interclass movement was prohibited. Though classed at the bottom, in reality, merchants could be fabulously wealthy (thanks to all that *daimyō* spending).

But the most striking feature of Tokugawa rule was its policy of *sakoku* (closure to the outside world). The shogunate feared foreign agitation (especially from Catholic missionaries) and expelled all Westerners (save for a handful of Protestant Dutch confined to an island off the coast of Nagasaki with whom trade was permitted) in the early 17th century. Overseas travel for Japanese was banned (as well as the return of those already overseas).

1707	1721	1868
Mt Fuji erupts, spewing ash over Edo 100km to the north-east. The stratovolcano remains active but with a low risk of eruption.	Edo's population grows to 1.1 million; meanwhile, London's population is roughly 650,000.	The Meiji Restoration initiates a new period of constitutional monarchy, with Tokyo as its capital.

Meiji Restoration

By the turn of the 19th century, the stagnating Tokugawa regime was losing its grip. It is questionable how much longer it might have held on, but as it happened, external forces were to hasten its demise. In 1853 and again the following year, US Commodore Matthew Perry steamed into Edo-wan (now Tokyo Bay) with a show of gunships and demanded Japan open up to trade and provisioning.

The humiliating acquiescence that followed fanned existing flames of anti-government sentiment into outright rebellion. A series of military clashes resulted in the abdication of the last shogun, Yoshinobu (1837–1913) in 1867. In 1868 authority was restored to the teenage emperor Mutsuhito (1852–1912, later known as Meiji) and a new government was formed in his name. The role of shogun, and the whole feudal system, was abolished. The emperor moved to Edo, which was rechristened Tokyo (Eastern Capital).

Above all, the new leaders of Japan feared colonisation by the West and moved quickly to modernise (in the image of the West), embarking on a grand project of industrialisation and militarisation. With *sakoku* over, a great exchange began between Japan and the West: Japanese scholars were dispatched overseas while Western scholars were invited to teach in Japan's nascent universities. By 1889 the country had a constitution, modelled after the government frameworks of England and Prussia.

The Meiji Restoration also brought about far-reaching social changes. The four-tier class system was scrapped; after centuries of having everything prescribed for them, citizens were now free to choose their occupation and place of residence. In the coming decades, hundreds of thousands would come to Tokyo from the provinces, to try their luck in a city that now dazzled with electric lights, street cars and white-collar jobs.

World War II

The early 20th century was, devastating earthquake aside, a time of great optimism in Tokyo. Old feudal-era loyalties finally buckled and party politics flourished for the first time. Western fashions and ideas, initially the domain of only the elite, began to trickle down to the emergent middle class. Cafes and dance halls flourished. Women began to work in offices, department stores and factories, enjoying a new freedom and disposable income.

But there were sinister undercurrents: the nation's new-found confidence was tied to its displays of military might on the world stage. Japan had won victories over China (1894–95) and Russia (1904–05) and embarked on modern, Western-style empire building with its annexation of Taiwan (1895), then Korea (1910) and Micronesia (1914). In 1931 the Japanese military manufactured a conflict with China, and then installed a puppet government in Manchuria. Nationalist fervour was quickly replacing democratic ideals.

Japan signed a pact with Germany and Italy in 1940; a year later, the country drew the US into WWII with an attack on Pearl Harbor. At first Japan scored rapid successes, pushing its battlefronts across to India, down to the fringes of Australia and into the mid-Pacific,

1923	1944–45	1964
Great Kantō Earthquake kills more than 140,000 and destroys an estimated 300,000 houses.	Allied air raids during WWII destroy large swaths of the city, including the Imperial Palace.	The Tokyo Summer Olympics mark Japan's postwar reintegration into the international community.

Decorative *obi* (kimono sash)

JOHN LEUNG / SHUTTERSTOCK ©

★ **Best in Print**

The Book of Tokyo: A City in Short Fiction (Comma Press; 2015)

Contemporary Japan: History, Politics and Social Change Since the 1980s (Jeff Kingston; 2010)

Low City, High City (Edward Seidensticker; 1970)

claiming European colonial territories for its own. But the decisive Battle of Midway in 1942 turned the tide against Japan and in the end the war was disastrous. Incendiary bombing in 1944 and 1945 destroyed half of Tokyo. In one night alone some 100,000 people were killed – more than were killed by the atomic bombing of Hiroshima – as fires swept through densely populated neighbourhoods of wooden homes.

The emperor formally surrendered on 15 August 1945 and American forces, under the command of General Douglas MacArthur, occupied the country. Japan was obligated to give up its territorial claims in Korea and China, adopt a new constitution that dismantled the political power of the emperor, denounced war and banned a Japanese military.

Postwar Period

The early postwar days in Tokyo were extremely rough: poverty and homelessness were widespread, black markets thrived and prostitution (out of desperation) was common. During the US occupation, which lasted until 1952 (and in Okinawa until 1972), American pop culture poured into Japan and along with it a yearning for the affluent and comfortable lifestyles portrayed on the big and small screens.

In the 1950s Japan took off on a trajectory of phenomenal growth that has been called miraculous. (Though many historians, both Japanese and American, say Japan's role as a forward base for the USA in the Korean War was the catalyst for this.) Construction and modernisation continued at a breakneck pace through the '60s and '70s, to reach a peak in the late '80s, when wildly inflated real-estate prices and stock speculation fuelled what is now known as the 'bubble economy'. Based on the price paid for the most expensive real estate in the late 1980s, the land value of Tokyo exceeded that of the entire US.

In 1991 the bubble burst, sending the economy into a protracted slump; stubbornly persistent stagnation turned Japan's 'Lost Decade' into decades. Economic woes are Japan's new normal – though this isn't necessarily apparent in central Tokyo, where there are always glistening new skyscrapers and packed restaurants.

1995	2011	2016
Doomsday cult Aum Shinrikyō releases sarin gas on the Tokyo subway, killing 12 and injuring more than 5000.	Massive earthquake and tsunami in north-eastern Japan kills nearly 20,000 and cripples a Fukushima nuclear power plant.	Tokyo elects its first female governor, Koike Yuriko; Emperor Akihito (b 1933) announces his wish to retire.

Brightly dressed young woman in Akihabara

Pop Culture

*From giant robots to saucer-eyed schoolgirls to a certain
ubiquitous kitty, Japanese pop culture is a phenomenon
that has reached far around the world. Tokyo is the
country's pop production centre; meanwhile, neighbourhoods such as Akihabara incubate subcultures that are
gaining more and more influence over the culture
at large.*

Manga

Whole generations have come of age reading classic manga, such as Tezuka Osamu's *Tetsuwan Atom* (Astro Boy; 1952–68) and *Black Jack* (1973–83); Toriyama Akira's *Dragon Ball* (1984–95); and Kishimoto Masashi's *Naruto* (1999–2014). Osamu (1928–89) is often known as *manga no kamisama* (the 'god of manga') for having brought a level of artistry and profundity to the form, raising it above mere pulp. ('Astro Boy' is a humanoid robot with empathic powers and a champion of robots' rights.) He was also the first to draw characters with big eyes; though this look has come to define Japanese manga and anime, Osamu was in fact influenced by early Disney works (such as *Bambi*) and the 1930s American cartoon character Betty Boop (animation's first pin-up).

Pop-Culture Districts

Akihabara ('Akiba') is considered the locus of *otaku* subculture, but there are other areas, too: Nakano, just west of Shinjuku, has a reputation as a more low-key, underground Akiba. Ikebukuro, north of Shinjuku, has many of the same anime and manga stores that you see in Akihabara – but they're full of goods that girl geeks love. Gundam fans should head to Odaiba to see 'life-sized' **Unicorn Gundam** (www.unicorn-gundam-statue.jp). There are also the temporary communities that come together around events such as Comiket.

Some series have been going on so long as to transcend generations: the titular character of *Doraemon* (1969–96; Fujiko Fujio), who is a blue robot cat from the future, is so iconic he's sometimes called Japan's Mickey Mouse. The best-selling manga of all time is Oda Eiichirō's *One Piece*, nominally about a band of misfit pirates. First serialised in 1997, it's still going – meaning one lucky generation might just get to grow old with their favourite manga.

Anime

Anime has a synergistic relationship with manga: many anime series are adapted from manga (*Full Metal Alchemist, Death Note* and *Jojo's Bizarre Adventure* are great examples; and of course there's a *One Piece* animated series). There are also hugely popular original anime series, such as *Mobile Suit Gundam* (1979–1980) and *Neon Genesis Evangelion* (1995–1996), that have since spawned larger media franchises, including manga series and feature-length movies. Both *Mobile Suit Gundam* and *Neon Genesis Evangelion* belong to the genre of anime and manga called 'mecha', meaning they feature robots.

While anime, like film, can be about anything really, the form has proven to be particularly outstanding at world-building and imbuing post-humans and machines with a certain pathos. Other classics include Ōtomo Katsuhiro's *Akira* (1988), a psychedelic fantasy set in a future Tokyo (actually 2019); Ōishii Mamoru's *Ghost in the Shell* (1995), with a sci-fi plot worthy of Philip K Dick involving cyborgs, hackers and the mother of all computer networks; and the works of Kon Satoshi (1963–2010), the Hitchcockian *Perfect Blue* (1997), the charming *Tokyo Godfathers* (2003) and the sci-fi thriller *Paprika* (2006).

Studio Ghibli (www.ghibli.jp) is Japan's most critically acclaimed and commercially successful producer of animated movies. Its films include *Nausicaä of the Valley of the Winds* (1984), *My Neighbor Totoro* (1988) and the Oscar-winning *Spirited Away* (2001), all directed by Miyazaki Hayao. In 2016 Miyazaki announced he was coming out of retirement to make one last film, to be called *How Do You Live?* Based on a 1930s novel of the same name, it will likely be released in 2020 or 2021.

One new director to watch is Shinkai Makoto: his 2016 *Kimi no Na wa* (Your Name) was both a critical and box-office smash – the second highest-grossing domestic film ever, after *Spirited Away*.

Otaku Culture

'Otaku' is the word used to describe super-fans of manga and anime. (It has since evolved into a general modifier for any kind of super-fan; a *densha* (train) *otaku*, for example, is a trainspotter). *Otaku* are famous consumers, proving their affection through the collection of merch; but theirs is also a subculture rich in creation and humour. A popular phenomenon is *dōjinshi*, amateur manga, which are often parodies or fan fictions of established series (and sometimes involving romantic or sexual scenes not found in the original). There are also those fans who go to great lengths to transform themselves into their favourite characters – an art known as cosplay (a portmanteau for costume play).

Bar, Shinjuku

Tokyo Cuisine

At its heart, Japanese food is highly seasonal, drawing on fresh local ingredients coaxed into goodness with a light touch. But it's also far more varied than you might imagine: it's not just sushi and sake; it's also gut-busting ramen and fiery shōchū (distilled liquor). Increasingly, Japanese cuisine is a global one – borrowing this and contributing that – enhancing its richness and variety.

The Japanese Restaurant Experience

When you enter a restaurant in Tokyo, you'll be greeted with a hearty *irasshaimase* (Welcome!). Then a waiter will likely ask you *nan-mei sama* (How many people?). Indicate the answer with your fingers, which is what the Japanese do. You may also be asked if you would like to sit at a *zashiki* (low table on the tatami), at a *tēburu* (table) or the *kauntā* (counter). Once seated you will be given an *o-shibori* (ideally a hot towel, but it might just be a wet wipe), a cup of tea or water (this is free) and a menu.

Ordering: more and more restaurants in Tokyo have English menus. If there isn't one and you can't work out what to order, there are two phrases that may help: *o-susume wa nan desu ka* (What do you recommend?) and *omakase shimasu* (Please decide for me). It's probably a good idea to set a price cap, like: 'Hitori de san-zen-en' (one person for ¥3000).

Japanese Spirits

Sake, aka *nihonshu* (日本酒) is the obvious drink of choice, but there are spirits worth sampling, too. Shōchū (焼酎) is a clear, distilled spirit usually made from potato or barley. It is potent (alcohol content of around 30%) and thus usually served diluted with hot water *(oyu-wari)* or mixed in a cocktail (the combination of *shōchū*, soda water and lemon juice known as a 'lemon sour' is popular).

Japan produces some of the finest whiskies in the world; Tokyo has a growing number of dedicated bars where travellers can sample the best of the major makers Suntory and Nikka and also from cult faves and small-batch producers like Chichibu. Also keep a lookout on bar counters for gin from Kyoto's new craft distillery Ki No Bi.

Most often the bill will be placed discreetly on your table with your food. If not, you can ask for it by catching the server's eye and making a cross in the air (to form a kind of 'x') with your index fingers. You can also say *o-kanjō kudasai*. Payment is usually settled at the register near the entrance. Credit cards are widely accepted at restaurants where the bill is likely to top ¥5000.

Izakaya

Izakaya (居酒屋) translates as 'drinking house'; it's the Japanese equivalent of a pub. An evening at an *izakaya* is dinner and drinks all in one: food is ordered for the table a few dishes at a time along with rounds of beer, sake or *shōchū*. While the vibe is lively and social, it's perfectly acceptable to go by yourself and sit at the counter. If you don't want alcohol, it's fine to order a soft drink instead (but it would be strange to not order at least one drink).

An orthodox *izakaya* is family-run with menu items, such as *shio-yaki-zakana* (塩焼魚; a whole fish grilled with salt), designed to go with sake. They might look a bit weathered – but that's usually a good sign. There are also large, cheap chains, popular with students, often have with a healthy (er, unhealthy) dose of Western pub-style dishes (like chips), and stylish chef-driven *izakaya* with creative menus. Classic starters to get you going (that any *izakaya* should have) include *sashimi mori-awase* (刺身盛り合わせ; a selection of sliced sashimi), edamame (枝豆; salted and boiled fresh soy beans) and *moro-kyū* (もろきゅう; sliced cucumbers and chunky barley miso). A night out at an average *izakaya* should run ¥3000 to ¥5000 per person, depending on how much you drink. Chains often have deals where you can pay a set price for a certain amount of dishes and free drinks.

Shokudō

Shokudō (食堂) are casual, inexpensive eateries that serve homey meals – similar to what you might call a greasy spoon cafe or a diner (in the USA). Some are scruffy; some are well-scrubbed, but much like *izakaya*, appearance has little to do with the food.

One thing to order here is a *teishoku* (定食), a meal set with one main dish, rice, miso soup and pickles. Other likely menu items include various *donburi* (どんぶり or 丼; large bowls of rice with meat or fish piled on top) and 'katsu' (カツ) dishes, where the main is crumbed and deep fried, as in *tonkatsu* (豚カツ or とんかつ; deep-fried pork cutlets) and *ebi-katsu* (海老カツ; breaded and fried prawns).

Tokyo's working and student population take a significant number of their meals at *shokudō*; you'll find them around every train station, and also in popular tourist areas. Some allow smoking, but otherwise these tend to be family-friendly joints, with plenty that kids will eat. Meals typically cost ¥800 to ¥1500 per person. Many have plastic food displays in the windows, which of course makes ordering simple.

Ramen

Ramen originated in China, but its popularity in Japan is epic. Your basic ramen is a big bowl of crinkly egg noodles in broth, served with toppings such as *chāshū* (sliced roast pork), *moyashi* (bean sprouts) and *negi* (leeks). The broth can be made from pork or chicken bones or dried seafood; usually it's a top-secret combination of some or all of the above. It's typically seasoned with *shio* (salt), *shōyu* (soy sauce) or hearty miso – though at less orthodox places, anything goes. Tokyo's classic style is a *shōyu*-flavoured broth with a subtle bitter smokiness that comes from *niboshi* (dried young sardines). Another popular style is *tsukemen*, noodles that come with a dipping sauce (like a really condensed broth) on the side.

Noodle restaurants (which include places serving udon, wheat noodles, and soba, buckwheat noodles) often use a unique ordering system: a vending machine. Select what you want, put your money in the machine and retrieve a ticket with your order printed on it to hand to the cooks behind the counter. Ramen should be eaten at whip speed, before the noodles get soggy; that's why you'll hear diners slurping, sucking in air to cool their mouths. If you're really hungry, ask for *kaedama* (another serving of noodles), usually only a couple of hundred yen more.

Kissaten

In Japan there is a distinction between a *kafe* (カフェ) and a *kissaten* (喫茶店), though they both primarily serve coffee. *Kissaten* is the older term, the one used before chains like Starbucks arrived in Japan and changed the game. Today the word is used to describe independently run coffee shops that either date from the early or mid-20th century – when Japan's coffee first wave hit – or at least look like they do. A *kafe*, meanwhile, could be a chain, anywhere that serves espresso drinks or that has a contemporary vibe.

Kissaten typically serve freshly ground, dark roast coffee, hand-poured or siphon-brewed, accompanied by adorably tiny single-serving pitchers of milk. (If all this attention to detail sounds suspiciously third-wave, know that Japan's classic *kissaten* were one of the inspirations behind the current coffee scene).

Many serve 'morning sets' (モーニング セット; *mōningu setto*) from 8am until around 11am that include thick, buttery toast, a hard-boiled egg and a cup of coffee, for about the same price as a cup of coffee (around ¥500) later in the day. It's a fantastic deal in a city like Tokyo, where a hot breakfast can be hard to find. The downsides: *kissaten* are often smokey and rarely have wi-fi. Some of our favourites are Berg (p125), Saböru (p144) and Kayaba Coffee (p145).

Japanese Tea

Here *o-cha* (お茶; tea) means green tea and broadly speaking there are two kinds: *ryoku-cha* (steeped with leaves) and *matcha*, which is made by whisking dried and milled leaves with water until a cappuccino level of frothiness is achieved. As *matcha* is quite bitter, it is served with *wagashi* (traditional sweets made from sugar, rice flour and bean-paste).

The complementary tea served in a standard Japanese restaurant is usually *bancha*, ordinary-grade green tea, with a brownish colour. (In summer, you might get cold *mugicha*, roasted barley tea, instead.) After dinner, restaurants often serve *hōjicha* (ほうじ茶), roasted green tea, which is weaker and less caffeinated.

To sample the more rarefied stuff – like *gyokuro* (玉露), the highest grade of loose-leaf green tea, shaded from the sun and picked early in the season – you'll have to seek out a teahouse or speciality shop. Long a city addicted to coffee, Tokyo is going through

Sushi in the Tsukiji Outer Market (p36)

★ **Food & Drink on Film**

Tsukiji Wonderland (Naotaro Endo; 2016)

The Birth of Saké (Erik Shirai; 2015)

Jiro Dreams of Sushi (David Gelb; 2011)

Tampopo (Itami Jūzō; 1985)

PATRICK WONG / SHUTTERSTOCK ©

something of a tea renaissance. There are now several salons serving single-origin *sencha* (medium-grade loose-leaf tea) – inspired by the third-wave coffee scene – and doing contemporary takes on Japan's centuries-old art of the tea ceremony.

Making Reservations

If you have your heart set on eating at a particular restaurant, you'll want to make a reservation. This is especially true for dinner, but if you want to take advantage of a fancy restaurant's bargain lunch special, you'll want to book for that, too. If you can that is: some restaurants only take bookings for dinner, or for the first seating, or not at all. Groups larger than four are required to book ahead at some places. Confusing, yes – even for Tokyoites. Some places have introduced online reservations systems (though it might only be in Japanese). Check restaurant websites for email addresses (most Japanese can read and write English better than they speak it). Open Table (www.opentable.com/tokyo-restaurants) has a small presence in Japan.

The big advantage of staying in a top-tier hotel is having a concierge who can do all the hard work for you. At some restaurants, a well-connected concierge may be your only hope. Tokyo restaurants have a real fear of no-shows and there is a prevailing belief that foreign tourists are more prone to flaking. Whether this is actually true or an urban myth is unclear, but some restaurants – particularly exclusive or popular places – will only take reservations from a concierge. If you speak Japanese and have a local phone number you might be able to get around this. This goes without saying, but please do show up. If you have to cancel, call the day before; otherwise, you may be expected to pay a no-show fee.

If you're planning to frequent just casual places, pay no mind to any of the above. You'll be fine, though you might have to queue for a bit at a popular ramen shop or wait for a table if you're a bigger party. Solo travellers, meanwhile, are in the best position: often you can squeeze into a counter seat at an otherwise fully packed restaurant.

Tips & Etiquette

As you'll quickly realise, Tokyo restaurants are often very small and run on a tight margin (hence the fear of no-shows; a missing party of four at a 12-seat restaurant is a big loss). Lunch is one of the city's great bargains; however, restaurants can only offer cheap lunch deals because they anticipate high turnover. Spending too long sipping tea after finishing your meal might earn you dagger eyes from the kitchen.

As long as you're not negatively influencing the bottom line, restaurants generally have a high tolerance for tourist gaffes. If you're enjoying the food, they're happy. The only really offensive thing you can do is to stick your chopsticks upright in a bowl of rice or pass food from one pair of chopsticks to another – both are reminiscent of Japanese funereal rites.

Snow at Kaiunbashi Bridge and First National Bank by Kobayashi Kiyochika, Mori Art Museum (p110)

SHIMIZU CORPORATION, TOKYO ©

Arts

Tokyo has an arts scene that is broad, dynamic and scattered – much like the city itself. Highlights include visiting the museums whose collections include some of the most celebrated works of classical Japanese art; seeing ukiyo-e *(woodblock prints) and* kabuki *– Tokyo's signature arts; and gawking at the fascinating creations of Japan's 20th-century architects.*

Classical Arts

Japan has a long artistic tradition of painting, metalwork, lacquerware, textiles and pottery. Early on, and during periods of openness, Japan imported styles, techniques and themes from its nearest Asian neighbours, China and Korea. (And being located at the eastern end of the Silk Road, meanwhile absorbed a whole continent's worth of influence). During times of retreat, Japan's artists refined these techniques, filtered styles through local sensibilities and tweaked themes to correspond with the times and materials at hand.

Traditional paintings – adorning folding screens, sliding doors and hanging scrolls – are done in black ink or mineral pigments on *washi* (Japanese handmade paper). Over the centuries, painting modes have included colourful, highly stylised scenes of courtly life *(yamato-e);* monochromatic suggestions of craggy mountains executed with a few lively brushstrokes *(sumi-e);* or flattened compositions of seasonal motifs, boldly outlined against a backdrop of solid gold leaf (works of the Kano school). Today, *nihonga* (Japanese-style painting) may reference any of the above.

Metalwork includes bronze statues of Buddhist deities and ritual elements as well as tea kettles and intricately designed hand guards for swords. Lacquerware – sometimes black, sometimes red and sometimes inlaid with mother-of-pearl or sprinkled with gold leaf – appears on boxes for storing sutras or writing implements and serving trays. Japan's skilled weavers, dyers and embroiderers come together to create the lavish kimono historically worn by the nobility and the actors on the *nō* and kabuki stages.

Pottery can be rough earthenware or delicate enamelled porcelain. Ceramics made for the tea ceremony often appeared dented or misshapen, with drips of glaze running down the side – and were prized all the more for their imperfections.

The Tokyo National Museum (p65) and the Nezu Museum (p46) are the best places to see classical artworks in Tokyo. For modern masters, visit the Crafts Gallery (p107); department stores such as Mitsukoshi (p161) sell contemporary artisan wares and kimono.

Art of the Floating World

The Edo period (1603–1868) was one of prolonged isolation and great creative experimentation – especially in the wealthy capital, Edo (pre-modern Tokyo). This is when two of Japan's most recognisable art forms emerged: kabuki and *ukiyo-e*.

Ukiyo was a play on words: spelt with one set of Chinese characters, it meant the 'fleeting world', our tenuous, temporary abode on earth and a pivotal concept in Japanese Buddhism for centuries. Change the first character, however, and you got the homophone, the 'floating world', which was used to describe the urban pleasure quarters of the Edo period (1603–1868). In this topsy-turvy world, the social hierarchies dictated by the Tokugawa shoganate were inverted: money meant more than rank, kabuki actors were the arbitrators of style and courtesans were the most accomplished of artists.

Ukiyo-e were literally pictures of the floating world, capturing famed beauties, pleasure boats and outings under the cherry blossoms. They were also postcards from the world beyond; at a time when rigid laws prevented much of the populace from travelling, woodblock prints presented compelling scenes from around Japan. The famous *ukiyo-e* artists, Katsushika Hokusai (1760–1849) and Utagawa Hiroshige (1797–1858) are best known, respectively, for their series *Fifty Three Stations of the Tōkaidō* and *One Hundred Famous Views of Edo*.

The vivid colours, novel composition and flowing lines of *ukiyo-e* caused great excitement in the West in the late 19th century, sparking a vogue that one French art critic dubbed *japonisme*. The best place in Tokyo to see *ukiyo-e* is the Ukiyo-e Ōta Memorial Museum of Art (p46); the Tokyo National Museum (p65) also has some on display.

19th- & 20th-Century Modernism

When Japan opened up to the world in the late 19th century, new forms and ideas came spilling in – oil painting, figurative sculpture, the novel – which was exciting, but also fraught. Making art now meant either a rejection or embrace of Western influence, a choice that was hard to divorce from politics.

This shift raised a number of questions: Could the old styles ever be modern (at a time when modernity was equated with the West)? Could works in Western mediums ever transcend mere imitation? What about some kind of hybrid – would that be a breakthrough, or an embarrassment? Some critics argue that these same questions haunt the arts to this day. In the 1950s and '60s avant-garde movements sought a clean break from the weight of all this history, and strove to create something new entirely. The National Museum of Modern Art (p107) traces the history of visual art in Japan from the Meiji Restoration onwards.

Literature, however, was perhaps the best medium in which to parse the profound disorientation that had settled upon Japan by the early 20th century. Works such as Sōseki Natsume's *Kokoro* (1914) and Kawabata Yasunari's *Yukiguni* (Snow Country; 1935–37) address the conflict between Japan's nostalgia for the past and its rush towards the future, between its rural heartland and its burgeoning metropolises. (These are themes still explored today: just watch *Your Name*.)

Murakami Haruki

Among contemporary novelists, Murakami Haruki (b 1949) is the biggest star, both at home and internationally. The release of his latest novel, *Kishidancho Goroshi* (Killing Commendatore; 2017; English release in 2018), created a media frenzy and fans lined up early outside bookstores to snag a copy. Of all his books, the one most Japanese people are likely to mention as their favourite is the one that established his reputation, *Norwegian Wood* (1987). It's a wistful story of students in 1960s Tokyo trying to find themselves and each other. Like the main character, Murakami once worked at a record store; the university in the novel is modelled after his Tokyo Alma Mater, Waseda University.

Tokyo Pop & Beyond

Love him or hate him, Murakami Takashi (b 1962) brought Japan back into an international spotlight it hadn't enjoyed since 19th-century collectors went wild for *ukiyo-e*. His work makes fantastic use of the flat planes, clear lines and decorative techniques associated with *nihonga*, while lifting motifs from the lowbrow subculture of manga (Japanese comics). As much an artist as a clever theorist, Murakami proclaimed in his 'Superflat' manifesto that his work picked up where Japanese artists left off after the Meiji Restoration – and might just be the future of painting, given that most of us now view the world through the portals of two-dimensional screens.

Today's younger artists, working in diverse mediums, have had trouble defining themselves in the wake of 'Tokyo Pop' – as the highly exportable art of the '90s came to be known. They have also to contend with what it means to make art in a post-Fukushima world. The Mori Art Museum (p110) stages exhibitions of established contemporary artists from both Japan and abroad. Scrappier 3331 Arts Chiyoda (p81) is a collection of galleries in Akihabara; even scrappier gallery complex Design Festa (p47), which puts on the twice-yearly art fair of the same name, is in Harajuku. For exhibition recommendations, see **Tokyo Art Beat** (www.tokyoartbeat.com).

Sanja matsuri (p10) at Sensō-ji (p88)

YUKIHIPO / SHUTTERSTOCK ©

Traditional Culture

Over the centuries, Japan's two most prominent belief systems, Shintō and Buddhism – together; they were not considered mutually exclusive – shaped the country's culture, having a profound effect on Japan's art and architecture, ritual and daily life. While few today consider themselves religious, the influence of Shintō and Buddhism remains highly visible – even in contemporary Tokyo.

Shintō & Shrines

Shintō, or 'the way of the gods', is the native religion of Japan. Its innumerable *kami* (gods) are located mostly in nature (in trees, rocks, waterfalls and mountains, for example), but also in the mundane objects of daily life, like hearths and wells. According to Japanese mythology, the celebrated sun goddess, Amaterasu, was the ancestress of the emperor. Historically, extraordinary people could be recognised as *kami* upon death, such as the Emperor Meiji who, along with is wife, is enshrined at Meiji-jingū (p40).

Kami can be summoned through rituals of dance and music into the shrines the Japanese have built for them, where they may be beseeched with prayers (for a good harvest or a healthy pregnancy, maybe, and in modern times for success in business or school exams). Sumo was once part of shrine festivities.

Shintō's origins are unknown. For ages it was a vague, amorphous set of practices and beliefs; however, in the late 19th and early 20th centuries, it was reconfigured by the imperialist state into a national religion centred on emperor worship. This ended with Japan's defeat in WWII, when Emperor Hirohito himself publicly renounced his divinity. Today just 3% of Japanese affiliate themselves with Shintō, but what exactly they believe is unclear.

Still, there are customs so ingrained in Japanese culture that many continue to perform them, regardless of belief. Shrines are still the place to greet the New Year, in a rite called *hatsu-mōde*; to celebrate the milestones of childhood, during festivals such Seijin-no-hi and Shichi-go-san; and where the lovelorn come to pray for a match. At the very least, many would say, doing such things can't hurt.

Temple or Shrine?

Centuries of coexistence means Buddhist temples and Shintō shrines resemble each other architecturally. The easiest way to tell the two apart is by the gate. Shrine have *torii* (a style of gate specific to Shintō shrines), usually composed of two upright pillars, joined at the top by two horizontal crossbars, the upper of which is normally slightly curved. In contrast, a temple *mon* (main entrance gate, also used in palaces and estates) is often a much more substantial affair, constructed of several pillars or casements, joined at the top by a multi-tiered roof.

In Tokyo there are grand, monumental shrines, such as Meiji-jingū, but also countless small ones, sometimes no bigger than a doll's house. They're maintained by local communities, who take up collections for their upkeep and leave fresh offerings, such as fruit, flowers or sake. The shrines are located at auspicious points, based on ancient geomancy, and for that reason aren't moved – even if it means constructions have to go up around them.

Matsuri: Traditional Festivals

Shrines continue to hold their annual *matsuri* during which local *kami* are welcomed into a portable shrine (called a *mikoshi*) and paraded through the streets, accompanied by much ceremony, chanting and merrymaking. Sanja Matsuri and Kanda Matsuri are two of the city's biggest events and draw huge crowds; but there are small neighbourhood festivals, too. They're mostly held between May and September.

Catching a *matsuri* is like stepping back in time: participants come dressed straight out of the Edo period (1603–1868), with some men wearing just short coats and *fundoshi* (the loincloths worn by sumo wrestlers). Many spectators arrive in colourful cotton kimono (called *yukata*). And while the younger generation normally shows little interest in traditional culture, everyone loves a *matsuri*. (Bonus: festivals have street-food vendors.)

Buddhism & Temples

It is said that Shintō is concerned with this life and Buddhism with the afterlife. So while shrines perform weddings, temples perform funeral rites and memorial services. The Buddhist festival of O-Bon, in mid-summer, is when the souls of departed ancestors are believed to pay a short visit. Families return to their hometowns to sweep gravestones, an act called *ohaka-mairi*, and welcome them. Only a third of Japanese today identify as Buddhist, but even non-believers might feel it ominous to skip such rituals.

In Tokyo, O-Bon traditions include Kōenji's Awa Odori, a folk dance parade, and lantern festivals. Temple bells ring out the end of the year on 31 December, during a rite called Joya-no-kane.

Kabukichō district gate, Shinjuku

SEAN PAVONE / SHUTTERSTOCK ©

Survival Guide

Directory A–Z

Customs Regulations

○ Japan has typical customs allowances for duty-free items; see Visit Japan Customs (www.customs.go.jp) for more information.

○ Some prescription medications that may be legal in your home country may be controlled substances in Japan (such as the ADHD medication Adderall). You may need to prepare a 'yakkan shōmei' – an import certificate for pharmaceuticals. See the Ministry of Health, Labour & Welfare's website (www.mhlw.go.jp/english/policy/health-medical/pharmaceuticals/01.html) for more details about which medications are subject to regulations and how to prepare the form.

Electricity

100V/50Hz/60Hz

Emergency

Ambulance & Fire	☎119
Police	☎110
Non-emergency police hotline for foreigners (8.30am-5.15pm Mon-Fri)	☎03-3503-8484
Medical Information Centre English Hotline (9am-8pm)	☎03-5285-8181

Health

Tokyo enjoys a high level of medical services, however few hospitals and clinics have doctors and nurses who speak English. Larger hospitals are your best bet. Expect to pay about ¥3000 for a simple visit to an outpatient clinic and from around ¥20,000 and upwards for emergency care.

Clinics

Primary Care Tokyo (プライマリーケア東京; ☎03-5432-7177; http://pctclinic.com; 3rd fl, 2-1-16 Kitazawa, Setagaya-ku; ◷9am-12.30pm Mon-Sat, 2.30-6pm Mon-Fri; 🚉Keiō Inokashira line to Shimo-Kitazawa, south exit) Fluent English-speaking, American-trained doctor who can address common health complaints.

Tokyo Medical & Surgical Clinic (東京メディカルアンドサージカルクリニック); ☎03-3436-3028; www.tmsc.jp; 2nd fl, 32 Shiba-kōen Bldg, 3-4-30 Shiba-kōen, Minato-ku; ◷9am-4.30pm Mon-Fri, to noon Sat; 🚇Hibiya line to Kamiyachō, exit 1) Staffed with English-speaking Japanese and foreign physicians. 24-hour emergency consultation is also available. Note: prices here are steep.

Emergency Rooms

Seibo International Catholic Hospital (聖母病院; ☎03-3951-1111; www.seibokai.or.jp; 2-5-1 Nakaochiai, Shinjuku-ku; 🚉JR Yamanote line to Mejiro, main exit) and **St Luke's International Hospital** (聖路加国際病院; Seiroka Kokusai Byōin; ☎appointments 03-3527-9527, general 03-3541-5151, international department 03-5550-7166; http://hospital.luke.ac.jp; 9-1 Akashi-chō, Chūō-ku; ◷international department

8.30am-5pm Mon-Fri; S Hibiya line to Tsukiji, exits 3 & 4) both have some English-speaking doctors.

Medications

Pharmacies in Japan do not carry foreign medications, so it's a good idea to bring your own. In a pinch, reasonable substitutes can be found, but the dosage may be less than what you're used to.

Insurance

Basic emergency coverage is adequate. Note that Japanese hospitals only take Japanese health insurance, so you will need to pay in full and get reimbursed. Worldwide travel insurance is available at www.lonelyplanet.com/travel-insurance. You can buy, extend and claim online any time – even if you're already on the road.

Book Your Stay Online

For more accommodation reviews by Lonely Planet authors, check out http://hotels.lonelyplanet.com/tokyo. You'll find independent reviews, as well as recommendations on the best places to stay. Best of all, you can book online.

Internet Access

o Free wi-fi can be found on subway platforms, at convenience stores, major attractions and shopping centres – though signals are often weak. Look for the sticker that says 'Japan Wi-Fi'. Download the Japan Connected (www.ntt-bp.net/jcfw/en.html) app to avoid having to login to individual networks; if you are unable to connect, try clearing your cache.

o Pocket wi-fi devices, which can be used by multiple devices, can be rented from the airport. Some services, such as Japan Wireless (www.japan-wireless.com), will ship to your hotel.

Legal Matters

o Japanese police have extraordinary powers compared with their Western counterparts. If you find yourself in police custody, insist that you will not cooperate in any way until allowed to make a call to your embassy. Police will speak almost no English; insist that a *tsuyakusha* (interpreter) be summoned; police are legally bound to provide one before proceeding with any questioning.

o It is a legal requirement to have your passport on you at all times. Though checks are not common, if you are stopped by police and caught without it, you could be hauled off to a police station to wait until someone fetches it for you.

o Japan takes a hard-line approach to narcotics possession, with long sentences and fines even for first-time offenders.

LGBT Travellers

o Gay and lesbian travellers are unlikely to encounter problems in Tokyo. There are no legal restraints on same-sex sexual activities in Japan apart from the usual age restrictions. Some travellers have reported being turned away or grossly overcharged when checking into love hotels with a partner of the same sex. Otherwise, discrimination is unusual. One note: Japanese people, regardless of their sexual orientation, do not typically engage in public displays of affection.

o Tokyo has a small but very lively gay quarter, Shinjuku-nichōme; outside this and a handful of other places (p175), however, the gay scene is all but invisible. For more advice on travelling in Tokyo, have a look at Utopia Asia (www.utopia-asia.com).

Money

○ These days pretty much everywhere in Tokyo accepts cards, but it's still a good idea to keep at least several thousand yen on hand for the few places that don't. Visa is the most widely accepted card, followed by MasterCard, American Express and Diners Club. Foreign-issued cards should work fine.

○ Most Japanese bank ATMs do not accept foreign-issued cards. Seven Bank ATMs at 7-Eleven convenience stores and Japan Post Bank ATMs at post offices accept most overseas cards and have instructions in English. Seven Bank ATMs are accessible 24 hours a day. Be aware that many banks place a limit on the amount of cash you can withdraw in one day (often around US$300).

○ With a passport, you can change cash or travellers cheques at any Authorised Foreign Exchange Bank (signs are displayed in English), major post offices, some large hotels and most big department stores. Note that you receive a better exchange rate when withdrawing cash from ATMs than when exchanging cash or travellers cheques in Tokyo.

Practicalities

Magazines *Time Out Tokyo* (www.timeout.com/tokyo), *Tokyo Weekender* (www.tokyoweekender.com) and *Metropolis* (www.metropolisjapan.com) are free English-language mags with city info.

Newspapers *Japan Times* (www.japantimes.co.jp) is a long-running English-language daily.

Smoking Tokyo has a curious policy: smoking is banned in public spaces but allowed inside bars and restaurants (though non-smoking bars and restaurants exist, too). Designated smoking areas are set up around train stations.

Weights & Measures The metric system is used along with some traditional Japanese measurements, especially for area (eg *jō* is the size of a tatami mat).

Opening Hours

Note that some outdoor attractions (such as gardens) may close earlier in the winter. Standard opening hours:

Banks 9am to 3pm (some to 5pm) Monday to Friday

Bars around 6pm till late

Boutiques noon to 8pm, irregularly closed

Cafes vary enormously; chains 7am to 10pm

Department stores 10am to 8pm

Museums 9am or 10am to 5pm; often closed Monday

Post offices 9am to 5pm Monday to Friday; larger ones have longer hours and open Saturday

Restaurants lunch 11.30am to 2pm, dinner 6pm to 10pm; last orders taken about half an hour before closing

Public Holidays

If a national holiday falls on a Monday, most museums and restaurants that normally close on Mondays will remain open and close the next day instead.

New Year's Day (Ganjitsu) 1 January

Coming-of-Age Day (Seijin-no-hi) Second Monday in January

National Foundation Day (Kenkoku Kinen-bi) 11 February

Spring Equinox (Shumbun-no-hi) 20 or 21 March

Shōwa Day (Shōwa-no-hi) 29 April

Constitution Day (Kempō Kinem-bi) 3 May

Green Day (Midori-no-hi) 4 May

Children's Day (Kodomo-no-hi) 5 May

Marine Day (Umi-no-hi) Third Monday in July

Mountain Day (Yama-no-hi) 11 August

Japanese Years

In addition to the typical Western calendar, Japan also counts years by the reigns of its emperors. The era until the retirement of Emperor Akihito on 31 April 2019 is called Heisei (pronounced hay-say); he ascended the throne in 1989 (Heisei 1); thus 2019 is Heisei 31. When the crown prince ascends the throne, a new era will be named.

Respect-for-the-Aged Day (Keirō-no-hi) Third Monday in September

Autumn Equinox (Shūbun-no-hi) 23 or 24 September

Health & Sports Day (Taiiku-no-hi) Second Monday in October

Culture Day (Bunka-no-hi) 3 November

Labour Thanksgiving Day (Kinrō Kansha-no-hi) 23 November

Emperor's Birthday (Ten-nō-no-Tanjōbi) 23 December

Safe Travel

● The biggest threat to travellers in Tokyo is the city's general aura of safety. It's wise to keep up the same level of caution and common sense that you would back home. Of special note are reports that drink-spiking continues to be a problem in Roppongi (resulting in robbery, extortion and, in extreme cases, physical assault).

● Twenty-four-hour staffed *kōban* (police boxes) are located near most major train stations.

Telephone

The country code for Japan is ☏81; Tokyo's area code is ☏03, although some outer suburbs have different area codes.

Mobile Phones

● Japan's mobile network runs on 3G and 4G, so overseas phones with either technology should work in Tokyo.

● Data-only SIM cards for unlocked smartphones are available at kiosks at both Narita and Haneda airports and at large electronics stores (such as Bic Camera, Yodobashi Camera etc). To work, they may require some fiddling with settings, so make sure you've got a connection before you leave the shop. Staff usually speak some English. B-Mobile's Visitor SIM (www.bmobile.ne.jp/english/index.html), which offers 5GB over 21 days for ¥3480, is a good choice.

● For visitors who anticipate needing to make voice calls, a rental pay-as-you-go phone is a better option. Rentafone Japan (www.rentafonejapan.com) offers rentals for ¥3900 a week (plus ¥300 for each additional day) and domestic calls cost a reasonable ¥35 per minute (overseas calls start at ¥45 per minute).

Public Phones

● Public phones do still exist and they work almost 100% of the time; look for them around train stations. Ordinary public phones are green; those that allow you to call abroad are grey and are usually marked 'International & Domestic Card/Coin Phone'.

● Local calls cost ¥10 per minute; note that you won't get change on a ¥100 coin. The minimum charge for international calls is ¥100, which buys you a fraction of a minute. Reverse-charge (collect) international calls can be made by dialling ☏0051.

Time

Tokyo local time is nine hours ahead of Greenwich Mean Time (GMT). Japan does not observe daylight saving time.

Toilets

● Public toilets (free, typically clean and with toilet paper) can be found in most train stations; convenience stores often have toilets you can use, too. The most common words for toilet in Japanese are トイレ (pronounced 'toi-re') and お手洗い ('o-te-arai'); 女 (female) and 男 (male) will also come in handy.

○ Some restrooms still have squat toilets; Western-style toilets are often marked with the characters 洋式 (*yōshiki*) on the stall door. 'Washlets', increasingly common, are heated-seat thrones that wash and dry your intimate areas at the touch of a button.

○ Larger attractions, train stations, department stores and shopping malls usually have at least one wheelchair accessible, gender-neutral toilet.

○ Separate toilet slippers are usually provided in establishments where you take off your shoes at the entrance; they are typically just inside the toilet door.

Tourist Information

Note that Tourist Information Centers (TICs) cannot make accommodation bookings.

Tokyo Tourist Information Center (☎03-5321-3077; info@tokyo-tourism.jp; 1st fl, Tokyo Metropolitan Government bldg 1, 2-8-1 Nishi-Shinjuku, Shinjuku-ku; ⏰9.30am-6.30pm; Ⓢ Ōedo line to Tochōmae, exit A4) Booking counters for tours,

money-exchange machines, wi-fi, and a shop with a range of souvenirs. Additional branches in Keisei Ueno Station, Haneda Airport and Shinjuku Bus Terminal.

JNTO Tourist Information Center (☎03-3201-3331; www.jnto.go.jp; 1st fl, Shin-Tokyo Bldg, 3-3-1 Marunouchi, Chiyoda-ku; ⏰9am-5pm; 📶; Ⓢ Chiyoda line to Nijūbashimae, exit 1) Run by the Japan National Tourism Organisation, this TIC has information on Tokyo and beyond. There are also branches in Narita Airport terminals 1 and 2.

Travellers with Disabilities

○ Tokyo is making steps to improve universal access (called 'barrier free' here), but still gets mixed reviews from travellers. Newer buildings have wheelchair access ramps, and more and more subway stations have elevators (look for signs on the platform, as not all exits have elevators). Hotels from the higher end of midrange and above usually have a 'barrier-free' room or two (book well in advance).

○ Accessible Japan (www.accessible-japan.com) is a great resource.

○ Download Lonely Planet's free *Accessible Travel* guide from http://lptravel.to/AccessibleTravel.

Tokyo Addresses

Tokyo is difficult to navigate even for locals. Only the biggest streets have names, and they don't figure into addresses; instead, addresses are derived from districts (*ku*), blocks (*chōme*, pronounced cho-may) and building numbers. Smartphones with navigation apps have been a real boon. Many restaurants and venues have useful maps on their websites.

Visas

Citizens of 68 countries, including Australia, Canada, Hong Kong, Korea, New Zealand, Singapore, USA, UK and almost all European nations will be automatically issued a *tanki-taizai* (temporary visitor visa) on arrival. Typically this visa is good for 90 days.

For a complete list of visa-exempt countries, consult www.mofa.go.jp/j_info/visit/visa/short/novisa.html#list.

Women Travellers

○ Tokyo is a relatively safe city for women travellers, though basic common sense still rules. Foreign women are occasionally subjected to some forms of verbal harassment or prying questions. Physical attacks are very rare, but have occurred.

○ Note that some budget hotels that target foreign travellers are in areas where prostitution occurs (such as Kabukichō); women, especially solo travellers, are more likely to be harassed in such places.

○ Several train companies have introduced women-only cars during rush hour to protect female passengers from *chikan* (men who grope women and girls on packed trains). There are signs (usually in pink) on the platform indicating where you can board these cars.

Transport

Arriving in Tokyo

Tokyo has two international airports. Narita Airport, in neighbouring Chiba Prefecture, is the primary gateway to Tokyo; most budget flights end up here. Haneda Airport, closer to the city centre, is now seeing an increasing number of international flights; this is also where most domestic flights arrive. Flying into Haneda means quicker and cheaper access to central Tokyo.

Both airports have smooth, hassle-free entry procedures, and are connected to the city centre by public transport.

Flights, tours and cars can be booked online at lonelyplanet.com/bookings.

Narita Airport

Narita Airport (NRT; 成田空港; ☏0476-34-8000; www.narita-airport.jp; 🛜) has three terminals (the new Terminal 3 handles low-cost carriers). Note that only terminals 1 and 2 have train stations. Free shuttle buses run between all the terminals every 15 to 30 minutes (from 7am to 9.30pm). Another free shuttle runs between Terminal 2 and Terminal 3 every five to 12 minutes (4.30am to 11.20pm); otherwise it is a 15-minute walk between the two terminals. All terminals have tourist information desks.

Bus

Purchase tickets from kiosks in the arrivals hall (no advance reservations necessary).

Friendly Airport Limousine (www.limousinebus.co.jp/en) Direct, reserved-seat buses (¥3100) depart from all Narita Airport terminals for major hotels and train stations in Tokyo. Schedules vary by route;

Shinjuku Bus Terminal (バスタ新宿; Busuta Shinjuku; ☏03-6380-4794; http://shinjuku-busterminal.co.jp; 🛜; Ⓡ JR Yamanote line to Shinjuku, new south exit) is the most frequent destination, with buses running 7am and 11pm. The journey takes 1½ to two

hours depending on traffic. At the time of writing, discount round-trip 'Welcome to Tokyo Limousine Bus Return Voucher' tickets (¥4500) were available for foreign tourists; ask at the ticket counter at the airport.

Keisei Tokyo Shuttle (www.keiseibus.co.jp) Discount buses connect all Narita Airport terminals and Tokyo Station (¥1000, approximately 90 minutes, every 20 minutes from 6am to 11pm). In the other direction, buses run 24 hours for early departures (¥1000; ¥2000 between midnight and 5am).

Train

Both Japan Railways (JR) and the independent Keisei line run between central Tokyo and Narita Airport terminals 1 and 2. For Terminal 3, take a train to Terminal 2 and then walk or take the free shuttle bus to Terminal 3 (and budget an extra 15 minutes). Tickets can be purchased in the basement of either terminal, where the entrances to the train stations are located.

Keisei Skyliner (www.keisei.co.jp/keisei/tetudou/skyliner/us) The quickest service into Tokyo runs nonstop to Nippori (¥2470, 36 minutes) and Ueno (¥2470, 41 minutes) stations, on the city's northeast side, where you can connect to the JR Yamanote line or the subway (Ueno Station only). Trains run roughly twice an hour, 7.30am to 11pm. Foreign nationals can purchase advance tickets online for slightly less (¥2200). The Skyliner & Tokyo Subway Ticket, which combines a one-way or round-trip ticket on the Skyliner and a one-, two- or three-day subway pass, is a good deal.

Keisei Main Line Limited-express trains (*kaisoku kyūkō*; ¥1030, 71 minutes to Ueno) follow the same route as the Skyliner, but make stops. This is a good budget option. Trains run every 20 minutes during peak hours.

Narita Express (www.jreast. co.jp/e/nex) N'EX trains depart Narita approximately every half-hour between 7.45am and 9.45pm for Tokyo Station (¥3020, 53 minutes) and Shinjuku (¥3190, 80 minutes); the latter also stops at Shibuya (¥3190; 75 minutes). At the time of writing, foreign tourists could purchase return N'EX tickets for ¥4000 (valid for 14 days; ¥2000 for under 12s). Check online or enquire at the JR East Travel Service centres at Narita Airport for the latest deals.

Taxi

Fixed-fare taxis run ¥19,500 to ¥22,500 for most destinations in Tokyo.

Haneda Airport

Haneda Airport (HND; 羽田 空港; ☏ international terminal 03-6428-0888; www.tokyo-air-port-bldg.co.jp/en; ☏) has two domestic terminals and one international terminal. Note that some international flights arrive at awkward night-time hours, between midnight and 5am, when only sporadic buses to central Tokyo will be running.

Bus

Purchase tickets at the kiosks at the arrivals hall.
Friendly Airport Limousine (www.limousinebus.co.jp/en)

Baggage Shipment

Baggage couriers provide next-day delivery of your large luggage from Narita and Haneda airports to any address in Tokyo (around ¥2000 per large bag), so you don't have to haul it on the trains. Look for kiosks in the arrival terminals. If you plan on taking advantage of this service, make sure to put the essentials you'll need for the next 24 hours in a small bag. Some tourist information centres also have courier counters for sending your bags back to the airport, or onto your next destination in Japan.

Coaches connect Haneda with major train stations and hotels in Shibuya (¥1030), Shinjuku (¥1230), Roppongi (¥1130), Ginza (¥930) and others; fares double between midnight and 5am. Travel times vary wildly, taking anywhere from 30 to 90 minutes depending on traffic. Night buses depart from the international terminal for Shibuya Station at 12.15am, 12.50am and 2.20am; Shinjuku Bus Terminal at 12.20am, 1am, 1.40am and 2.20am; and Tokyo Station at 1.05am and 2am.

Train & Monorail

Note that the international and domestic terminals have their own stations; when travelling to the airport, the international terminal is the second-to-last stop.
Keikyū Airport Express (www.haneda-tokyo-access.com/en) Trains depart several times an hour (5.30am to midnight) for Shinagawa (¥410, 12 minutes), where you can connect to the JR Yamanote line. From Shinagawa, some trains continue along the Asakusa subway line, which serves Higashi-Ginza, Nihombashi and Asakusa stations.

Tokyo Monorail (www.tokyo-monorail.co.jp/english) Leaves approximately every 10 minutes (5am to midnight) for Hamamatsuchō Station (¥490, 15 minutes), which is a stop on the JR Yamanote line. Good for travellers staying near Ginza or Roppongi.

Taxi

Fixed fares include Ginza (¥5900), Shibuya (¥6600), Shinjuku (¥7100), Ikebukuro (¥8900) and Asakusa (¥7200).

Getting Around

Bicycle

Tokyo is by no means a bicycle-friendly city. Bike lanes are almost non-existent and you'll see no-parking signs for bicycles everywhere (ignore these at your peril: your bike could get impounded, requiring a half-day excursion to the pound and a ¥3000 fee). Still, you'll see people cycling everywhere and it can be a really fun way to get around the city. Some hostels and

Climate Change & Travel

Every form of transport that relies on carbon-based fuel generates CO_2, the main cause of human-induced climate change. Modern travel is dependent on aeroplanes, which might use less fuel per kilometre per person than most cars but travel much greater distances. The altitude at which aircraft emit gases (including CO_2) and particles also contributes to their climate change impact. Many websites offer 'carbon calculators' that allow people to estimate the carbon emissions generated by their journey and, for those who wish to do so, to offset the impact of the greenhouse gases emitted with contributions to portfolios of climate-friendly initiatives throughout the world. Lonely Planet offsets the carbon footprint of all staff and author travel.

ryokan have bikes to lend. See Rentabike (http://rentabike.jp) for places around town that rent bicycles.

Boat

Tokyo Cruise (水上バス, Suijō Bus; ☎0120-977-311; http://suijobus.co.jp) Water buses run up and down the Sumida-gawa (Sumida River) roughly twice an hour between 10am and 6pm connecting Asakusa with Hama-rikyū Onshi-teien (¥980, 35 minutes) and Odaiba (¥1260, 70 minutes). Tickets can be purchased immediately before departure, if available, at any pier.

Tokyo Mizube Cruising Line (東京水辺ライン; ☎03-5608-8869; www.tokyo-park.or.jp/waterbus) Water buses head down the Sumida-gawa from Asakusa to Ryōgoku (¥310), Hama-rikyū Onshi-teien (¥620) and Odaiba (¥1130), and then back up again. Schedules are seasonal, and infrequent in winter. Tickets don't have to be reserved in advance but can be purchased just before departure.

Taxi

❂ Taxis in Tokyo feature white-gloved drivers, seats covered with lace doilies and doors that magically open and close – an experience in itself. They rarely make economic sense though, unless you have a group of four.

❂ All cabs run by the meter. Fares start at ¥430 for the first 1km, then rise by ¥80 for every 280m you travel (or for every 105 seconds spent in traffic). There's a surcharge of 20% between 10pm and 5am (including fixed-fare taxis from the airport). Most (but not all) taxis take credit cards.

❂ Drivers rarely speak English, though fortunately most taxis now have navigation systems. It's a good idea to have your destination written down in Japanese, or better yet, a business card with an address.

❂ Train stations and hotels have taxi stands where you are expected to queue. Otherwise, you can hail a cab from the street, by standing on the curb and sticking your arm out. A red light means the taxi is free and a green light means it's taken.

Train & Subway

❂ Tokyo's extensive rail network includes JR (Japan Rail) lines, a subway system and private commuter lines that depart in every direction for the suburbs, like spokes on a wheel. Major transit hubs include Tokyo, Shinagawa, Shibuya, Shinjuku, Ikebukuro and Ueno stations. Trains and subways run 5am to midnight.

❂ Tokyo has 13 subway lines, nine of which are operated by Tokyo Metro (www.tokyometro.jp) and four by Toei (www.kotsu.metro.tokyo.jp). The lines are colour-coded, making navigation fairly simple. Unfortunately, journeys that require transfers between lines run by different operators cost more than journeys that use only one operator's lines.

❂ Figure out the best route to your destination with the Navitime for Japan Travel app (www.navitimejapan.com); you can download routes to be used offline, too.

❂ Most train and subway stations have several different exits. Try to get your bearings and decide where to exit while still on the platform; look for the yellow signs that indicate which stairs lead to which exits. If you're not sure which exit to take, look for street maps of the area usually posted near the ticket gates, which show the locations of the exits.

Tickets

Fares start at ¥133/170/180 for JR/Tokyo Metro/Toei and go up depending on how far you travel.

○ Purchase paper tickets or top up train passes at the touch-screen ticket-vending machines outside station ticket gates. These have an English function.

○ To purchase a paper ticket, you'll need to work out the correct fare from the chart above the machines. If you can't work it out, just buy a ticket for the cheapest fare.

○ All ticket gates have card readers for Suica and Pasmo train passes; simply wave your card over the reader.

○ If you're using a paper ticket or a one-day pass, you'll need to use a ticket gate with a slot for inserting a ticket. Make sure to pick it up when it pops out again.

○ You'll need your ticket or pass to exit the station as well. If your ticket or pass does not have sufficient charge to cover your journey, insert it into one of the 'fare adjustment' machines near the exit gates.

Key Routes

Ginza subway line Shibuya to Asakusa, via Ginza and Ueno. Colour-coded orange.

Train & Subway Passes

Prepaid re-chargeable Suica and Pasmo cards (they're essentially the same; JR issues Suica and the subway issues Pasmo) work on all city trains and subways and allow you to breeze through the ticket gates without having to work out fares or transfer tickets.

Purchase one from any touch-screen ticket-vending machine in Tokyo (including those at Haneda and Narita airports). A ¥500 deposit and a minimum charge of ¥2000 is required (¥1000 for Pasmo); the deposit is refunded when you return the pass to any ticket window.

The only reason not to get a Suica or Pasmo is to take advantage of Tokyo Metro's 24-hour unlimited ride pass (adult/child ¥600/300). Note that this is only good on the nine subway lines operated by Tokyo Metro; purchase at any ticket machine at a Tokyo Metro subway station.

Hibiya subway line Connects Naka-Meguro, Ebisu, Roppongi, Ginza, Akihabara and Ueno. Colour-coded grey.

JR Yamanote line Loop line stopping at many sightseeing destinations, such as Shibuya, Harajuku, Shinjuku, Tokyo, Akihabara and Ueno. Colour-coded light green.

JR Chūō line Central express line from Tokyo Station to points in west Tokyo (Nakano, Kichijōji and Mitaka), via Shinjuku. Colour-coded reddish-orange.

JR Sōbu line Local express line running between west Tokyo (Nakano, Kōenji, Kichijōji and Mitaka) through Shinjuku to eastern suburbs, including Ryōgoku. Colour-coded yellow.

When to Travel

○ Trains and subways run 5am to midnight.

○ The morning rush (7am to 9.30am) for trains going towards central Tokyo (from all directions) is the worst, when 'packed in like sardines' is an understatement.

○ Until 9.30am women (and children) can ride in women-only cars, which tend to be less crowded.

○ The evening rush (around 5pm to 8pm) hits trains going out of central Tokyo – though as many work late or stay out, it's not as bad as the morning commute.

○ The last train of the night heading out of the city (around midnight) is also usually packed – with drunk people. Friday night is the worst.

○ Trains going the opposite directions during peak hours (towards central Tokyo in the evening, for example) are uncrowded, as are trains in the middle of the day.

Language

Japanese pronunciation is easy for English speakers, as most of its sounds are also found in English. Note though that it's important to make the distinction between short and long vowels, as vowel length can change the meaning of a word. The long vowels (ā, ē, ī, ō, ū) should be held twice as long as the short ones. All syllables are pronounced fairly evenly in Japanese. If you read our pronunciation guides as if they were English, you'll be understood.

To enhance your trip with a phrasebook, visit **lonelyplanet.com**.

Basics

Hello.	こんにちは。	kon·ni·chi·wa
Goodbye.	さようなら。	sa·yō·na·ra
Yes.	はい。	hai
No.	いいえ。	ī·e
Please.	ください。	ku·da·sai
Thank you.	ありがとう。	a·ri·ga·tō
Excuse me.	すみません。	su·mi·ma·sen
Sorry.	ごめんなさい。	go·men·na·sai

What's your name?
お名前は　　o·na·ma·e wa
何ですか？　nan des ka

My name is ...
私の　　　　wa·ta·shi no
名前は…です。na·ma·e wa...des

Do you speak English?
英語が　　　ē·go ga
話せますか？ha·na·se·mas ka

I don't understand.
わかりません。wa·ka·ri·ma·sen

Accommodation

Where's a ...?	···はど こですか？	... wa do·ko des ka
campsite	キャンプ場	kyam·pu·jō
guesthouse	民宿	min·shu·ku
hotel	ホテル	ho·te·ru
inn	旅館	ryo·kan
Do you have a ... room?	···ルームは ありますか？	...rū·mu wa a·ri·mas ka
single	シングル	shin·gu·ru
double	ダブル	da·bu·ru

How much is it per ...?	···いくら ですか？	... i·ku·ra des ka
night	1泊	ip·pa·ku
person	1人	hi·to·ri

air-con	エアコン	air·kon
bathroom	風呂場	fu·ro·ba
window	窓	ma·do

Eating & Drinking

I'd like to reserve a table for (two).
(2人)の　　　(fu·ta·ri) no
予約をお　　　yo·ya·ku o
願いします。 o·ne·gai shi·mas

I'd like (the menu).
(メニュー)　　(me·nyū)
をお願いします。o o·ne·gai shi·mas

I don't eat (red meat).
(赤身の肉)　　(a·ka·mi no ni·ku)
は食べません。wa ta·be·ma·sen

That was delicious!
おいしかった。oy·shi·kat·ta

Please bring the bill.
お勘定　　　　o·kan·jō
をください。 o ku·da·sai

Emergencies

Help!	たすけて！	tas·ke·te
Go away!	離れろ！	ha·na·re·ro
Call the police!	警察を呼んで！	kē·sa·tsu o yon·de
Call a doctor!	医者を呼んで！	i·sha o yon·de
I'm lost.	迷いました。	ma·yoy·mash·ta

I'm ill.
私は病　　　wa·ta·shi wa
気です。　　byō·ki des

Where are the toilets?
トイレは　　toy·re wa
どこですか？ do·ko des ka

Transport & Directions

Where's the ...?
···はどこ　　... wa do·ko
ですか？　　des ka

What's the address?
住所は何　　jū·sho wa nan
ですか？　　des ka

Can you show me (on the map)?
(地図で)教えて　(chi·zu de) o·shi·e·te
くれませんか？ ku·re·ma·sen ka

When's the next (bus)?
次の(バス)は　tsu·gi no (bas) wa
何時ですか？　nan·ji des ka

Behind the Scenes

Writer Thanks

Rebecca Milner

Thank you to my mom and dad, who walked all over the city with me (sometimes logging over 10 miles a day!) to update this edition. I loved having your company and your insights. And to Chikara, as always, for your patience and acceptance.

Acknowledgements

Climate map data adapted from Peel MC, Finlayson BL & McMahon TA (2007) 'Updated World Map of the Köppen-Geiger Climate Classification', Hydrology and Earth System Sciences, 11, 1633–44.

Illustration p66-7 by Michael Weldon.

This Book

This guidebook was researched and written by Rebecca Milner. The previous edition was written by Rebecca Milner and Simon Richmond.

Destination Editor Laura Crawford

Product Editors Kate Chapman, Shona Gray

Senior Cartographer Diana Von Holdt

Book Designer Jessica Rose

Assisting Editors Katie Connolly, Gabrielle Stefanos, Sarah Stewart

Cartographer Julie Dodkins

Assisting Book Designers Nicholas Colicchia, Wibowo Rusli

Cover Researcher Naomi Parker

Thanks to Ronan Abayawickrema, Naoko Akamatsu, Grace Dobell, Liz Heynes, Anne Mason, Kirsten Rawlings

Send Us Your Feedback

We love to hear from travellers – your comments keep us on our toes and help make our books better. Our well-travelled team reads every word on what you loved or loathed about this book. Although we cannot reply individually to postal submissions, we always guarantee that your feedback goes straight to the appropriate authors, in time for the next edition. Each person who sends us information is thanked in the next edition, the most useful submissions are rewarded with a selection of digital PDF chapters.

Visit lonelyplanet.com/contact to submit your updates and suggestions or to ask for help. Our award-winning website also features inspirational travel stories, news and discussions.

Note: We may edit, reproduce and incorporate your comments in Lonely Planet products such as guidebooks, websites and digital products, so let us know if you don't want your comments reproduced or your name acknowledged. For a copy of our privacy policy visit lonelyplanet.com/privacy.

Index

Tokyo Bay at dusk

DUANE WALKER / GETTY IMAGES ©

Tokyo City Maps

Harajuku, Aoyama, Shibuya & Ebisu

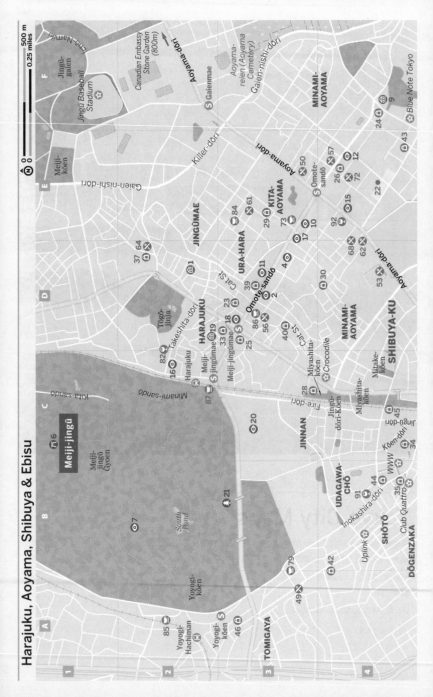

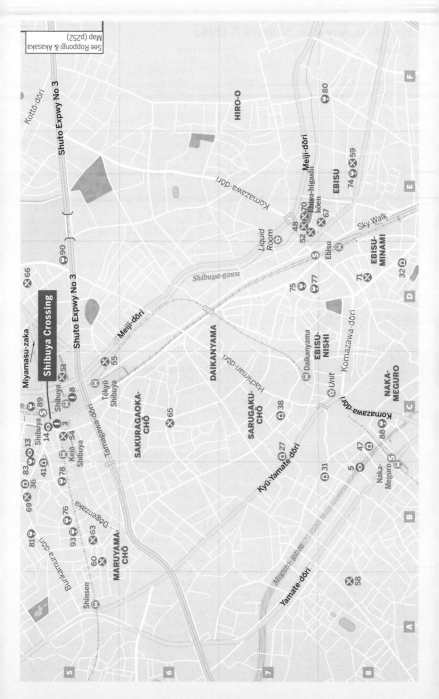

See Roppongi & Akasaka Map (p252)

Kotto-dōri

Shuto Expwy No 3

HIRO-O

Komazawa-dōri

Meiji-dōri

70
48
52
67
Ebisu-higashi
kōen
EBISU
74 59

Liquid
Room

90

66

Shibuya-gawa

Sky Walk

Ebisu

S

75
77

71

EBISU-
MINAMI

32

D

Shuto Expwy No 3

Meiji-dōri

Daikanyama

DAIKANYAMA

Komazawa-dōri

Shibuya Crossing

Miyamasu-zaka

51
8
Shibuya

Tōkyū
Shibuya

55

Hachiman-dōri

EBISU-
NISHI

Unit

NAKA-
MEGURO

89
S
Shibuya
14
3
13
Keiō 54
Shibuya
78
41
83
36

Tamagawa-dōri

65

SAKURAGAOKA-
CHŌ

SARUGAKU-
CHŌ

38

27

Kyū-Yamate-dōri

31

47
5

88

Naka-
Meguro S

69
76

Dōgenzaka

81
93
63

Bunkamura-dōri

60

MARUYAMA-
CHŌ

Shinsen

Meguro-gawa

Yamate-dōri

58

A

Harajuku, Aoyama, Shibuya & Ebisu

Marunouchi, Nihombashi, Ginza & Tsukiji

Marunouchi, Nihombashi, Ginza & Tsukiji

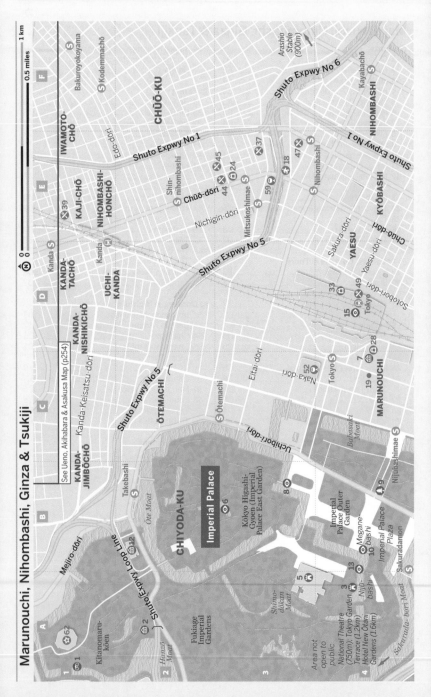

CHŪO-KU

IWAMOTO-CHŌ

Bakuroyokoyama

Kodemmachō

Shuto Expwy No 6

Arashio Stable (900m)

NIHOMBASHI

Kayabachō

KAJI-CHŌ

Shuto Expwy No 1

Shuto Expwy No 1

Edo-dōri

39

Shin-nihombashi

45

24

37

47

18

Nihombashi

KYŌBASHI

NIHOMBASHI-HONCHŌ

Chūō-dōri

44

59

Mitsukoshimae

Sakura-dōri

YAESU

Chūō-dōri

Nichigin-dōri

Kanda

Kanda

Yaesu-dōri

Sotobori-dōri

KANDA-TACHŌ

UCHI-KANDA

Shuto Expwy No 5

33

49

15

Tokyo

D

KANDA-NISHIKICHŌ

See Ueno, Akihabara & Asakusa Map (p254)

KANDA-KEIJŌ

Kanda-Keisatsu-dōri

KANDA-JIMBŌCHŌ

Shuto Expwy No 5

Takebashi

ŌTEMACHI

Eitai-dōri

Naka-dōri

52

7

28

Tokyo

19

MARUNOUCHI

Shuto Expwy Loop Line

12

Mejiro-dōri

Uchibori-dōri

Ōte Moat

ŌTEMACHI

Babasaki Moat

Kōkyo Higashi-Gyoen (Imperial Palace East Garden)

6

Nijūbashimae

CHIYODA-KU

Imperial Palace

8

9

Shuto Expwy Loop Line

2

Hanzō Moat

Kitanomaru-kōen

62

1

Shimo-dōkan Moat

5

13

3

National Theatre (750m); Tokyo Garden Terrace (1.2km); Hotel New Otani Gardens (1.6km)

Fukiage Imperial Gardens

Area not open to public

Imperial Palace Outer Garden

Megane-bashi

10

Imperial Palace Plaza

Nijū-bashi

Sakuradamon

Sakurada-bori Moat

N

0

0.5 miles

1 km

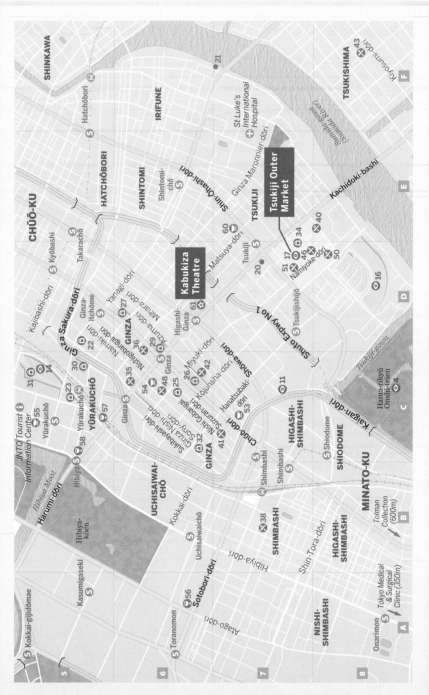

Kabukiza Theatre

Tsukiji Outer Market

SHINKAWA

CHŪŌ-KU

SHINKAWA

Hatchōbori

HATCHŌBORI

Kyōbashi

Takarachō

Kajibashi-dōri

Sakura-dōri

Ginza

IRIFUNE

SHINTOMI

SHINTOMI-chō

Shintomi-chō

Shin-Ōhashi-dōri

TSUKISHIMA

Kiyosumi-dōri

Sumida River (Sumidagawa)

St Luke's International Hospital

Ginza Marronnier-dōri

Kachidoki-bashi

TSUKIJI

Tsukiji

Matsuya-dōri

Namiyoke-dōri

Tsukijishijō

Shuto Expwy No I

Higashi-Ginza

Ginza Itchōme

Yanagi-dōri

Mihara-dōri

Azuma-dōri

Ginza

Namiki-dōri

Nishiginbangai-dōri

Miyuki-dōri

Hanatsubaki-dōri

Kōjunsha-dōri

Suzuran-dōri

Showa-dōri

Chūō-dōri

HIGASHI-SHIMBASHI

Shiodome

SHIODOME

Kaigan-dōri

Hama-rikyū Onshi-teien

Hama-rikyū Onshi-teien

JNTO Tourist Information Center

Yūrakuchō

YŪRAKUCHŌ

Ginza Nishi-dōri

Sony-dōri

Sukibayashi-dōri

Nishi Gobangai

GINZA

Shimbashi

Shimbashi

HIGASHI-SHIMBASHI

Shimbashi

MINATO-KU

Hibiya Moat

Hibiya

Hibiya-dōri

UCHISAIWAI-CHŌ

Kokkai-dōri

Uchisaiwaichō

SHIMBASHI

HIGASHI-SHIMBASHI

Shin-Tora-dōri

Tolman Collection (600m)

Harumi-dōri

Hibiya-kōen

Hibiya-dōri

Sotobori-dōri

Atago-dōri

NISHI-SHIMBASHI

Tokyo Medical & Surgical Clinic (350m)

Kasumigaseki

Kokkai-gijidōmae

Toranomon

Onarimon

Roppongi & Akasaka

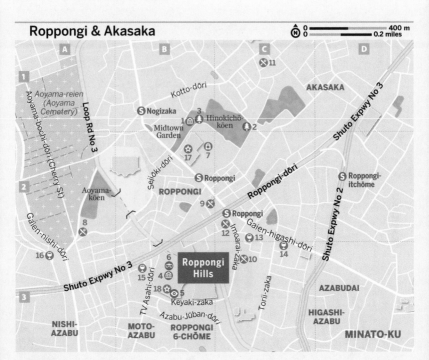

Roppongi & Akasaka

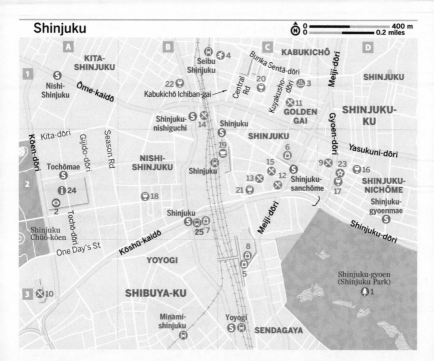

Shinjuku

Ueno, Akihabara & Asakusa

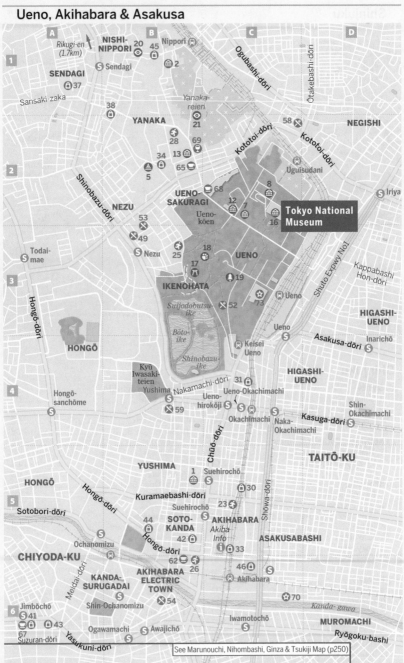

Rikugi-en (1.7km)

NISHI-NIPPORI
A1 20 45
Nippori
B
C
D

Ōgubashi-dōri

Ōtakebashi-dōri

SENDAGI
S Sendagi
2
37

Sansaki-zaka

YANAKA
38
Yanaka-reien
21
28
69
34 13
65
5

Kototoi-dōri
58
Kototoi-dōri
NEGISHI

Uguisudani
8
UENO-SAKURAGI
68
12
7
16
Tokyo National Museum
S Iriya

NEZU
53
49
S Nezu
Ueno-kōen
25
18
17
19
UENO

Todai-mae S

Shinobazu-dōri

HONGŌ

Shuto Expwy No1

Kappabashi Hon-dōri

IKENOHATA
Suijōdobutsu-ike
52
73
S Ueno
S Ueno

HIGASHI-UENO
Inarichō
Asakusa-dōri S

Bōto-ike

Shinobazu-ike

Keisei Ueno

HIGASHI-UENO

Shin-Okachimachi

Kyū Iwasaki-teien
Yushima
Nakamachi-dōri
31
Ueno-Okachimachi
Shin-Okachimachi

HONGŌ
Hongō-sanchōme S
Ueno-hirokōji
59
Okachimachi S
Naka-Okachimachi
Kasuga-dōri S

TAITŌ-KU

YUSHIMA
1
Suehirochō

HONGŌ
Hongō-dōri
Kuramaebashi-dōri
30

Sotobori-dōri
Suehirochō
23

SOTO-KANDA
44
AKIHABARA
Akiba Info
42

Ochanomizu S
Hongō-dōri
62 26
33
46 S

CHIYODA-KU
KANDA-SURUGADAI
AKIHABARA ELECTRIC TOWN
54
S Akihabara

Shin-Ochanomizu S

70
Kanda-gawa

MUROMACHI

Jimbōchō
S 41
43
67
Suzuran-dōri
Ogawamachi
S Awajichō
Iwamotochō S
Ryōgoku-bashi

Meidai-dōri
Yasukuni-dōri

See Marunouchi, Nihombashi, Ginza & Tsukiji Map (p250)

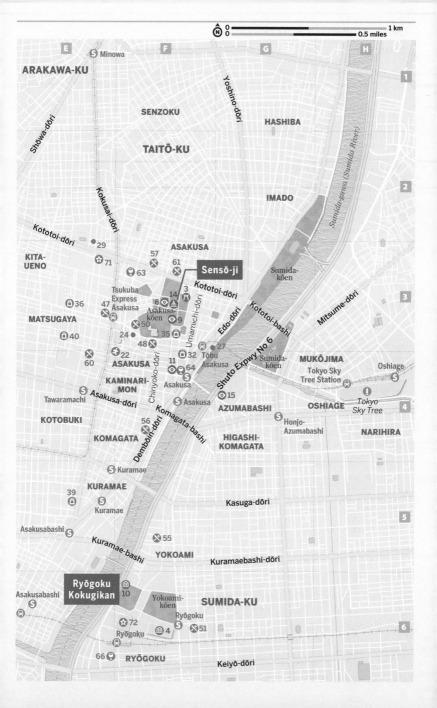

0 1 km
0 0.5 miles

ARAKAWA-KU

Minowa

SENZOKU

TAITŌ-KU

Yoshino-dōri

HASHIBA

Shōwa-dōri

IMADO

Sumida-gawa (Sumida River)

Kokusai-dōri

Kototoi-dōri

29

KITA-
UENO

71

57

ASAKUSA

63

61

Sensō-ji

Kototoi-dōri

Sumida-
kōen

MATSUGAYA

36

Tsukuba
Express
Asakusa

47

3

6

14

Kototoi-bashi

Mitsume-dōri

Asakusa
kōen

9

Edo-dōri

Umamichi-dōri

40

24

50

35

48

32

Tōbu
Asakusa

27

Sumida-
kōen

MUKŌJIMA

Tokyo Sky
Tree Station

Oshiage

60

22

ASAKUSA

11

64

Shuto Expwy No 6

Oshiage

KAMINARI-
MON

Asakusa

OSHIAGE

Tokyo
Sky Tree

Tawaramachi

Asakusa-dōri

Asakusa

15

AZUMABASHI

Honjo-
Azumabashi

NARIHIRA

KOTOBUKI

56

Komagata-bashi

HIGASHI-
KOMAGATA

KOMAGATA

Dembōin-dōri

Chinyoko-dōri

Kuramae

KURAMAE

39

Kuramae

Kasuga-dōri

Asakusabashi

Kuramae-bashi

55

YOKOAMI

Kuramaebashi-dōri

Ryōgoku
Kokugikan

10

Yokoami-
kōen

SUMIDA-KU

Asakusabashi

72

Ryōgoku

Ryōgoku

4

51

66

RYŌGOKU

Keiyō-dōri

Ueno, Akihabara & Asakusa